T0329660

The Impossible Advantage

ANDREAS **BUCHHOLZ**, WOLFRAM **WÖRDEMANN**
AND NED **WILEY**

The
Impossible
Advantage

WINNING THE COMPETITIVE GAME BY
CHANGING THE RULES

A John Wiley & Sons, Ltd., Publication

Based on a German work entitled *Speilstrategien im Business: Die Regeln des Wettbewerbs verändern* by Andreas Buchholz and Wolfram Wördemann, copyright © Campus Verlag 2008, published by Campus Verlag.

Designations used by companies to distinguish their products are often claimed as trademarks. All brand names and product names used in this book are trade names, service marks, trademarks or registered trademarks of their respective owners. The Publisher is not associated with any product or vendor mentioned in this book.

This publication is designed to provide accurate and authoritative information in regard to the subject matter covered. It is sold on the understanding that the Publisher is not engaged in rendering professional services. If professional advice or other expert assistance is required, the services of a competent professional should be sought.

Other Wiley Editorial Offices

John Wiley & Sons Inc., 111 River Street, Hoboken, NJ 07030, USA
Jossey-Bass, 989 Market Street, San Francisco, CA 94103-1741, USA
Wiley-VCH Verlag GmbH, Boschstr. 12, D-69469 Weinheim, Germany
John Wiley & Sons Australia Ltd, 42 McDougall Street, Milton, Queensland 4064, Australia
John Wiley & Sons (Asia) Pte Ltd, 2 Clementi Loop #02-01, Jin Xing Distripark, Singapore 129809
John Wiley & Sons Canada Ltd, 6045 Freemont Blvd. Mississauga, Ontario, L5R 4J3 Canada

Wiley also publishes its books in a variety of electronic formats. Some content that appears in print may not be available in electronic books.

Library of Congress Cataloging-in-Publication Data

A catalogue record for this book is available from the Library of Congress

British Library Cataloguing in Publication Data

A catalogue record for this book is available from the British Library

ISBN 978-0-470-71712-7

Typeset in 11/15 pt Times by SNP Best-set Typesetter Ltd., Hong Kong
Printed and bound in Great Britain by TJ International Ltd, Padstow, Cornwall, UK

This book is printed on acid-free paper responsibly manufactured from sustainable forestry in which at least two trees are planted for each one used for paper production.

Contents

About the authors

Andreas Buchholz, Wolfram Wördemann and Ned Wiley all began their professional careers at Procter & Gamble, where they occupied executive positions in marketing. Buchholz and Wördemann are management consultants for the development of 'topline' growth strategies, and have published numerous articles in the professional press, including the *Harvard Business Manager*. Wiley is the managing director of a new media operation of the Axel Springer group.

Foreword

This is a book written by marketing experts for entrepreneurs. Not for corporate employees seeking to work their way up the ladder, but for those who, whatever their status, look upon business as a creative and even risky task. It presents a Game Strategy which is based on an understanding of how to change, rather than follow the conventions of the marketplace. As the authors themselves suggest, this Game Strategy is designed for contrarians, 'for people who think big and free.' So be forewarned. This is *not* a handbook for the grey flannel bureaucrat.

But as the authors also argue, they have devised a truly democratic tool. You don't have to be rich or prestigious, you don't have to sit on a world-beating new technology in order to apply these guidelines. You don't even have to have gone to business school. Its recommendations are applicable to the most dynamic independent corporate mogul or to a assistant beginning in the marketing division of Procter & Gamble, where the three authors began their careers. As the authors point out, the wisdom in this work is not limited to marketing or to business. They present a philosophy and a practical method for dealing creatively with challenges,whatever their origin. In fact, the authors suggest that political campaigns are perfect places to begin the study of their theories of Role Games and patterns.

Most surprising about the ideas in *The Impossible Advantage* is that they haven't been widely spread among business and management schools for years. The authors have combed the literature and believe that their ideas have never before been presented as we have them in this book. I believe them, because if the ideas presented here had been revealed even in a less comprehensive form, they would long ago have been applied as one of the basic methods of problem solving at training schools all over the world.

This is one of those books which is almost obvious in the retrospective, but hard to imagine beforehand. Of course Ryanair owed its success to the way in which it created an entirely new concept for airline operations! They changed the rules of the Game. Of course the Swatch turned the entire chronologue industry on its head. Building your business on a cheap plastic watch broke every convention of the tradition-laden international watch industry. The analysis we are given as to why Ryanair or Swatch were in fact rule changing products are so logical, you wonder why you didn't think of them yourself.

The basic point of this book is that simple: '... those players that take control of the rules in a competitive game enjoy a remarkable advantage over other players that strictly play by the rules.'

I knew that when I was ten years old. I used to tip over the Monopoly board every time my brother got too far ahead and demand that we start again. I usually got slugged in return. That was the risk-taking part of the strategy. But somehow I knew that the rules on the back of the box didn't always serve my interests. What I didn't know was how to turn this audacious behavior into a strategy for business success.

To correct that deficit, the authors take us through their strategy step-by-step. We start out learning exactly what a game is and is not. We then learn about the origin of rules and what they say about our culture. The authors then explain the concept of Game Masters, the persons and institutions who make up the rules. We are also introduced to the concept of the Game Changer, the person who turns the rules on end.

This is where it gets exciting. The authors point out that games in the marketplace are different from set piece games such as sporting competitions or Monopoly for that matter. In the marketplace, some of the players are also Rule Makers. 'They are changing the rules of a game to their own advantage *while they are playing it*. Compared to ordinary players, they enjoy an advantage that would be nothing less than "impossible" in any formal game or competition.'

Formality versus flexibility. This is not a theory about *breaking* formal rules enforced by a higher authority. It is a strategy for *changing* the 'collection of prevailing ideas, concepts and conventions which competitors believe they must respect if they are to win.' Amazingly, large percentages of business respondents believe that to be successful, they must abide by the established rules of the marketplace, whatever they are. Thus, Game Changers enjoy 'An Impossible Advantage.'

This book takes you through the methods of gaining this 'impossible advantage' in considerable detail. They provide both analysis of how the market functions and of how to devise a strategy for success. It is from this standpoint, a hands-on guidebook for success. At the same time, it is peppered with fascinating historical background, from how the rules for soccer football were set by a group of persons in a room in England in the 1870's to how an Indian-born economics Professor provided insights based on Game Strategy to help integrate poor countries into the globalized economy.

In fact, while the authors work hard to remain true to their marketing origins, they have written a book well-designed to help us understand many of the perplexing challenges of the globalized age. For most of its history, human society has generally been a fairly disorganized undertaking. Formal rules of business, government and national behavior are generally less than 300 years old. Game Changers were more widespread than were Game Masters for most of human history.

And that was the problem. As the industrial revolution gained steam, society could no longer tolerate the proliferation of Game Changers who had guided its affairs until then. Modern science and technology demands standardization and discipline. Wars are no longer friendly fights among rival Barons. They became catastrophic in their destructive effects. Game Changers became frowned upon. The Game Masters took over and the corporate bureaucrat was born.

The past twenty years have witnessed both dramatic advances in science and technology and an amazing release of human energy which accompanied the end of the Cold War. Whether they know it or not, the Game Masters are being swept away. Both political and industrial structures are changing fast. The result is confusion and at times conflict. Our 21st Century world is in desperate need of creative methods for understanding the new rules of a new age.

The Impossible Advantage will not answer all of the questions being thrown at us at the moment. But it can give us a very important framework for analyzing the confusion which has overtaken our societies and for helping understand how to overcome it. I wish specialists and general readers alike an enlightening journey through these chapters. I am sure you will enjoy it.

John C. Kornblum
Berlin, January 2009

John Kornblum served as an American diplomat for more than 30 years before retiring in 2001 as Ambassador to Germany. Since then he has served as Chairman of Lazard Freres Germany (2002–2008) and as a private advisor to a number of German and American firms. He has also served on the Advisory Boards of Bayer, Thyssen-Krupp Technologies, Motorola Europe and Russell Reynolds. Ambassador Kornblum lives in Berlin.

The surprising limitation of the World's Number One business strategy

There are almost as many business strategies as there are stars in the sky, but throughout the 1980s, one of these strategies took root in the business landscape in a manner never seen before. We refer to the concept of 'Positioning'. First introduced by Al Ries and Jack Trout in the 1970s, Positioning began its rise to prominence with their 1981 classic book, *Positioning – The Battle for Your Mind.*

The dominant role of Positioning as a business strategy is perhaps no better demonstrated than in a simple Google search. At the time of publication, a search for the keyword 'Positioning' returns six times as many results as the term 'business strategy', four times as many as the name of the US president and about as many as the high profile 'climate change.' Not bad for something originally conceived as an aid in the development of advertising campaigns!

WHY THERE ARE LIMITS TO THE POWER OF POSITIONING

Positioning has achieved this status of distinction because of its undeniable success. Brands have been built and companies founded on the basis of solid and distinctive Positionings. When it all first started about twenty years ago, the few corporations using smart Positioning techniques were able to achieve a lasting head start in the Competitive Game. The three authors of this book all started their careers at one of the world's most respected 'schools of marketing,' Procter & Gamble. Positioning was – and remains – at the heart and soul of P&G's marketing and advertising planning process. Nothing can be started without a succinct, precise summary of a brand's fundamental Positioning, over which seemingly endless energy is expended in refining, polishing and perfecting, producing in the end a crystal-clear brand strategy statement.

Is Positioning still as powerful as it used to be? For the very reason that Positioning is now pretty much a standard tool in marketing, we are facing a situation today where you can expect that the majority of your competitors are as skilled in developing clever Positioning strategies as the marketing professionals in your own company. In other words, the concept of Positioning has substantially contributed to taking the Competitive Game to a higher level. Your own company, for instance, is undoubtedly playing the Game in the marketplace on a higher level these days than ten or twenty years ago – but so are most of your competitors. That is why we believe that it is time to stretch our strategic thinking a bit *beyond Positioning*.

It has always been the most natural thing in the world to compare competition with a game – just like football, basketball, baseball, tennis or chess. If we take that metaphor seriously, 'Positioning' is very much what the players do in any type of game to achieve a strategic or tactical advantage over competitors. Football players 'position' themselves, as do tennis players or chess players. Using the 'game' metaphor leads us to making an important statement about Positioning – and about its inherent limitation.

'Positioning' is what players do to achieve a competitive advantage. But when choosing their Positioning on the field (or marketplace), the players must respect certain limitations, namely the rules of the Game. These rules are accepted as part of the untouchable framework conditions in a game. In that sense, the rules of the Game limit your Positioning options as a player.[1]

It is as simple as that. The 64 squares of a chess field limit the Positioning possibilities of a chess player. Obviously, no chess player in the world – no matter how ingenious he may be – can position his figures *beyond* those 64 squares. That's what the rules of the chess game define – and not even in our fondest dreams

---

[1] We recognize that Trout and Ries referred to a 'Positioning in the consumer's mind' as opposed to a 'Positioning in the marketplace.' However, the term as generally used today is more likely to be the latter.

would we try to shake or break or reinvent those rules. What about the Competitive Game in business life?

As consultants and business executives we have observed over many years how companies in the most diverse business sectors deal with these 'laws and rules' of the 'Competitive Game' in the market. The vast majority act much like this chess player: they blindly respect the rules – as if they knew they were sure to lose if they shake, break or change them. At first glance, this makes a lot of sense, but then again, once in a while you come across a company or corporation that does *exactly the opposite*. By changing the rules of the Game, they liberate themselves from any limitations that stand in the way of dramatic and sustainable growth. By shaking or changing the rules, you can fundamentally 'rock your market,' dethrone competitors and achieve a sustainable leadership position. Most interestingly, it seems that any company can do this – even if they do not have a breakthrough product innovation or a market leader position or unlimited funds.

THE RULE MAKER'S 'IMPOSSIBLE' ADVANTAGE

Quite logically, those players that take control of the rules in a Competitive Game enjoy a remarkable advantage over other players who strictly play by the rules. In any formal game or competition, this would be unheard of, bizarre, virtually impossible. The rules are 'taboo' for the players – it is as simple as that. However, the Game in the marketplace is different: the players are also making the rules. Well, at least some of them do while the vast majority of players in the marketplace are happy with just playing along. They do not know much about the rules, let alone the fine art of changing them to their own advantage. Have you ever wondered what the 'laws and the rules' in *your* market really are and where they are coming from? Nobody has ever articulated or expressed these rules – neither in spoken words nor in writing. So why do we all believe we need to respect them and that we will fail in the Competitive Game if we don't? Where do the rules come from? How does winning and losing in the marketplace depend on the rules of the Competitive Game – as opposed to more tangible competitive factors like product quality and innovation? How can you find out whether the rules of the Game are helping your company or whether they stand in the way of success? Most importantly, how can *one company* – yours, for instance – change the rules of the Game in *your* market to *your* own benefit?

This is the new aspect of business success that our book will address. To the best of our knowledge, it is the first publication of this kind. Go through the tons of business literature, methods and strategies, principles, insights and panaceas of the last twenty years. You won't find much – if anything – about the rules of the Game in the marketplace. And most certainly, you won't find out anywhere else why and how *any* company has the opportunity to change them to their own advantage.

GAME CHANGING STRATEGIES START WHERE POSITIONING STOPS

It was our realization that the ubiquitous concept of 'Positioning' had several inherent limitations that was the impetus for our development of what we call 'Game Strategy.' The fundamental premise of Game Strategy is that participants in the market can in fact change the so-called rules of the market, *while the Game is being played.* These participants are actually able to intervene in the underlying processes and rules governing the market, take control of them and turn them to their own advantage.

Game Strategy recognizes that the rules of the market can be changed and turned into powerful levers for growth and market success. In this way, Game Strategy is ultimately able to produce significant changes in the prevailing power relationships in the market.

In this book, we will demonstrate through concrete case histories across a broad range of product and service categories how individual firms are able to overturn apparently inviolable market rules, and in so doing dethrone previously all-powerful market leaders. We will also show how not only large and powerful companies are able to change the rules of the marketplace, but also smaller firms or even newcomers.

This book will show you four specific kinds of Game Strategy through which you, too, will be able to alter, modify and change the rules to your own advantage.

The 'Positioning' concept implicitly respects the laws and the rules of the market as part of the untouchable framework conditions in the Competitive Game. 'Game Strategy' goes further,

challenging those rules and laws, modifying them and turning them into powerful levers for growth, and thereby shifting the market's prevailing power relationships.

Game Strategy is something all firms, large, small or medium sized, can use to their advantage. It does not require breakthrough technical innovation or extraordinary levels of marketing and sales investments. It *does* require a fresh, new way of thinking.

SIX PREJUDICES TO IGNORE

In most situations in life we are used to following rules that somebody else defined – and only rarely do we assume the role of the 'rule maker.' From earliest childhood, most of us have been taught and trained to follow rules – and were punished if we broke them and frustrated if we tried to change them. All of life's experiences teach us the same thing: 'If you want to win the Game, you have to follow the rules.'

Game Strategy works only when you are prepared to challenge previously accepted rules and laws, and do so with absolutely no 'taboos' in your thinking. You have to ignore mental prejudices, such as these:

1. 'The only ones who can change the rules of the Game are the big players, the market leaders, the guys with huge resources and all the time they need. That's not our situation. We don't have either the capital or time needed. At the end of it all, we would end up stretched way beyond our limits.'
2. 'The rules in our market have evolved over years, or decades, or even centuries. They are what they are, and that's that. As a single company, all on our own, we can't do much about it.'
3. 'By the rules of the Game, I'm talking about legislation, namely the political, regulatory and legal framework conditions in the marketplace. That's why we have lobbyists, whose job is to represent our interests to the politicians. Our lobbyists will do whatever is possible in the political arena.'
4. 'Why should I risk everything by trying to change the rules of my market? We have more than enough problems in trying to sell our current products and services. That's where we have to put 100% of our focus.'

5. 'Sure, it would be great to revolutionize the market, but to do that you've got to have a technological breakthrough or a truly groundbreaking product innovation. There's just no realistic chance of that. So we had better play it safe.'

6. 'Lots of people have tried to change the rules of the market and all they have to show for it is a big black eye. Too risky. If we try it, things will spin out of control, and then the competition and the media will finish us off. We just cannot afford to take that risk.'

By and large, these reservations are very understandable. However, they all impose drastic limits to the kind of thinking and perspective needed to realize truly outstanding potential in the marketplace. Only if you accept no taboos in your thinking will you be able to recognize and capitalize on all of the opportunities the market offers.

Our analysis and conclusions are all based on real case histories and supported by our collective experience as managers and consultants across a broad range of business sectors. The Game Strategy thought process is applicable to managers in all sectors, at all levels of the organization and across all professional disciplines. We have consciously avoided a lot of the marketing and management jargon all too often used in this field, in order to encourage a range of managers from different disciplines to get personally involved with the critical issue of marketplace growth.

After reading this book, we hope you will have a very different view of your market, your competition, your own position in the market and certainly your own growth potential. Above all, we hope to have offered you a new way of thinking, able to give you the inspiration needed to steer the way to dramatic growth in the years ahead. With this in mind, let's get ready to find out how Game Strategy works!

It's time to think radically about growth

A recent survey showed that over 80% of all managers in companies of any size believe it is critical to understand and follow the rules of the Game in the marketplace, if they want to count among the winners. While that may be true, our observation is that the biggest winners are those that do the exact opposite. Firms that throw the conventions of the market overboard and invent their own game. These companies – we call them 'Game Masters' or 'Game Changers' – are the ones who come up with the real marketplace breakthroughs and achieve astonishing growth – not just a few tenths of a market share point but big, even leadership, shares. Here's the good news: the art of these Game Masters is something you can learn. There are tried and tested strategies for success that in principle 'anyone' can employ. All you have to do is change your entire way of thinking!

Let us start with an example from the airline business, in Europe, in 1985. Tony Ryan is an Irish entrepreneur who has just founded a new airline, called (what else?) Ryanair. His aim is to challenge the national flag carrier Aer Lingus. Tony's company gets big quickly – unfortunately, so do its debts. After three years of trying, Ryanair stands on the brink of bankruptcy. Tony then hires a chartered accountant by the name of Michael O'Leary to tackle this problem. After having a quick look at the sad state of affairs, Michael tells Tony to close the books and call it a day. What he doesn't count on is Tony's strength of will: he refuses to fail and hires O'Leary as CEO, giving him a simple brief: 'Turn it around.' The rest, as they say, is history.

SOMEONE COMMITTED TO BREAKING ALL THE RULES

O'Leary didn't have any time to lose, but what he did was nothing less than lay the foundations for a completely new market in Europe: budget air travel.

Borrowing from the US success story of Southwest Airlines, O'Leary created this market in Europe out of not a lot more than 'thin air.' He started from scratch, throwing out almost all the 'rules and laws' of the traditional airline business.

First, O'Leary asked himself a lot of questions: Where is it written in stone that airlines have to fly from major metropolitan centers? Nowhere, so he decided that Ryanair should fly exclusively from second-tier airports in provincial cities and towns. Who needs complicated route structures? Ryanair routes are without exception point to point. Who says that only long distance routes are profitable? O'Leary built an extremely efficient 'shuttle' service on short routes. Why do you need to have a fleet made up of different types of aircraft? Ryanair concentrates on one single model of airplane. What's the point of business class? Why have an airport lounge? Why do you need check-in terminals at the airport, employing expensive staff? To cut down on staffing, Ryanair runs almost all of its booking through the Internet or a call center. Why does everyone seem to believe that on-board service is a 'must'? To further reduce staff, Ryanair avoids any kind of in-flight entertainment or free meals. Under O'Leary, the company even got rid of free peanuts, not because they were particularly expensive, but rather because they increased cabin cleaning costs. Which law says that an airline has to make money on the transporting of passengers? Ryanair makes its profit on ancillary businesses: O'Leary established partnerships with firms in the tourism business. He rents out the space on the back of his seats to advertisers instead of having a seatback pocket. He sells meals, snacks and drinks. Most recently, he has announced plans to launch a fee-charging, in-flight Internet telephone service. This collection of related businesses represents a full 16% of total revenues, and is projected to rise to 25%. O'Leary even dreams of one day giving away the flight tickets! You pay for the other bits and pieces, but the flight is on Ryanair.

In a nutshell, Ryanair broke with just about every single established convention and rule in the market. O'Leary reinvented flying and his new low-cost airline market operates according to totally different rules and laws. As a result, the new type of airline transports double the number of passengers for half the cost of traditional carriers. A flight from London to Linz (or from Frankfurt to Fuerteventura for that matter) costs about 10 euros. That's flying at the price of a taxi, assuming, of course, that you only take the cab to the corner store.

Budget Air Travel Runs Wild

Here is a boom like nothing we've seen for a long time. One of the world's most traditional markets was so fundamentally reinvented that it defied the laws of global competition. September 11, 2001 plunged the entire global tourism industry into a deep crisis. To everyone's amazement, that is exactly when the low-cost airline boom began. Like mushrooms, budget flyers sprang up out of the ground all across Europe and proved to an astonished financial world that – in sharp contrast to traditional 'premium' airlines – they could make fistfuls of profits during a major economic downturn. When things were at their absolute nadir – 2003 – Ryanair placed an order with Boeing for 100 brand new planes at a cost of over sixty billion dollars O'Leary was able to negotiate a hefty 40% discount and smiled when commenting on the event: 'During the time after September 11, 2001, I was the only one who called Boeing wanting to place an order.'

The big, state-owned airlines were put in a tremendous squeeze. It was therefore no surprise when they responded by creating their own low-cost copycats – like Lufthansa with GermanWings – but all to no avail: the original low-cost airlines, with faster turnarounds and city-to-city 'shuttle' services, just had too much of an advantage on the short haul routes. At one point, British Airways considered throwing in the towel, and concentrating exclusively on long haul routes. It looks like 'David' is putting the big, national 'Goliath' under quite a bit of pressure!

Then came the ultimate symbolic triumph in the battle with the national airlines: just a week after the Irish government privatized Aer Lingus, O'Leary made a takeover bid for the national carrier to a tune of about 1.5 billion euros. Panic spread through the Irish government, who at first refused to relinquish their 25% share in the flag carrier.

At this point, low-cost airlines were no longer a niche market, but the growth motor for the entire sector. By 2004, in Europe alone, there were 54 low cost airlines, with a collective market share of 30 to 35%. By 2010, low-cost carriers are projected to account for about 40% of the market. The greatest beneficiary of this trend is the company that started it all: Ryanair, with an annual turnover today of over 2.7 billion euros and a pre-tax profit of 480 million euros. Before the end of this decade, Ryanair is a serious contender to become the largest airline in Europe, by almost all standards of measurement.

The Revolution Gains Momentum and Affects Adjacent Markets

Provincial airports used to be pleasant, sleepy little places, with a lot of historical charm. Not since budget carriers came to be. The former US Airforce base at Hahn in northern Germany has announced an expansion plan costing 200 million euros. The German federal government wants to revive old decommissioned rail connections to Hahn at a cost of 100 million euros. And here's one crazy fact: not only is the operator of the main Frankfurt airport, Fraport, involved with Hahn's revival, but so is Lufthansa, through its participation in Fraport. The media has loads of fun with the fact that Lufthansa is actually helping its low-cost competitors to grow even larger.

Lots of other industries have been affected, in some surprising areas. Take, for instance, the bus business: the manufacturers' association reports declines in new registrations for tour and city buses in the range of 10%. The leading German newspaper, *FAZ*, reports 'Low-cost airlines are a plague on the bus industry.' Even the national railways cannot avoid the effect of budget flyers: first class luxury train service from Cologne to Hamburg had to be downgraded to a normal service. According to the head of the German railways, Hartmut Mehdorn, since the arrival of budget air travel, the luxury train simply no longer made economic sense.

Tour companies are also complaining: the CEO of Alltours, Verhuven, said that it is 'absurd' when a train ticket from Düsseldorf to Frankfurt costs more than a plane ticket from Düsseldorf to Rome. His solution is government price controls in the form of 'national minimum air ticket prices' together with a ban on all forms of subsidies for low-cost airlines – this from the man running one of the leaders in the low-cost travel sector.

One of the other side-effects of the structural change caused by the boom in low-cost air travel has been *unprecedented competition among airports*. Airport authorities across Europe are fighting furiously to secure low-cost airlines. The appeal of these carriers is the highly profitable 'nonaviation' business: duty-free shops, restaurants, boutiques and parking garages. These businesses represent together almost 30% of an airport's total revenues. Who would have thought it possible: *airports fighting tooth and nail for low-cost carriers!* The winners, the ones who secure slots for the budget carriers, will have to introduce new standards of speed and efficiency, probably through outsourcing. Now that business travelers have discovered the advantages of low-cost carriers, even the biggest airports are going to have to get downright dirty to compete with their cheaper provincial rivals. 'Any airport not slotting low-cost airlines is going to find it tough going in the future,' according to one industry source.

Not surprisingly, local politicians are also jumping on the budget airline bandwagon as a means to enhance the attractiveness of their locations. Take, for example, Weeze am Niederrhein, not exactly a household name, but near the Dutch border and the beneficiary of an array of state subsidies geared to attract low-cost carriers and thereby maintain jobs in an otherwise economically distressed region.

The low-cost airline boom shows no sign of relenting. On the contrary, it is now migrating from Europe to Russia, Asia and Africa. Especially in Asia, low-cost travel is the foundation for air travel as a whole, offering accessible flights to a huge emerging middle class for whom flying used to be a dream beyond their reach. Asia has over 130 cities with a population in excess of a million, but without a single international flight connection: these are the first targets of the low-cost carriers. Growth is so dramatic that infrastructure lags far behind. Indian and African operators are forced to hire staff from abroad and build airports on 24-hour construction schedules. Of course, now the low-cost carriers face new challenges, in the form of exploding fuel costs and a worldwide economic downturn. But the airline business will never be the same again.

Get Your Mind Ready for Game Strategy

If you want to benefit from Game Strategy, you must be prepared for a different way of thinking. You need to be inspired by something greater than next quarter's financials. You have got to *crave a greater measure of growth* than you have committed to in your ordinary annual business plan. What does it take to achieve a real breakthrough in the market or turn around a disastrous sales decline? Let's assume you don't have a secret, groundbreaking innovation in the pipeline and you don't have a limitless supply of capital. Now what? Do you still have a real-istic chance of marketplace success? Yes, you most certainly do! There are lots of examples of companies that have done just that, including some that started out very small indeed. Newcomers, too. Our conclusion is that no company should accept there is a good reason why they *cannot* be the next success story in their market.

One thing ought to be clear at this point: if you want dramatically greater growth in the marketplace, you obviously cannot just continue with the same strategies, the same tools and the same kind of thinking that was good enough to get you to where you stand now. Start by thinking differently and not just differently from the competition, but literally liberate yourself from your past thinking routines and past strategy templates.

If you want breakthrough growth, you have got to go beyond conventional business thinking and today's standard strategy routines. If they have not generated the next great idea in the past, how can they provide the crucial, decisive inspiration the future demands?

How Rule Breakers Change the Competitive Game

Michael O'Leary is going well beyond 'Positioning' his airline: instead of simply playing along with the other competitors, he created entirely new conditions in the market and started a new game based on his own rules. He put himself above all of the laws and conventions that had defined the airline business for decades, threw out the rules of the market and *created the conditions* for a spectacular success story. Nothing, but nothing, was sacred to O'Leary.

Why take off from the big airports in metropolitan centers? Why have complicated route structures? Why have expensive administration, why check-in terminals? Who needs business class or airport lounges? Why not make money with additional services? Why can't flying be for free?

That is what makes 'Game Masters' different: they measure their goals against the rules of the Game and then defy those rules or establish new ones. That doesn't mean they pigheadedly go against all norms and standards, but they are prepared to do so when the conventional rules of the Game stand in their way and limit opportunities to grow their business. That is what distinguishes them from the other players in the market, the ones who slavishly adhere to accepted rules. The entire crew of distinguished managers in the European airline industry behaved in a time-honored fashion for decades, and many of them did very well in the process. Then from out of the blue comes Ryanair and turns the Competitive Game upside down.

Rule breakers and Game Changers tend *not* to be the old hands in the market, but rather are newcomers and outsiders. Up to the end of the 1990s, the head of Lufthansa, Jürgen Weber, insisted that there was no market for low-cost airlines in Germany. O'Leary scoffed back, 'How the devil does he know that? I'll bet the Germans will crawl over broken glass to get them.'

Revolutions Need 'Game Changing Ideas' More Than Anything Else

When O'Leary started out, he didn't have a lot going for him: no technological innovation, not a single patent, no meaningful financial capital. In fact, he was looking at a huge mountain of debt. He didn't possess any marketing dominance and he wasn't much more than a speck of dust on the market's radar screen.

Even the idea of low-cost air travel wasn't new, but something as old as the twelve-year Irish whiskey O'Leary was known to imbibe on occasion. He 'borrowed' the idea from Southwest Airlines in Texas. For twelve long years this idea had been aging in the cellar of the industry, but none of the old hands took any notice of it.

O'Leary wasn't smarter, more intelligent, more creative or more experienced than other airline managers. What he did possess was a large measure of audacious, free, radical thinking. He had a combination of fresh perspective and an ingrained lack of respect for rules of any kind. As a university student, he had his Mercedes registered as a taxi in order to drive on the bus lanes of Dublin's streets. O'Leary is a notorious contrarian. It is not for nothing that leading business magazines characterize him as the 'mad Irishman,' the 'Irish Asterix,' the 'pirate of the sky.'

It's Time to Venture Beyond Conventional Business Strategies

There are lots of proven business strategies. They all claim to show how to generate growth – most of the time, however, they do this within the 'accepted' parameters of the marketplace. But where are the textbooks, where are the strategy experts, the business gurus who have ever asked, 'What are the rules of the marketplace game? Who made them? How do they influence the Game in the market? Who uses them and who suffers from them? Who can influence them, and how exactly do you do that?'

Game Strategy starts where most business strategies stop, with the rules of the market, and goes on to demonstrate how those rules can be reinvented, deliberately and systematically.

Game Strategy focuses some very bright spotlights on the rules of the Game. That is something new. Our reason for doing this is simple: the biggest success stories come from companies that break the accepted rules of the Game and, in so doing, achieve tremendous growth.

Game Strategy should not be viewed as a *substitute* for other proven strategic approaches. It should be looked on as a way to create a dramatic shift in the market, without any need for limitless resources.

Game Strategy is designed for contrarians, for people who think big and free. Its source of inspiration is a radical and free approach. Game Strategy helps you to dissolve old thought patterns and unleash your mind. Who among us is completely free of templates, blinkers and tunnel vision? What we offer you with Game Strategy is an array of exciting case histories, we will show you how you can form, dominate, steer, change or even reinvent the marketplace game. The skills we put on offer are not only useful, but downright fun!

GAMES AS A STRATEGIC MODEL

Let's start at the beginning, with what seems like a very simple question, but which in fact turns out to be extremely complex: *What is a game?* Every child knows what it means to play, but for some reason it takes philosophers, encyclopaedists, academic experts in culture and behavioral theory, mathematicians and Nobel Prize winners to arrive at a halfway reasonable definition. Not surprisingly, a lot of these attempts to define play become academic, turgid and inaccessible; they lose all of the freshness, spontaneity and creativity that should be at the heart of playing.

Fortunately for this book – and for our strategic model – a pragmatic rule of thumb and one-line definition is sufficient:

A Game is any form of competition governed by rules.

That's just fine. To get started you don't need a more detailed definition. This single sentence is enough, because it gets to the essence of the matter: the rules of the Game. Those rules are what differentiate games from other 'unruly' forms of competition – primitive battles, for example, fought according to the 'law of the jungle.'

Competition in the marketplace is 'regulated' as we will see despite occasional complaints about unscrupulous 'predatory capitalism'. Obviously, this is a dramatic distortion of the truth. By and large, no one doubts that the often cited 'rules and laws of the marketplace' also apply today. The rules of the Game fulfill the fundamental function of providing that degree of 'order' that permits the Game to function at all.

A Brief Trip Back in Time to the Origin of the Rules of the Game

In dimmest pre-history, the 'law of the jungle' prevailed, while today regulated competition applies. How did this change come about? *Where do games and rules come from?*

Scientists have made a connection between the origin of games and the origin of culture more broadly. Human evolution is based on four essential factors: (1) the development of language; (2) the invention and use of tools; (3) the mastery of fire and (4) the development of explicit rules that define living together in society. Cultural historians speak of *'Homo ludens'* – the playing man – and contrast him with *'Homo sapiens'*, the 'wise man'. As part of the process of becoming human, the primitive 'laws of the jungle' are gradually replaced by social rules. The individual must subordinate his own interests to the interests of the group in which he lives. Conflicts of interest are handled in a 'regulated' manner.

The discovery of games and their rules represents a cultural and historical achievement, and ultimately a milestone on the long evolutionary path from apes to man. There is still a long way to go from there to classical, formal games, such as board games or those involving dice and athletic competitions. The first board game on record dates to the year 2800 BC and takes us to ancient Egypt. The first recorded athletic competition was the Olympic Games, held for the first time in Greece in 776 BC.

The rules of the Game for the marketplace are as old as the marketplace itself. As soon as man built cities, he also founded markets, with a kind of behavioral code that 'regulated' the commercial games of the time. During the Middle Ages, market practices were controlled by trade guilds. Even today, some fragments of these old codes of honor survive – in the ethics of the Hanseatic trader or the Italian *correttezza commerciale*.

The Second, Higher Level of Games

Over time, the rules of the Game became highly differentiated and formalized, in order to create an orderly competitive framework. The rules served to regulate the ways and means to deal with negotiations, conflicts of interest and competition generally. The rules of the Game regulated the behavior of all parties involved with the Game.

This historical cultural principle requires one logical premise. The rules of the Game *must be beyond the reach and control of the players.* What is the point of a system of order when the competitors – or a select, privileged few among them – can take control of the rules, change them according to their own preferences, possibly even during a competitive event? That would reduce the concept of order to an absurdity. For this reason, it is only logical to require that *the rules of the Game are 'taboo' for the competing parties.*

Even the world's most individual, free-spirited and dare we say egomaniacal players respect the taboo surrounding games. Imagine the tennis zealot John McEnroe, the football fanatic Zidane or the ear-biting boxer Mike Tyson: They may have objected strenuously to *interpretations* of the rules of the Game, but they never questioned the rules themselves. Have you ever heard of a top athlete who wanted to destroy, revolutionize or reinvent the rules of their game? Of course not; the rules of the Game enjoy an almost 'sacrosanct' status among the competitors.

However, what about competitors in the marketplace? In general, they have a comparable respect for the 'rules and laws' of the market. Everyone wants to do their best, to play the best possible game and demonstrate their competitive strengths according to the rules. Companies invest fortunes in market and trend research in order to better understand the rules and laws of the market, and then orient themselves to those rules. Touching the rules and laws of the market is something that lies within the taboo zone for most managers and entrepreneurs. By and large, that is a good thing.

Accordingly, there must be a second, higher level of the Game, a kind of 'meta-level,' on which the rules of the Game are conceived, fashioned, administered and controlled. In the case of classic, formal games, control of the rules rests in the hands of an external authority. It is called FIFA for football, FIDE for chess or FIA in Formula 1 racing. These organizations have the power to define, modify, change, overthrow or reformulate the rules of the Game. In the vocabulary of Game Strategy, they are called 'Game Masters.'

In classic, formal games, the Game Masters and Rule Makers sit on a second, higher level. That second level becomes the supervisory, control and power level of the Game.

A First Visit to the Second Level: How Rule Makers Make the Rules

To learn more about what happens on this somewhat mysterious second game level, let's take the example of football. Football is thought to have originated in the early Middle Ages in England. Two neighboring villages tried to put a ball through the opposing village's town gate. The football field was the level expanse separating the two villages. At first, there were no rules to the Game.

Now let's put ourselves on the second game level and fast-forward through the historical origins of football rules, looking over the shoulders of the 'Rule Makers' of the time. It all started when a few Cambridge students defined the first football regulations. From that point on, a team consisted of between 15 and 20 players. In 1863, football enthusiasts founded the 'Football Association' (FA) and devised an extensive body of rules. In 1866, the offside rule was changed: a player was subsequently judged offside only when he came into possession of the ball with fewer than two opponents in front of him. During the same period, corner kicks and free kicks were introduced. In 1870, the number of players was reduced to 11 on a side. One year later, the English Football Association prohibited the handball. At that point, American Football split off as a separate sport and eliminated scoring of goals with the foot; in its place, the touchdown was introduced. The penalty kick followed in 1891 and various types of penalties for intentional and willful foul play were established in 1897, as was the notion of 'extra time.' In 1896, the Jena Rules specified that the playing field had to be free of trees and bushes. Since 1924, a corner kick was allowed to go directly into the goal. Since 1970, we have had yellow and red cards. In 1996, for the first time a 'golden goal' was introduced in the European Championship, meaning that the football match ended with the first goal scored in extra time.

This excursion to the second level demonstrates how 'strange' it is to us. During a game, most people focus entirely on the first level, the playing field. This *interior perspective* of the Game is something we are all familiar with. From the second level of the Game, however, we have a completely new vantage point, the *exterior perspective* of the Game. This change in perspective is extremely exciting, because:

From the Interior Perspective, the Rules of the Game always seem to be fixed – even irrevocable rules of nature. But from the second game level, the Rules of the Game appear to be the exact opposite: they become creative control and steering instruments.

Just imagine: in 1870, the members of the London Football Association sat around and came up with the rules of football. They were the Game and Rule Makers, and brought with them all of their ideas, ideals and vision. Even more specifically, what was going on when an Irishman by the name of William McCrum invented the penalty kick in 1891? How did he decide it should be precisely 11 meters – why not 13 meters, 15 meters or 30 meters? How many football games around the world would have turned out differently, if William McCrum would have defined the penalty kick differently – or if he never invented that rule al all?

Of course, this is all speculation, but it does dramatically demonstrate what distinguishes a Game Master from a normal player. Game Masters look at the rules of the Game as instruments that permit them to shape the Game according to their own ideas.

It is completely different for the typical football player or fan. He concentrates entirely on the interior perspective of the Game. He is entrapped by the Game and the emotions it inspires. As a general rule, he opposes any changes in the rules, which are holy for him. Just try sometime discussing with a football fan whether football doesn't need a major rules revision. More likely than not, you'll see his face covered with blood, sweat and tears. For him, the rules are untouchable: they are within the taboo zone.

How Game Masters Deliberately Steer and Control the Game

The example of football shows just how powerful the second game level can be. Taking the matter one step further, you can see that the Game Masters and Rule Makers actually become strategic thinkers and planners. They design their regulations in an entirely calculating manner, because they want to take the Game in a certain direction. They grasp the structures and mechanisms of competition, and are able to change or dramatically shift the balance of power among the competitors.

One example is Formula 1 racing, which is not just a fascinating and hugely popular sport, but also a billion dollar global business. On the second game level you find two Game Masters: the operating firm SLEC, built around the legendary founder, Bernie Ecclestone, and the FIA, racing's umbrella organization.

These Formula 1 authorities are always engaged in constantly revising the enormously complex set of rules and regulations for the sport. Just about every year, a complete new package of rules is issued. Legitimate business interests naturally govern the Rule Makers. They analyze the sport and develop it further, so that it continues to remain exciting to the mass market and attractive to new prospects. We can observe one specific interest that drives the Rule Makers, which is critical to our thinking, namely Formula 1 racing should be first and foremost a 'competition for the best driver' as opposed to a 'competition for the best high-tech engineers.' The Formula 1 authorities want to give a chance to smaller, private teams – such as the 'Red Bull' team – in addition to the big automotive concerns like Renault, Fiat, Daimler, Honda, BMW, Toyota and Ferrari. The major automobile producers have exactly the opposite interest: in order for Formula 1 racing to justify the huge investments required, they want it to serve as a showcase to demonstrate their engineering excellence. This can be seen in the example of the Tyrrell team during the early years of the Formula 1, which put a six-wheeled monster on the track. Or later in the 1970s when Renault introduced the first turbocharged engines, producing over 1000 hp and permitting them to dominate the Formula 1 sport throughout the 1980s.

Today, Formula 1 Rule Makers are steering against the 'competition of engineers,' who find their room for maneuvering constantly shrinking. The permissible rpm's for motors was cut to 19,000 in 2007, and all vehicles have to use the same type of tire. In the future, all electronics will be standardized. Then come aerodynamics. In every case, the goal appears to be a kind of homogenized technology.

If the engineers of the leading automotive firms were permitted to use their high-tech expertise to the fullest, it is quite possible to imagine there would be a significant shift in the balance of power among the various racing stables. Would the smaller, private teams be able to keep up? Would even an exceptional driver for a 'small' team ever be able to make up for the technological edge of the big firms?

In classic, formal games, the 'Game Masters' use the rules as instruments to regulate the Game as they please, that is to realize their specific (hopefully) legitimate interests and objectives.

Detecting the Game Master's 'Impossible' Advantage

The Game Master sits on the second game level in the case of classic, formal games. He enjoys absolute authority over the Game. His power is such that he can generate a dramatic shift in the balance of power among the players, as we saw in the Formula 1 example.

We can observe something comparable to the two game levels in the marketplace, where politics actively intervenes in market activities. When politicians conceive of new legislation that affects certain aspects of the market-place game, they are behaving like Game Changers. They influence marketplace events in a more radical and far-reaching manner than any of the other players could ever hope to do. Take as an example health legislation reform: for the leading pharmaceutical companies, the players on the first game level, legislation is always one of the fixed, immutable general parameters (except insofar as it can be influenced indirectly by political lobbying). However, for politicians – in their role as Game Changers – laws are exactly the opposite, namely creative instruments of control, through which they can support specific political interests. This instance of 'political regulation' is entirely understandable in the context of game thinking.

In general, political intervention is usually a side issue in a free market economy. It is part of the formal rules of the Game. However, there is also a vast range of informal rules, ultimately established by each business sector itself. In all sectors, there are established conventions that just about everyone adhere to. A successful airline must operate from the major airports. An airline has to offer meal service on board, a business class and a check-in counter. Such conventions appear to be the rules of the Game, because leading airlines around the globe have accepted them for decades. It is almost as if they were unwritten laws, and those who ignore them do so at their own peril.

> **The Rules of the Game in business is that collection of prevailing ideas, concepts and conventions that competitors believe they must respect if they are to win.**

Everyone knows that these laws of the airline business were originally established by the sector itself, but that doesn't change the point that, after a long time, they gain the status of natural laws … at least until Michael O'Leary put those rules to the test, one after another, and then threw them all overboard.

The Competitive Game in the marketplace is unique insofar as some of the players are also the Rule Makers. They are changing the rules of a game to their own advantage *while they are playing it*. Compared to ordinary players, they enjoy an advantage that would be nothing less than 'impossible' in any formal game or competition.

Now that's a real difference: in classic, formal games it is impossible to imagine that the players could 'fiddle with' the rules. Players never have access to the rules of the Game. Guys like Kimi Räikkönen, Fernando Alonso or Michael Schumacher have a lot of ways to become the world Formula 1 champion, but they do not have access to the rules governing Formula 1 racing. A chess grandmaster, however gifted he may be, will always have to limit his genius to the 64 squares on the board – even for him, changing the rules of the Game is strictly taboo.

This is precisely where the marketplace differs. Here, the Game Masters are simultaneously the players. We recently polled a number of managers across a range of business sectors, asking them: 'Do you believe that your firm has a meaningful influence on the rules and laws of the market?' Astonishingly, over 80% replied in the negative. We can conclude that they never even think strategically about how they could change the Game in their market to their own advantage. From the perspective of game thinking, this result is nothing short of shocking. It means that more than 80% of all firms are content to leave the rule making to others – even to their own competitors.

Our Thesis: The few Game Masters and Rule Makers in the marketplace always have an advantage over the majority of rule-respecting players. In the long term, they will emerge as the 'logical' winners.

Game thinking supports the somewhat radical notion that there are 'logical' winners in the market and, by consequence, 'logical' losers. Everyone talks about the marketplace game and its players and rules, and the metaphor makes a lot of common sense. It is also fairly evident that the majority of firms have no ambition to make rules or create the Game – and that some very few of them do, including some that start from a disadvantaged position, like Ryanair. The theory persists: there are 'logical' winners and 'logical' losers in the marketplace, and more often than not, the 'logical' winner, according to the model, is also the actual winner.

FOUR CLASSICAL GAME STRATEGIES

The Game Master in the marketplace doesn't have to start out larger or more powerful than the other players. On the contrary, often it is the big companies that cling to the tried and trusted rules of the Game, while entrepreneurial personalities from small or medium-sized companies have got the courage to challenge the accepted rules of the market. Simple players and Game Masters are distinguished from each other first and foremost in their way of thinking. While most players will spare no effort to find new and creative solutions for their business, at the end of the day they do this while respecting what they regard to be the rules and laws of the market.

This way of thinking prevails across all industries and sectors – and there is nothing wrong with it. It does leave considerable room for maneuvering in order to win. You can execute almost all classical business and marketing strategies within the constraints of given market conditions: product improvements or new pricing plans; line extensions; innovation; marketing, sales and communication campaigns; distribution drives; opening new markets – none of these go beyond the rules of the Game for the market in question. For that reason, it is pretty hard to criticize or condemn the thinking and action of the typical player.

However, Game Strategy starts with a completely different premise: that rules and laws for any market, and parameters in general, *by definition* pose fundamental limitations to the range of possibilities. For this reason, Game Masters look at the entire collective range of supposed general conditions when developing their strategies.

The Game Master wants to change the Game itself. He wants to control the basic market, its dynamics and the competitive confrontation. He wants to revise the rules of the market, steer them in a particular direction and turn them to his advantage.

The Game Master is able to subtly change the dynamics of the market. His decisions and actions cause changes in the underlying market mechanisms, values and structures. In all this, the Game Master is driven by the desire to create precisely those conditions he requires to generate exceptional growth.

You can find Game Masters or Game Changers at the level of global mass markets, as well as regional and specialty markets. Even relatively small players can be the source of fundamental change that creates a revolution in a billion dollar sector, as we saw in the case of Ryanair. In other cases, the Game Master can make fine, delicate 'microsurgical' moves, at first glance hardly visible, which ultimately result in considerable impact.

The actions of the Game Master can be classed in four typical or 'archetypical' strategic variations:

Game Strategy 1: Redefining the Measures of Performance

Today, most players in the market do all they can to be 'the best' in their sector or category. What does 'best' mean? How do you define what people regard as 'the best' – and who defined it? Every market and virtually every market segment is characterized by a different measure of quality and performance. Over time, those measures may change. The vast majority of game players readily accept these measures irrespective of how and when they came into being over the past years, decades or even centuries.

The Game Master, on the other hand, is fully aware of the fact that the measure of quality and performance in any game ultimately decides who will become the winners or losers. That is why Game Changers readily challenge existing 'measures of quality,' shaking them and, where possible, changing them to their own advantage. Our case histories demonstrate how this can trigger a massive shift in the power relationships among the competitors. Interestingly, more often than not you do not need a dramatic technological innovation or a 'big bang' marketing and sales campaign to make this happen. More about this is found in the chapter 'First Game Strategy: Redefining the Measures of Performance.'

Game Strategy 2: Reshaping the Market Landscape

Today, all game players take part in 'segmenting' the market – thus leaving minor structural changes on the surface of the larger market landscape. Most players do this with the objective of identifying a 'niche' where they enjoy relative freedom from competitive pressure. Segmentation is all about dividing the market into smaller and smaller units, until it falls apart into mere 'fragments.' 'Positioning', as it is most commonly understood, is about finding the optimum 'position' within the complex market environment.

The Game Master thinks and acts differently. He seeks to change the face of the market landscape with an entirely different objective: he wants to redirect the fundamental dynamics of the Competitive Game. Our case studies will show how individual companies can deliberately change market structures to their own sustainable advantage. In this way, they can avoid negative market trends, create booming new categories and build structural barriers able to defend against their most dangerous competitors. They achieve all this without major product innovations or massive financial resources. More can be found in the chapter 'Second Game Strategy: Reshaping the Market Landscape.'

Game Strategy 3: Restaging the Competitive Confrontation

Today, 'Positioning' yourself usually involves defining your own role in the market game. Typical game players try to adopt the role of innovation leader, for instance, or quality leader or price leader – or leader of something. This fairly straightforward approach is part of how most players understand the concept of 'Positioning.'

The Game Master looks far beyond his own role. He wants to 'stage' the entire competitive confrontation, the big 'Who versus Who'. He employs one of the most archetypical staging techniques used over the past thousand years – ever since biblical writers staged the legendary conflict 'David versus Goliath' using an underlying black and white so-called 'Game Pattern': 'small and good versus big and evil.' Our case studies will show how today's companies can use similarly powerful Game Patterns to radically shift power relationships among the competitors by focusing the attention of the entire market (including the media) on the big competitive showdown.

You will read more about how this is done in the chapter 'Third Game Strategy: Restaging the Competitive Confrontation.'

Game Strategy 4: Taking the Game to the Next Level

Today, even the best player is at his wit's end when the market game loses some of its original energy, when the market is declining or the Game gets stuck in a routine. Some categories just become a bit dusty over the years and decades, others are 'ailing', tumbling or even die out. In all these cases, even the best 'Positioning' doesn't stand a chance. What good would it do to position yourself successfully as the uncontested number one in a market that is falling to pieces?

The Game Master takes the market game back to the drawing board. There, he attempts to analyze and define the 'Original Idea' of his category. He then proceeds to reinvent that idea without respect for any sacrosanct beliefs, traditions or conventions. In this manner, the Game Master can take the market game to the next level, infusing it with an entirely new and fresh dynamic. As a result, he is able to dethrone the previous market leaders and assume that role himself. Our case studies will demonstrate that doing so does not necessarily require technological product innovations or huge financial investments in order to succeed.

You will read more about this in the chapter 'Fourth Game Strategy: Taking the Game to the Next Level.'

Even Radical Thinking Has Its Limits

In this book you will read case histories of Game Masters who were able to bring about astonishing changes in the market because they demonstrated that some of the presumed fixed 'general conditions' were in fact movable levers for growth and success.

Naturally, not all rules of the Game can be changed and not all limiting conditions can be 'levered' in this manner. There are even some small, apparently unimportant, rules of the Game that end up being incredibly intractable. Think about Coca-Cola. When Dr John Stith Pemberton introduced Coca-Cola in 1886, his recipe for the beverage specified that it have a 'brown' color. That ended up becoming an established convention that today enjoys the status of a rule of the Game: 'Authentic cola has to be brown.' Referring to our earlier definition of the rules of the Game in the market, the brown color of cola is a convention that has become a rule of the Game, precisely because it is accepted by the entire market.

In the recent past, Coca-Cola tried twice in vain to launch a 'nonbrown' Cola: first a transparent drink that looked something like mineral water and then a golden colored drink. These were two remarkable flops. In 1994, the British billionaire Richard Branson launched his 'Virgin Cola,' building on the success of Virgin Records and Virgin Airlines. What was the color of his drink? Brown, of course! Although Branson has a reputation as one of the most notorious contrarians and rule breakers on the planet, he submitted without hesitation to certain rules of the Game when he launched his Cola.

In free markets, the things that are known as rules and laws of the market are often nothing more than conventions that represent an informal consensus among the market's participants. That is why they are subject to change. However, in certain isolated cases, such as with brown cola, the time for that change has yet to come.

WANTED: A 'HIGHLY INFECTIOUS' GAME CHANGING IDEA

A single question is holding you back from the four practical strategy chapters of this book: what equipment do you need? What do you need to be a successful Game Changer in the marketplace? What is the most important prerequisite, the most important tool, the most critical resource needed to break the rules or to start a completely new game? Prevailing opinion sees four requirements, which we will prove to be massive misconceptions:

1. A leading market position, the status of market founder or even a monopoly? Not necessary!
2. A significant technological innovation that sets new standards? You can be a Game Changer without one!
3. Extensive financial resources to fund massive new product or marketing offensives? Good to have, but not needed!
4. A sophisticated network of influential people, opinion leaders and contacts among government authorities? Not a prerequisite either!

You may have noticed that three of these four factors involve 'power.' We are not denying that 'power plays' so often described and decried in the media are often inseparable from the reality of the market economy. The real and higher art of Game Strategy, however, is based on 'winning over' voluntary and believing allies, as opposed to flagrant use of 'market muscle.' The game strategist gets everyone else to adopt his ideas of the Game. This immediately makes it clear what is the most important resource of the Game Master: *his Game Changing Idea*. The idea must convince, grip, fascinate and excite. It must 'infect' the other players – be they customers, dealers, investors, experts, journalists or other opinion leaders. None of them can be bought or intimidated or forced to act under duress. They want to be convinced and excited before they allow themselves to be brought into a new game.

Above all, the Game Changer needs a convincing Idea to win over committed allies among the other market participants, like customers, retailers, investors, media and opinion leaders. Once they buy into your idea and behave accordingly, you can gradually change the nature of the Competitive Game.

How One Man Changed the Game in a Multibillion Dollar Market

The following example involves a single man who was able to revolutionize a billion dollar market with nothing more than a 'highly infectious' idea. He turned the rules of the Game upside down, changing marketplace dynamics in a fundamental manner.

In 1988 the United States Food and Drug Administration (FDA) published a study declaring 'fat' to be the nutritional Public Enemy number one. This was the origin of the 'low-fat' megatrend. The food industry split into two huge camps: on one side was the 'bad' protein and fat camp, to which the meat, dairy products and egg industries belonged; on the other side was the 'good' camp, in which carbohydrates dominated: bread, pasta, cereals. No fewer than 160 million Americans changed their behavior to suit the new rules of the Game. They instinctively followed the new logic, 'fat makes you fat.'

When a 580 billion dollar market shifts, it is rather like two of the planet's massive tectonic plates separating and then drifting apart with incredible force. No one could have expected that, in such a situation, a single player could successfully introduce a counter-revolution.

However, that is exactly what happened. It all started with a simple but provocative idea, introduced by Dr Robert C. Atkins in his bestseller *Dr Atkins' Diet Revolution*, in which he questions the entire prevailing world view of the nutritional market: 'Fat is not the nutritional Public Enemy number one, but rather Public Friend number one' was the essence of his message 'and carbohydrates are not our friends, but in truth our most dangerous enemies.' Atkins undertook a frontal assault on the rules of the Game of the market. He restaged the competition between the two camps in the market. The previous good camp (represented by the carbohydrate industry) became a negative signal and the previously negatively perceived camp (protein and fat) a positive one. The roles of friend and foe were reversed. Good became evil and evil became good.

Portrait of a Game Changing Idea

Dr Atkins' idea had its roots in the science of biological evolution: the ancestors of men were above all meat eaters, and indeed for a period of more than two million years. Darwin would have said that human metabolism had developed on the basis of consumption of animal flesh and its conversion to energy. A mere 10,000 years ago *Homo sapiens* invented agriculture and shifted his diet largely to grains and thereby carbohydrates, but 10,000 years in evolutionary terms are a blink of the eye. On a 1 meter measuring stick representing two million years, it would be equivalent to not more than half a centimeter. How is it possible, Atkins asked, that human metabolism could adjust to grains and the conversion of carbohydrates to energy? Atkins' idea can be summarized as follows: 'If we consume nothing but carbohydrates, we are going against the grain of our own biological nature. We are forcing our metabolism to adopt an unnatural behavior.' The organism gets its own revenge – as punishment, our society gets fatter and fatter.

Atkins supported his idea with scientific argumentation: he who eats too many carbohydrates drives up his blood sugar level, dramatically increasing the sensation of hunger. The body first burns sugars (= carbohydrates) and fat stays on the hips. Avoid carbohydrates, and you will force the metabolism to shift to active fat burning. With the Atkins Diet, people get their energy above all from stored fat – and in that manner they become slender. Many disciples of the ideas of Atkins report that they have very fast initial success – sometimes a weight loss of up to four kilograms (almost nine pounds) per week.

You may have a totally different nutritional philosophy, but nevertheless you can probably identify with the 'highly infectious' fascination that enabled Atkins to spread his idea like wildfire across the USA and many other parts of the developed world.

How the Idea Triggered a Structural Change in the Food Industry

At the turn of the 21st century, Atkins unleashed a kind of hype never before seen, ultimately influencing the purchase and consumption behavior of a hundred million Americans and a great part of the world. Atkins' books even pushed Harry Potter off first place in the bestseller lists in England, the home of the magical apprentice! In the course of just a few years, the 'low-carb' business in the US alone was worth over 20 billion dollars, including the diet books themselves, if you can go by the industry reports of 'LowCarbiz'. By comparison, the entire US bread industry at the same time had sales of about 11.4 billion dollars. That means that for every dollar spent in the US on bread, two went for low-carb products; 40% of the US population had some experience with low-carb nutrition. Low-carb was more than just a diet: it had become a personal philosophy. All of a sudden, you could regenerate at a 'low-carb' resort hotel, while personal physicians across the country joined together in 'low-carb doctors' associations.'

Suddenly, as if by magic, the declining egg and pork industries were blossoming again. Egg prices almost doubled annually. Beef, cheese, nuts – in all fat and protein rich segments the growth motor was humming again. Managers in these sectors rejoiced, as did industry associations and journalists. At the same time, the carbohydrate-based industries were mercilessly hounded into the cellar. Bread consumption dropped by 7%, from 147 pounds per person to 137 pounds annually. 'Our products have an image problem,' said Judi Adams, President of the Wheat Foods Council, and invested at the time four million dollars a year to get that problem under control. What did she mean by an *image problem*? 'Fear of extinction' would be a better way to describe it. With a sense of desperation, the bread and pasta industries pounded on the doors of science and demanded for their customers the *first carbohydrate-free bread.* Sound like an oxymoron? Bread is grain and grain essentially consists of carbohydrates. To take the carbohydrate out of bread would be a bit like depriving light of brightness or taking oxygen out of the air we breathe. Why and how would anyone want to deprive a food of its own primordial nature? Science was being asked to deliver the absurd: grain products without carbohydrates.

'If consumer demand is so great, we don't have much of a choice,' said Albert Haase, a manager in the bakery chain Breadsmith, with 175 outlets. 'The US consumer wants everything with zero carbohydrates,' confirmed Mian N. Riaz, University Professor and nutritional expert. He initiated costly research projects for the industry to replace carbohydrates with protein. This paradoxical challenge has a number of issues. Bread without carbohydrates just tastes bad. Proteins don't mix easily with water and they tend to become as hard as stone after a short while. Somehow, all that doesn't seem to matter to consumers anymore.

Over 100 million Americans jumped into the new game, creating such enormous pressure that even the giants in the food industry finally had to give in: Unilever, PepsiCo, Kellogg's, Heinz, Hershey's – all of them brought out low-carb product lines. Put yourself in the position of Kellogg's. Cereals are pure grain products, that is, pure carbohydrates. All of a sudden, food chemists are working furiously to bring the first 'low-carb' cornflakes to the market. And how about beer, which primarily – besides water – consists of malted barley, which is a carbohydrate? The brewing industry, too, bowed to the 'low-carb' idea and offered the first 'low-carb' beers'. Once Atkins had dictated the new rules to the food industry, in came the public authorities. The Institute of Medicine is the final authority for nutritional recommendations in the USA. It decreased its Recommended Daily Allowance (RDA) for carbohydrates from 300 to 130 grams for adults, thereby giving a further boost to the consumption of meat, sausage, bacon, cheese and eggs.

Then the US restaurant business jumped on the low-carb bandwagon. Just check out the menus of the 'Ruby Tuesday' restaurant chain, with more than 650 outlets, and you will find over 30 special low-carb dishes.

The market value created by low-carb food products merits special consideration. Market research firm A.C. Nielsen reported that the weekly food shopping cart of the average US household contains about $59 worth of products. However, if you want to live strictly according to the principles of low-carb diets, the same shopping cart would cost you $99, or about +70% more. Other researchers have put the low-carb price premium at between +80 and +100% versus 'normal' products. No wonder that the low-carb revolution ploughed deep furrows in the food market's landscape. In the course of just a few years, more than 250 low-carb specialty stores sprung up out of nowhere. There are even low-carb shopping centers. WalMart, the second biggest company in America, was publicly considering building a low-carb supermarket chain.

Dr Atkins himself received a kind of 'personal knighthood' as an icon of contemporary culture, with a mention in the Oxford English Dictionary.

What We Can Learn from the Atkins Case

Some of our readers will think, 'Yes, sure, but that kind of thing could only happen in America.' Maybe so. However, it is exactly this kind of extreme example that is at the core of our thesis: more than anything else, ideas cause revolutions in the marketplace. In the extreme case, the infectious power of an idea is strong enough to change the fundamental structure of a market or shift its dynamics in a totally different direction. In the Atkins case, it was 100 million consumers, in America alone. Indirectly, he forced multinational companies to alter their product line-ups.

His ideas spurred researchers to absurd kinds of product developments. Retail giants like WalMart speculated about entirely new retailing concepts.

How much capital or market power would you need to repeat a comparable revolution in the food industry? What kind of once-in-a-century innovation could do the same? Which public authority could enforce it? The answer is fairly clear. No company in the world could repeat a comparable structural shift with only financial capital or market influence. There are no resources, no innovations that can take the place of an infectious idea. A famous media company once attempted to estimate the cost of media coverage for the low-carb message if Atkins had to spend advertising or marketing funds for it. The amount was in the several hundred million dollars, close to the billion mark. Dr Atkins didn't need this money. A powerful idea that can fascinate and 'infect' the rest of the market – including the media – blazes its own trail.

In conclusion, one last bit of information to bring this case history back from the stratosphere down to the ground of sober facts. Atkins might have revolutionized a billion dollar market, but ironically, he failed as an active player, entrepreneur and manager. In 1989, Atkins founded his own company to market low-carb products: Atkins Nutritionals. He and his employees (he died in 2003) built this up over the following 16 years to respectable annual sales of 215 million dollars, which is, however, only about 1% of the estimated value of the low-carb market. It seems like one of the ironies of destiny that in this booming market – in 2005 – the Atkins firm finally declared bankruptcy. Other low-carb firms in the market were far more successful than Dr Atkins and founded true low-carb empires, some of them with annual sales surpassing 100 million dollars.

OUR PLEA FOR FREE, OPEN AND RADICAL THINKING

At this point, we have one simple request for our readers: for the rest of this book, forget the next quarter's sales targets, put aside all conventional business strategies and focus 100% on a bigger mission: how to push the 'possiblilities of the market' to their limits with a truly Game Changing Idea.

From here on we'd like you to raise yourself to the second level of the Game, and start to critically analyze what others consider to be the 'rules and laws' of the market game.

Managers of small and medium sized firms often get hung up on doubts about whether they have a realistic chance of becoming Game Changers or 'Rule

Makers,' or whether it isn't a better idea to just leave that to the market leader or some multinational competitor. Managers from large companies may suffer from the opposite syndrome: thinking that they already understand all they need about rule making in the market.

For this reason, we have split our plea to each of these groups of managers. If you are part of a large company, skip the next section that is aimed at small and medium sized firms (and vice versa of course!).

Dear Small or Medium Sized Company: Don't Leave Rule Making to Your Bigger Competitors!

We recently sponsored a management conference at which a very successful entrepreneur from a medium sized company came straight to the point:

'If I understand you correctly,' he called out to the auditorium, 'you are saying that as a medium sized firm we have got to change the rules of the Game in order to create exceptional growth. Do you have any idea what that means for us? Our competitors are international companies. They are the Rule Makers! We've got all we can do just to keep up with their innovations and create an acceptable price–performance relationship for our products. We've got to focus on selling our products! What's the point of thinking abstractly about the Game of the market or philosophizing about the rules of the Game for someone in our position?'

In all fairness, we respect this point of view. That said, it doesn't have much to do with the 'player' and 'winner' spirit that we are advocating. Just think about how many success stories in recent business history would never have taken place if all medium sized companies also thought in a medium size manner. The Ryanair success story happened under extremely unfavorable conditions – and by a medium sized firm that was on the brink of bankruptcy! How much simpler it would have been to argue: 'Re-inventing a new market just isn't on the cards right now. We are close to broke. We've got zero market power. We are fighting for our lives.'

Turn the question around and ask: 'What would a model rule breaker and contrarian like Michael O'Leary make out of your company? How would he open up thinking and break the marketplace rules?'

In most markets, thousands if not millions of small and medium sized companies stand up against a few dozen major companies and global players. However, it is exactly those medium sized firms that are the economic motor and the driving innovating force in the market, giving jobs often to more than three-quarters of all employees.

It would be truly alarming if the top managers of small and medium sized firms were to surrender without a struggle to the dozen or so large firms. That is not the way winners think.

Those of us that look at the Rules of the Game of the market as a taboo leave Rule Making to the other players – and that includes their own competitors.

Dear Big Company Manager: Pre-empt the 'Idea Leadership' in Your Market!

Now our plea to those company managers who already consider themselves and their firms to be the 'market makers:' 'Your point about changing the Game is correct and interesting,' we were recently told by a manger from the software industry. 'Actually, your description fits us perfectly. We are the Game Changers in our market. We always have been. We know how markets are made. We don't need to follow the rules of the Game. We make them.'

We said: 'In your company about 1300 managers and management trainees are working in a market-oriented manner: among them product developers, marketing people, market and trend researchers, the sales force. Ask them how markets are made. Ask them how you can change the rules of the Game in competition. How you can intervene in the functioning of the market and competition?' In all likelihood, you will hear the same answers: 'We have to be innovation leaders; we have to offer more quality for a lower price; we have to initiate marketing and sales campaigns.' Big companies often have too much faith in technical progress and expensive resource battles to be able to win in competition.

Game Strategy deals with using idea leadership to exert influence, drive and control in competition. That is a strategic, creative, elegant and economic art, which, frankly, is far too seldom practiced consistently by large corporations. For this reason, we are firmly convinced that the principles and concepts of Game Strategy are just as relevant to large corporations as they are to managers of small and medium sized companies.

You've Got to Really *Want* to Do This!

Victors in real life are often fascinating exactly because they are willing to challenge the rules and laws that others take for granted. Look at Arnold Schwarzenegger as an example: seven times Mr Universe in bodybuilding. Since 1984 an

American citizen and one of the best known and remunerated actors in Hollywood. Since 2003 Governor of the State of California. On February 22, 2004 Arnold created media uproar when he openly challenged the rules of the Game according to the United States Constitution. Article II, Paragraph 1 of the Constitution of the United States of America, in force since 1787, states that all US citizens born outside the US are not eligible to be elected President of the United States. With a refreshing lack of concern for convention, Schwarzenegger asked US Senator Orrin Hatch to propose a constitutional amendment permitting all American citizens to be eligible for the highest office, as long as they had resided in the United States for at least 20 years.

As an immigrant, the American rules of the Game explicitly discriminated against Schwarzenegger. The American Constitution made it impossible for him to become President. Instead of resigning himself to accept his destiny out of respect for the US Constitution, Schwarzenegger challenged the very pillars of the US legal system. You can judge this as grandly courageous or a delusion of grandeur – whatever it is, it shows the spirit that is at heart of all great players and athletes. Even if at first they do not succeed, what makes the winner is his attitude!

So What Comes Next?

So much for the preamble. Now we turn to examining the four classic game strategies in greater detail. Each of the strategic ideas will be illustrated by practical case histories, from the business-to-consumer sector as well as business-to-business.

You can expect inspiration, observations, extrapolations and experiences that will help you develop new growth plans. However, because we always insist on freeing you from conventional ways of thinking, there aren't going to be any templates or best practices, no methodical grids or palliative 'recipes for success.' Sorry, but inspired and fresh thinking just don't go together with methodical formalism.

Are you ready? OK, let's get started with our crash course for Game Changers!

First Game Strategy: redefining the measures of performance

Today, most players in the market go to extremes to be 'the best' in their sector or category. What does 'best' mean? How is 'best quality' or 'best service' defined? Every market and virtually every market segment brings forth a different measure of quality and performance and, over time, those measures may change. The ordinary market player readily accepts these measures irrespective of how and when they came into being over the past years, decades or even centuries, no matter whether they are right or wrong in any objective sense. The ordinary market player is content to simply find out 'what counts' for customers, the trade, the media or opinion leaders, and then to immediately enter the 'rat race' to deliver 'the best' of whatever that measure of all things may be.

The Game Master, on the other hand, is fully aware of the fact that the measure of quality and performance in any game ultimately decides who will become the winners or losers. That's why Game Masters always challenge existing 'measures of quality,' shaking them, and where possible changing them to their own advantage. Our case histories demonstrate how this can trigger a massive shift in the power relationships among the competitors. Interestingly, more often than not you do not need a dramatic technological innovation or a 'big bang' marketing and sales campaign to make this happen.

Picture a man named Smith who takes a holiday in Australia. He visits an Aborigine festival and encounters the long woodwind instrument that the natives call the Didgeridoo. He decides to buy one for a souvenir. Economists contend that in each and every purchase decision, consumers try to maximize their utility. That presents a bit of a problem for Mr Smith: Which is the best Didgeridoo? Are long ones better than short ones? Thick ones better than slender ones? How about the type of wood or where it comes from and how it is fashioned or decorated? Or maybe what is the condition of the hollow space inside? Smith obviously wants the best possible instrument for his money, but he hasn't a clue which quality standard he should apply. At the end of the day, with a shrug of his shoulders, Smith goes for the one that he judges to have the 'nicest' design.

The 'Chicken or Egg' Dilemma

Experts could have told Mr Smith that the shape of the 'air column' of the Didgeridoo is responsible for its tonal range, and on that basis the quality of the instrument. Smith doesn't know that, but he is no dummy. He uses 'design' as his criterion of what he perceives as 'superior quality', simply because he knows no other. However, he would have undoubtedly been receptive to learning about a better one – if only an expert had been around to tell him what Didgeridoo quality really is all about.

It is easy to generalize from this insight. Smith is a customer in thousands of markets, and in hardly any of them does he feel like an expert. Smith purchases butter, coffee, aspirin or dental floss. Once he bought a hedge clipper. Then he bought a car insurance policy and a new printer for his PC. Since he is also the manager of a large company, in the course of his job he purchases advertising and consulting services, IT services, office furniture, leasing contracts, office premises. No single person can hope to be sufficiently 'expert' in all these markets and know precisely how quality and performance is measured in each.

How do the manufacturers of these products and providers of these services behave? They send their market researchers to the customers to ask which quality and performance criteria they use in a purchase decision. Since Smith is a pretty honest kind of guy, they would have learned in the case of the Didgeridoos that 'design' was his Number One purchase factor. In all probability, a few thousand other clueless tourists would have given the same answer, so that the Didgeridoo manufacturer decides: 'We bow to the wishes of our customers and will shift our product development focus toward "Designer Didgeridoos".'

Fundamentally, here is a variation of the classic 'chicken or egg' dilemma: is the customer so convinced of the quality standards he applies that the manufacturer must accept them? Or should the manufacturer – in his role as an expert – offer the customer more qualified standards needed to properly evaluate quality? Our Didgeridoo example brings us to the following thesis:

In countless markets, the customer doesn't feel like an expert. In order to make the best choice from several alternatives, he either must know the correct quality standard – or be prepared to learn it!

What Separates Game Changers from Mere Players

It is only fitting and proper that every company closely studies the needs, wishes, standards and criteria of their customers, and orient themselves accordingly. We recently attended a Procter & Gamble Alumni reunion in London. One of the highlights was a talk by A.G. Lafley, the company's current CEO. Asked what he thought was the greatest challenge for the future, Lafley said modestly, 'Procter & Gamble must understand its consumers better.' This is coming from the head of one of the largest and most successful consumer products companies in the world, whose market and consumer research budget is close to a billion dollars every year. For that reason, it makes sense for most firms to use P&G as an example and to learn more about their target prospects than they know today.

A good player in the market thinks like this: 'In order to be successful, I must investigate the needs, quality standards and purchase criteria of my target prospects and devise my product line-up accordingly.'

Essentially, this is also the attitude of the Game Master. He knows he has to keep his ear close to the customers if he is to offer them what they want. Even Game Changers would never simply ignore customer wishes.

But what he *doesn't* do is accept those wishes as part of the market's 'general framework conditions;' rather, he challenges the criteria of his customers. The Game Master intuitively understands the 'chicken or egg' dilemma and the resulting purchase decision conflict ('How am I supposed to measure quality and performance?') that plagues thousands of the choices of our friend Mr Smith.

The Game Master knows that customers are often unsure how they should evaluate and compare quality and performance. Because they want to maximize their own utility, there is an

opportunity to establish new, credible quality criteria and standards in the market that replace the old ones.

It takes an extra dose of spiritual freedom to think in this manner, but that is exactly the entire point of Game Strategy: *to start thinking where others usually stop.*

The case histories in this chapter will show how certain firms, even when starting from an inferior market position, ripped out the old standards, established new ones and triggered a dramatic power shift in the marketplace. In principle, even smaller companies can weaken, destabilize or oust their larger competitors from positions of dominance. They don't need a revolutionary product or innovative service. Doesn't this only apply in so-called 'lifestyle' markets? Wrong, the strategy is equally successful in the 'business-to-business' sector. You cannot always change the standard of the market. However, on those occasions when it *is* feasible, that can give you one of the most powerful levers of all in the Game of the market.

Most players view accepted market quality standards as part of the general framework conditions of the Game. The Game Master recognizes that by changing or even replacing existing quality standards and performance measures there is a significant chance to change the power relationships in the market dramatically.

INFLUENCE THE CRITERIA OF THE 'CUSTOMER JURY'

Imposing new standards is a classical Game Strategy because it changes the conditions in the marketplace, forcing competitors off balance. You are operating on the second level, and in that way fulfill a 'sovereign' function as only a Game Master can. To show how this works, let's conduct a small experiment.

Imagine that you and your company are participating in a classic, formal competition. Sitting in front of you is a jury such as that of a beauty contest or the show 'American Idol,' except that this jury consists of customers, dealers, trade journalists and other opinion leaders from your market.

Let's say that, unfortunately, this competition isn't going very well for your company. You are in a kind of middling position, but think you are being underrated. You question the *validity of the standards* that the jury is using. Competitors that you have good reason to judge to be inferior find themselves far above you in the rankings. As long as the judges persist in applying the wrong standards, your company doesn't have a chance of showing its real strengths.

Imagine you are given an 'impossible advantage' over your competitors: to speak to the jury about their criteria. You appeal for a new, qualified standard of measurement, and successfully convince the jury. What happens? Under the new standard, some competitors move up in the rankings and others move down. By intervening in the rules of the Game, you were able to trigger a significant power shift in the competition and propel yourself to the top of the league. If your new criteria are indeed qualified and your company was previously underrated, this is entirely legitimate. This experiment illustrates the ultimate consequence of Game Strategy. You can influence the rules of a competition in which you are taking part as one of the competitors.

The quality and performance standards in a competition 'regulate' the Game. Redefine the Measures of Performance and you can create new winners and losers.

Performance Measures in Competition Are Never Perfect

A competition with no clear standards of performance can never work, first and foremost because there can never be any clear winners and losers. The standards must be simple, easy to understand and pragmatic, such as in football, where *only goals count for victory.* That is what it says in the rules. Of course, everyone knows that the number of goals scored doesn't provide a complete picture of performance on the pitch, and in fact can be an unfair rating. Haven't we all heard sports commentators say that the losing team played the more beautiful, elegant and in sum better game? They had longer ball possession, they played more fairly and they won the most one-on-one contests. Maybe they had bad luck and a 'lucky goal' or even an own-goal decided the match. However, what counts in a game is always only that portion of the Game that is measured and counted, such as goals in football.

It is even clearer in the context of a more complex competition just how difficult it is to perceive and evaluate performance. How does the Oscar jury actually rate films and why do Hollywood productions win most of the time? The standards of evaluation in competition reflect the value system of the culture that defines them. How does the Nobel Prize committee select the next winner of the literature prize? What is the relative importance of the first, second and third criteria? By modestly changing or shifting the criteria, a new favorite suddenly rises to the top of the rankings.

> **The standards and measures ('what counts to win?') in a competition always provide an incomplete picture of the performance of the players. Furthermore, standards are often shaped by cultural or ideological factors. Despite this incompleteness and deficiency, the standards 'regulate' who wins or loses.**

In markets, too, there are no 'objectively correct' or complete standards. What customers define as a 'top performance' is often a reflection of their culture, value system or current taste. Most clients of advertising agencies today focus above all on 'creativity'. Does that make sense or not? For years, 'megapixels' were the ultimate standard for digital cameras. Is that correct or naive? In the real estate market, it always comes down to three things: location, location, location. Isn't that just a bit one-sided? The purchaser of a luxury wristwatch makes his choice on the basis of 'fine mechanical complexity'. Remarkable! In almost all aspects of life we spend money in order to make complicated things easier, simpler, more comfortable. However, for high-end wristwatches, the exact opposite is true: *the more complicated it is, the higher the price.* This is despite the fact that extremely complex watches are more accident-prone, require more maintenance and sometimes are even less precise in their measurement of time.

You must forget the illusion that the criteria that decide a competition are in any way sensible, fair, logical or self-evident. In the market for fashion blue jeans, it seems that the degree of 'artistic destruction' is the primary value standard. A brand new and qualitatively perfect pair of jeans can today cost at most 150 euros, but a pair of *ripped and torn* jeans attracts customers willing to pay up to 1500 euros at the clothing store. Is that just a somewhat pathological syndrome of modern lifestyle? Not at all. Markets have always had astonishing standards of quality. Centuries ago, farmers at the local market would select a horse if it had a good set of teeth. *Good teeth, good horse.* Quality measures can be very one-sided at times. Finally, a word on competition in the marriage market: young men from the Padong-Karen tribe in Thailand look for a wife who has a long neck. 'Long like a swan' is the ideal, and from early childhood an ever-taller stack of gold neckbands gradually stretches the necks of young girls. *The longer the neck, the more desirable the woman.* That notwithstanding, we doubt that one of these swan-necked Karen women would stand much of a chance in a beauty contest in the Western world. Other cultures, other standards – that pretty much sums it up.

A glance at such curious, bizarre value standards should help you to loosen up your thinking and get rid of any slavish respect for the rules of the Game.

Quality and Performance Measures Are Valid Even When They Are *False*

When putting standards to the test, it is important to determine first whether they are 'correct' or 'valid'. A quality standard can be said to be valid in a real-life market game when it is part of the Game's experience. A standard can be 'objectively correct' but nevertheless 'invalid'. Alternatively, it can be 'objectively false' but still 'valid.'

When the market for digital cameras was born in the 1990s, the 'megapixel' quickly became the dominant standard of quality. 'The pixel craze sweeps the nation,' wrote one newspaper at the time. The manufacturing industry started a kind of arms race: from the first 2-megapixel cameras in 1999 to the 40-megapixel camera for more than 20 000 euros. Megapixels became a source of stratospheric added value. It was only after a few years that it finally began to dawn on the market: this 'megapixel standard' was only *one aspect* of digital photo quality. There were murmurs of amazement throughout the media landscape when a test institute announced: 'Cameras with seven megapixels often make better pictures than others with ten megapixels,' because the higher resolution often results in greater image distortion. Which model, however, would the majority of consumers choose when a seven-megapixel camera is sitting on the same shelf alongside one with ten megapixels, possibly for a comparable price and with the same additional features? Exactly. A false standard can result in making the objectively inferior product the winner and making the objectively superior product the loser. The megapixel, despite its inadequacy as a criterion, 'regulates' the competition.

The criteria and measures the customer uses to measure quality and performance in the market can often be shown on closer examination to be inadequate, one-sided, unfair, irrational or

**mistaken. This gives the Game Master the opportunity to intro-
duce new and more qualified standards.**

In general, the Game Changer will do that only when a new standard helps him
cast his company and its products or services in a better light.

HOW TO MAKE STRONGER OPPONENTS PLAY *YOUR* GAME

Both of the following case histories present companies that realized they were at
a disadvantage because of the unfavorable standards of their customers. Both
chose the 'radical' path and were determined to cast out these standards, putting
in their place new ones that were simultaneously more qualified and more favorable. The first success story concerns a newcomer to the market, who through a
classical Game Strategy was able to dramatically shift the balance of power in his
favor.

*Flashback: When the first German private television broadcaster
started in a garage. ...*

It is almost impossible to imagine a world without private television channels. However, as was true in most European markets at the time, Germany
had only state-owned television channels up until the 1980s. When on January 1,
1984 the first private channel was founded as RTL, the young company
found itself facing two national superpowers that had dominated television
entertainment for more than two decades: ARD and ZDF. The freshly minted
private channels, first RTL, then SAT1 and ProSieben, started by developing
programming targeted at a younger audience. They had to fight for their lives,
because unlike the state-owned institutions, largely financed by mandatory
viewer license fees, the privates had to rely entirely on advertising revenues. So
alongside their powerful opponents, they had to knock on the doors of the advertising industry and fight for ad spending. There was an extremely difficult competition for the larger budgets, since ARD and ZDF enjoyed huge reach to all the
country's living rooms, while the private channels were serving a much smaller
and younger niche audience. The small private channels appeared to be mired in
a hopeless battle. The major advertising accounts went to the state-owned institu-

tions, leaving the small private startups with nothing more than the small change that was left over.

This is the kind of situation when the thought comes almost by reflex: 'So that's it. The state-owned channels actually do have far more viewers. So obviously they will also get the lion's share of advertising spending.' It all seemed pretty hopeless for the private channels.

RTL Challenges the Quality Measure for Broadcasting Services

From a Game Strategy perspective, the standards of the customers, in this case the advertising industry, had to be put to a critical test. Remember that in the market at the time there was a very simple standard for evaluation and comparison of television channels, namely *total 'reach' of the programs among the entire population*. Those channels that reached the most households were able to demand the highest advertising prices and took the lion's share of the billion dollar advertising market.

The market imposed a pragmatic and entirely plausible standard of performance – one with the power to 'regulate' competition. On the basis of the standard valid at the time, there was no way for the private channels to win the competition.

An ordinary player in the market would have simply accepted this as a fact of life. He would have taken the view that the standards of the customer were just one of those unchangeable general parameters that you had to go by. A typical player might have decided to adjust his programming in order to reach the mass of the population better, struggling to get just a little bigger piece of the advertising pie.

The Game Changer thinks more radically. He has the confidence to put the market's 'rules of the Game' to a critical test. His conclusion would have been: 'Why do we have to accept a measure of performance according to which we will always remain the loser – now as much as in the long term future? This performance standard, which makes us look so awfully small and unimportant, isn't carved in stone and isn't an inalterable natural truth. Maybe there's a way to introduce a more qualified standard that makes RTL and the other private channels look a lot better?'

The brilliant head of RTL, Helmut Thoma, was exactly that kind of Game Changer. He recognized that the 'total audience reach' criterion, which appeared to be a fixed general condition, was in reality nothing more than a convenient, traditionally accepted rule, to which he could offer a qualified alternative that would put RTL in a far more favorable light.

RTL Introduces a Game Changing Idea

Thoma assumed the role of a Game Changer in order to advocate a new 'measure of all things' for the advertising industry, and one according to which even his powerful competitors were forced to measure themselves.

His new criterion was a refined modification of the old one. Instead of measuring 'reach to the entire population,' Thoma asserted it was more important and decisive to measure reach among an *advertising receptive age group*, which he went on to define as 14- to 49-year-old younger people. In this manner, Thoma defined a new measurement standard, according to which the advertising industry was to divide its billions among the various channels on offer. He made the audience of his channel into the 'measure of all things' and declared all viewers older than 49 simply irrelevant.

> **The old performance measure: Reach to the total population.**
> **RTL's successful new measure: Reach to the 'ad receptive age group' of 14 to 49 years.**

The new criterion was meant to apply henceforth to *all* channels, also to his state-owned rivals. Now realize that at that time 70% (!) of the ARD–ZDF viewers were *over 50 years old.* This 70% was suddenly eliminated from the competition, as if they had never existed. In so doing, Helmut Thoma succeeded in making 70% of the reach of his opponents invisible and thereby neutralized 70% of their strength. In comparative rankings of TV channels, RTL & Co. entered with 100% of their viewers (since the private channels hardly had any viewers over 50), while ARD and ZDF had only 30% of their public at the starting line, which now began with the age segment 14 to 49. One could say, Thoma defined the new 'measure of all things' so that his own strength came to the fore, simultaneously putting the greatest weakness of his competitors squarely in the spotlight. ARD and ZDF suddenly appeared nothing less than 'ancient.'

In this way, the private channels killed two birds with a single stone. First, with the criterion 'ad receptive age group' they catapulted their market share over the heads of the state-owned channels. Second, they were able to sell their advertising time at a much higher price, because they could guarantee reaching the 'receptive' target viewers far better than the big channels.

The revolutionary and spectacular aspect of this strategy is precisely that it appears so unrevolutionary and unspectacular. This seemingly unimportant point is exactly what made the strategy so strong. It was simply ignored by ARD and ZDF for a long time, permitting a dramatic power shift in the market to occur below the radar screen.

In all fairness, it must be acknowledged that Thoma had borrowed a page from the playbook of the American channel ABC. In 1957, those in charge recognized that ABC was strong among 18- to 49-year-olds, but weak in terms of total reach when compared with the leading networks CBS and NBC.

The Private Channels Dethrone Their State-Owned Competitors

The new measure of all things turned the competition on its head and in just a few short years, the private channels became market leaders in the truest sense of the word. Since 1992 independent research institutes have issued their famous TV ratings on the basis of 'advertising relevant target audiences'. What sticks out is that with the new standard, (focus on 14- to 49-year-olds) RTL reaches double (!) the market share of ARD and ZDF, with a corresponding effect on the distribution of advertising spending. If one were to apply the old standard (reach to the entire population), RTL would today be at about the same level as its state-owned competitors.

The new standard created a dramatic power shift in favor of the private channels, and the state-owned competitors couldn't do a thing about it. The competition was decided after almost a quarter century according to a criterion that RTL itself established: 'Advertising agencies and the advertising industry at large are convinced that only 14- to 49-year-olds are the only ones doing any consuming,' summarized Camille Zubayr, head of media research for ARD in the spring of 2006.

Critical Assessment of the 'Ad Receptive Age Group'

It is nothing short of fascinating to observe how the small players can dictate the rules of the Game to the big ones. First, Thoma won over the advertising industry as his ally. Then he brought the market research institutes into the Game. Finally, even the state-owned channels had to accept the new rules.

If you put the new rules to the test, how in the world was Thoma able to justify that citizens over 50 were no longer 'advertising relevant'? Why does your 'advertising receptive' life end precisely with your 50th birthday? Thoma came up with a simple explanation: after 50, customers are so brand-loyal and so dominated by engrained habits that advertising can no longer influence them. If a critic should persist, he would growl: 'Denture creams – we are happy to leave those to the other channels.' Hang on a second: *denture cream for a 50-year-old?* In what century is he living? *At fifty advertising doesn't matter any more?* That may be a bit cheeky and irreverent, but frankly it is also nothing less than absurd. More than 30 million people in Germany (out of a total population of 82 million) are over 50. The net income of this age group is 10% higher than the income of younger target audiences. Over-50s watch TV one and a half hours longer every day than the younger people who are deemed advertising receptive. In the 50-plus age category you can find present and former prime ministers, Angela Merkel and Gerhard Schröder, Arnold Schwarzenegger and even Mr Thoma himself. There is absolutely nothing to support the assertion that consumers in this target group are bogged down in a fixed routine of brand preferences. The generation of 50- to 70-year-olds controls the largest financial capital of their lives. Over-50s in Germany own a fortune of a half trillion euros, 90 billion of which they are free to spend every year, because at their age they no longer need to keep the piggy bank full. Over half of this age group agree with the statement: 'I prefer to enjoy life, rather than always having to save.'

And yet, Mr Thoma was able to force through and maintain his new standard. According to estimates of the ProSiebenSat1 media sales firm SevenOne Media, over 80% of all advertising campaigns are aimed at the 'ad receptive' audience.

At the end of the day, the 'advertising receptive target' concept was actually born as a response to what RTL judged to be an almost 'hopeless' competitive situation relative to the giant public broadcasters. But in the words of RTL's marketing director at the time, Uli Bellieno, 'Sometimes an act of desperation can be a stroke of genius'.

A Classic Example of Game Strategy

The essence of this Game Strategy lies in introducing new measures of performance, according to which all of the competitors must orient themselves.

The RTL example demonstrates in an ideal manner how this works. Here are eight of the most important hallmarks and characteristics of the strategy:

1. *Attack those rules of the Game that stand in the way of your success.* Intuitively and without further reflection, many managers simply would have accepted the original standard according to which channels were measured by 'total reach' as *part of the natural rules of the sector.* The Game Changer Thoma identifies this rule as the Number One barrier to sustaining growth and business success. He concludes that this historical standard for advertising spending is neither objectively correct nor carved in stone, and therefore has the potential to be changed.

2. *Leveling the grounds for above-average growth opportunities.* It is precisely these apparently untouchable general parameters that reveal themselves to be the most powerful levers for growth and marketplace success. With a new standard, RTL engineered a massive power shift and laid the groundwork for becoming the new market leader. The private channels were able to dethrone their state-owned competitors and put them squarely into second place.

3. *The most important resource is a Game Changing Idea, something that anybody can come up with!* RTL changed the rules of the market, without any major investments or innovations. Thoma's most important resource was his idea that the advertising billions should be distributed according to a *sharper, more narrowly targeted criterion,* which at least gave the appearance of being more *qualified* than the original standard.

4. *The new rule becomes 'valid' once you win over allies who play by your new rule.* A Game Changing Idea is something abstract and virtual in nature, until, of course, it wins over converts. The success of RTL was predicated on being able to win over the advertising industry. Later came the market research institutes and the media. As more and more participants in the market became 'infected' by the new rule, it became 'valid', that is to say, a part of the market reality that is still relevant and accepted today. Even now, experts estimate that 80% of all media plans in Germany are tailored according to the advertising receptive target audience.

5. *The 'equal opportunity' principle.* Even 'smaller' players are able to impose new rules of the Game that reflect their interests and which larger competitors ultimately have no choice but to accept. Because a convincing idea can win

over willing and committed players, there is absolutely no reason at all to accept the notion that bigger firms have a better chance than smaller ones. Good ideas are a democratic gift. So even small and medium size companies can successfully employ this Game Strategy.

6. *No extraordinary economic resources are needed.* One of the most common misconceptions is that challenging the rules of competition is like trying to spin a monstrous wheel and will need a massive effort. Wrong. Game strategies are no more difficult than any other business strategies. They do not necessarily devour larger budgets. They are in no way 'uneconomical.' RTL was on an educational mission in the market. The private channels only had to persuade their clients of the new criterion *once and one time only,* in order to be able to profit by it for a quarter century.

7. *Changing rules does not even necessarily imply a particularly high risk of backlash or failure.* There is an additional myth that Game Strategy – precisely because it is radical and challenges the general parameters of the marketplace – bears with it greater risks than conventional business strategies. The RTL example clearly refutes this mistaken prejudice. Had the RTL chief Thoma failed in his attempt, then absolutely nothing would have happened. The previously accepted measurement criterion would simply have remained in force.

8. *Changing rules can lead to sustainable success over years and decades.* The concept of Game Strategy may raise the false suspicion that it only concerns short term market successes. There is the temptation to believe that 'a game is only a game.' However, the RTL example proves the opposite. The 'advertising relevant target audience' has in the meanwhile been the measure of all things for over 20 years now, despite having obvious weaknesses. On closer examination, the focus on 14- to 49-year- olds is both naïve and anachronistic, but a standard does not have to be 'perfect' in order to be valid for a very long period of time.

ATTACK ON AN 'INVINCIBLE' MARKET LEADER

When standards for quality and performance change, yesterday's victors find themselves dramatically weakened, while competitors from the second tier are suddenly thrust to the fore. The example of RTL gave a first glimpse of the fact that this is entirely achievable also in markets outside of so-called 'lifestyle' sectors, where supposedly rational business decision makers and media planners make supposedly rational economic choices. The following example also comes from the business-to-business sector, this time in the pharmaceutical market. The target is doctors, who bear the responsibility for decisions that can affect health, and even life and death. We have chosen this rather 'serious' market to demonstrate that even here intuitively 'logical' quality standards can be challenged by a Game Changer whose plan is to destabilize a seemingly invincible market leader. Naturally, the Game Changer must respect ethical responsibility, and the health sector is certainly no exception.

Tackling an Apparently Unbeatable Market Leader Head On

Advantix is an antiparasite product for house pets from the pharmaceutical company Bayer – at the time a new and promising product with a new and unique efficacy profile that offered great hopes to the department responsible for its invention. Advantix was developed in order to solve a competitive problem that many managers have encountered in their careers. The new entry was up against a long-standing market leader that had built a powerful and deeply entrenched position in the marketplace over the course of years and decades. This market leader is called Frontline and in much of the world it enjoyed a position of absolute market dominance. Veterinarians appreciated Frontline because it was an excellent and highly reliable product that had been proven over many years. Dog owners were satisfied as well: they would take their pets to the vets' offices ready to request Frontline. Its superb effectiveness against parasites – so-called *killing power* – was at that time the measure of all things.

Why the Classical Marketing Approach Was Bound to Fail

In order to generate significantly greater growth, the Advantix team had to find a way to wrest major share away from the market leader. But how? According to classical marketing wisdom, the key was for Advantix to 'differentiate' itself from its competitor, to develop a unique selling proposition that would enable the brand to carve out its own distinctive profile.

That is precisely what the Advantix team proceeded to do. The first attempt capitalized on the fact that Advantix not only eliminated fleas and ticks, but also mosquitoes. In this manner, Advantix offered 'triple protection' against pests. This difference is only meaningful in certain climates and geographies, especially those where certain types of mosquito can carry life-threatening diseases. This is a classic unique selling proposition that – for reasons we will explain later – did *not* produce the desired breakthrough.

A second product edge possessed by Advantix is the fact that it eliminates, or better said 'repels,' a large part of ticks and fleas (80% or more) right from the first contact with the dog's fur. The Advantix marketing experts positioned this characteristic in a highly graphic and effective manner as the 'hot-foot effect.' Just as you would quickly pull your hand back from a hot stove, the majority of ticks and fleas fled from the dog's fur when it had been previously treated with Advantix. This is textbook marketing but, sorry, not a winner. The new approach was unable to make significant inroads into Frontline's dominant position.

'The hot-foot effect just wasn't getting us anywhere,' we were told by one of the product development experts from Bayer. 'The vets kept asking us, what kind of *added value* resulted from it. Frontline offers optimum killing power. No one wants any more than that. That's why vets can't see any strong enough reason to change to Advantix.'

Applying Game Strategy

In many markets there is a 'gold standard,' a measure of all things that is unsurpassable. For orange juice it is 'freshly squeezed juice.' In the antiparasite market the closest thing to that is '100% killing power.' In the absolute, of course, no parasite treatment can promise 100% killing power, but in the eyes of the veterinarians, Frontline came about as close as you possibly could to this magic number. As a result, the market leader was 'unbeatable.' Obviously, Advantix could tout their unique advantages, but as long as its opponent owned the gold standard, it was impossible to dethrone.

Approaching the dilemma from the perspective of Game Strategy, our solution was to put the gold standard to the test, to make it waver and, if possible, to replace it with a new, more qualified criterion. At least theoretically, this thinking offered a chance to attack the market leader's stronghold. At first glance, this way of thinking may appear questionable or even far-fetched: 'What do you mean a new gold standard? It is nothing less than absolutely logical and natural that as far as parasite treatments are concerned, killing power is what counts. If not that, then what else …?'

Unmasking 'Killing Power'

You really have to understand in depth the inner workings of the 'killing power' criterion, and to do so we spent many hours with Bayer's experts, analyzing precisely how ticks and fleas actually pester, bother and pose threats to dogs. 'The dog brings the parasites back with it from the woods,' one of the product developers explained to us. 'For example, ticks sit for a while on top of the fur, and then burrow into the coat and bite tightly on to the skin of the dog, transmitting their poison into the animal's bloodstream. This is how dangerous diseases are carried. But if the animal is protected by Frontline or Advantix, then the parasite dies before it can cause any real harm.' 'How long does it take for the parasite to die once it comes in contact with the dog?' 'Most die within a few minutes or hours, and the last ones after about 48 hours.' 'Does that mean that the parasites can have up to 48 hours to deliver their poison before dying?' 'Hmmm, well, yes, most standard medical studies use a time interval of 48 hours when measuring the effectiveness of tick preparations,' explained the experts.

This information was nothing less than a jolt. The parasites that attack the dog don't die immediately, but *survive for up to 48 hours*, able to bite the dog and infect it with dangerous diseases, before finally succumbing to the treatment. From this simple fact an important conclusion can be drawn. *You cannot blindly accept killing power as the measure of all things – even if it was close enough to 100%! What does killing power matter as long as a 48-hour window of risk remains, especially considering that, theoretically, a single tick is enough to transmit a dangerous disease during this survival period?*

Advantix Defines a New Gold Standard

By critically challenging killing power we were led directly to another more discriminating and thereby more highly qualified criterion, namely absolute risk of infection! '100% protection from infection' had the potential to become the new 'measure of all things'. Absolute 100% infection protection is obviously never attainable, neither with Advantix nor with any other competitor, but gradually approaching it is entirely within the realm of feasibility. In this way, the alternative gold standard can be applied to demonstrate Advantix's competitive edge over Frontline, and the competition suddenly can be viewed in a completely different light:

- We know that Advantix has a wide reaching repellant effect. At least 80% of all parasites are immediately driven from the dog's coat and die. This means that only *20 out of 100* parasites at most are able to reach the '48-hour window of risk' and can thereby be reliably eliminated.
- Since the market leader Frontline doesn't have any repellant effect, you have to presume that 100 out of 100 parasites are able to make it to the '48-hour window of risk.'

Now it becomes clear. Although Frontline can demonstrate a close to optimal killing power, it is evident that Advantix is significantly better than Frontline at controlling the risk of infection.

It is possible to go even further and challenge the entire proposition of the market leader. Isn't it a tremendously disturbing thing to consider that up to *100 out of 100* parasites are able to reach the animal before being killed after several hours? For a lot of people, the Advantix effect, through which at least 80% of the danger is eliminated right from the start, seems a lot more plausible. In focus group discussions with veterinarians, one participant said: 'I imagine a burglar in my house. It would be a lot better to scare him off at the door, as opposed to letting him in and then trying to arrest him 48 hours later.'

From all this we concluded that *if Bayer can succeed in establishing '100% infection protection' as the new gold standard – and there is no objective reason to think this is not plausible – then Advantix has a fair chance of becoming the preferred choice of vets, and to significantly weaken Frontline's stronghold position.*

Facts in Support of the New Strategy

It is not enough to depict Advantix's competitive edge *theoretically* or with some graphic analogies. Veterinarians demand facts, documentation and studies. Indeed, a well-known independent American research team was able to demonstrate – admittedly with a relatively limited sample – that certain animals that had been treated with Frontline had nevertheless significant levels of parasitic bacteria in their blood, which is to say they had been infected. The researchers conducted exactly the same study with dogs that had been previously treated with Advantix. The result: absolutely no parasitic bacteria in the blood of these dogs.

The old gold standard of performance: '100% Killing Power'
The new gold standard of performance, as advocated by Bayer:
'100% Infection Protection'

To summarize what we have learned, originally, *killing power* was the measure of all things, not only to scientists and researchers but also to veterinarians and consumers. No one dared to question this classic rule of the Game because it positively radiated the deceptive appearance of a rule of nature. As long as killing power remained the measure of all things, Advantix would never be able to seriously challenge or weaken the market leader. Its own unique selling propositions (such as 'triple protection' or the 'hot-foot effect') might have been enough to generate modest growth in the shadow of the market leader. However, they were simply not enough to challenge or confront that leader, to penetrate his stronghold, let alone to dethrone him. The most important and perhaps only possible opportunity for Advantix lay in turning the Game around: *establish a more qualified gold standard,* against which Frontline, too, had to be measured.

SURPRISING ESCAPE FROM A PRICE WAR

The previous case histories demonstrate how a new measure of performance can generate a significant competitive edge and weaken an opponent. Now we shift our focus to another critical aspect. How to escape from a price battle in a mass market, by moving 'up market' to a premium price position.

When a High-Class Player Cannot Win a Low-Price Competition

Some games are simply more 'sophisticated' than others and demand more skill from the players. Professional players almost always defeat amateurs in these games, such as in a complicated game of cards. Other games are trivial, banal and unsophisticated. Here, children, inexperienced and not particularly bright players can compete, and often have the same chances of winning as do experienced, talented professionals (think of the card game 'War').

The same applies in the marketplace. When banal, underdeveloped quality standards prevail, then the competition takes place at a very low level. Price tends to dominate the Game and premium players are rarely able to gain an edge over low-cost providers. When the majority of customers have no clear standard by which they can identify or appreciate a high-quality product, then providers of such products are unlikely to be able to sell much. They have little opportunity to use their strengths against the mass market sellers.

In order to go a bit deeper into the dilemma facing a high-class player in a trivial competition, let's imagine for a moment that the 'measure of all things' for winning the Nobel Prize for literature was 'commercial success.' If that were the case, then Joanne K. Rowling, the best-selling author of the Harry Potter novels, would have made several trips to Stockholm, probably more than half a dozen of them. Outstanding writers like Orhan Pamuk or Harold Pinter, on the other hand, perhaps because they do not appeal as much to a mass audience, would fail according to this commercial criterion. Their outstanding literary performances would be invisible in this competition and totally unrecognized. In this fabricated example, it would be right to contend that the competition takes place on a very low level indeed and that the world's most gifted authors couldn't win!

To summarize, in a low-class market game, a premium player often can't win – no matter how great the quality of his products or services may be. The strength of Game Strategy is to address this dilemma and to suggest a strategic way around it. One possible solution would be to propagate and establish a new, more highly qualified standard: a premium criterion that has the goal of raising the Game of the market to a higher level. How this works is illustrated in the following case study from the optical care market.

Thesis: Premium quality and premium performance will only be appreciated if there are firmly established premium criteria in the market.

A Classic Case of the Premium Player's Dilemma

Our story is about Zeiss, a respected German optics firm with a 150-year tradition of quality and innovation. The first microscope was produced there around 1850, and still today the company produces outstanding specialty microscopes for modern microsurgery. At one point Zeiss developed the most sophisticated telescopes in the world and today produces telelenses for the Mars expeditions. Zeiss has always produced lenses for cinema cameras and today sends its finest lenses to Hollywood. They are true premium players in the best sense of the word.

Ironically, in the down-to-earth and far less technologically complex business of eyeglasses Zeiss had never been able to truly exploit and capitalize on their competence edge. As can happen in many markets today, a downward spiral in prices brought with it merciless consequences. The winners were low-cost producers, including imports from Asia with unbeatable prices and well-accepted quality. National and international 'mass-market' brands were putting pressure on Zeiss's eyeglass business.

The Problem: a Market That Doesn't Appreciate Top Quality!

The management team at Zeiss invited us to work with them to find a solution to this difficult market situation. We experienced at first hand the degree to which the medium sized Zeiss organization is totally focused on technological top quality. Not only for microsurgery, space expeditions or Hollywood, but also for eyeglasses, Zeiss is firmly positioned as a premium producer.

Inspired by a century and a half of experience with the art of seeing, the Zeiss development labs came up with innovations straight out of a James Bond thriller. A typical example is that Zeiss engineers developed a video tower called 'Video Infral' that made it possible for opticians to film the 'vision process' of the customer's eye and to measure it precisely under different conditions. The measures were translated into precise mathematical algorithms that were beamed over the Internet to Zeiss production facilities where the glass lenses were ground. The grinding and focusing of eyeglasses involves a precision of hundredths of a millimeter. The slightest deviation can produce significant strain on the eye. With its innovative tower to measure vision, Zeiss enjoyed an undeniable technological advantage. The dilemma was, to put it crudely, nobody cared much. The optician's business is primarily about selling chic designer branded frames for glasses that offer the customer a sense of well-being and permitting them to express their personalities. At such an emotional moment, who gets excited about the technical advantages of superlative lenses? The magic Video Infral ended up as a tough and tedious sideline business – with little appreciation from opticians and their customers.

The Game Strategy Analysis

While Zeiss was occupied at the highest technological level with the *measurement of sight,* the market was ticking away at a much more modest level. In particular, customers paid attention to three purchase decision factors. Eyeglasses must be above all (1) antireflective coated, (2) scratch resistant and (3) super thin (therefore super light). Nothing more. These are the fundamental quality standards that lead all opticians and that guide the overwhelming majority of their customers.

We met with Zeiss management and described the problem in the context of Game Strategy. Our analysis can be summarized as follows: 'Right now, the Game in the market is being played at a very low level. The three predominant purchase criteria are related "only" to the physical characteristics of the glass material. These are relatively low-qualified standards, since even cheap producers in Asia can be relied upon to deliver solid processing of glass. On the other hand, your strengths are in the precise measurement of sight. That's something completely ignored by the market today – both by opticians and their customers. As long as you allow the Game to be played at this low level, you are not going to have much success as a premium producer.'

> **The existing quality measures in the market for eyeglasses were rather unsophisticated, because they were reduced to physical characteristics of the glass material. That is why the Game was being played at a low level.**

We illustrated this analysis with the example of the Nobel Prize committee, which led to the following conclusion. In order for Zeiss to stand out from the other market participants as a premium producer, the company must establish a new and intuitively aspirational premium performance criterion.

The Game Changer's Way of Thinking

How's this for a striking contradiction? Eyeglasses have to do with the 'art of seeing.' They support a highly sophisticated and complex physiological process, but, on the contrary, the market game revolves around the common criterion of *glass processing*, for which low-cost producers are trusted just as much as Zeiss. A new kind of 'quality' standard had to be established, and on a far higher level. There is a possible connection in the fact that perfect vision is the result of the *interplay between the defective eye and the corrective lens.* Eye and glass – the living and the artificial – must cooperate, interact and harmonize, perfectly.

It is on this higher level that the new premium criterion must be defined. The essence of the new premium criterion can be captured in the intriguing Game Changing Idea:

'Relaxed Vision' is a new measure of performance for eyeglasses, defining for the first time the opposite extreme to unnatural, strained, stressed-out vision that millions of consumers experience and suffer from day by day (especially the more mature consumers using reading glasses).

Let's remember that the eye is a 'muscle' – and one that's working 16 hours a day or more looking at computer screens, reading documents, files, books and magazines, watching TV or driving the car at night. Over the years, that muscle loses some of its power and specifically some of its ability to adapt as quickly and efficiently. You start wearing glasses to help the eye to work as perfectly as ever.

Now, who would you trust to deliver relief from that kind of eye fatigue? What about any one of these mass-market manufacturers that know everything about glass processing? Wouldn't it be a lot easier to trust a premium producer like Zeiss – one who has researched the art of natural and relaxed vision for over 150 years?

The 'Relaxed Vision' Tower Unfolds Its Magic

By establishing the new premium criterion, the Video Tower suddenly takes the spotlight in the entire sales approach toward opticians. The name of the futuristic column was changed from 'Video Infral' to 'Relaxed Vision Tower' and became a central part of the Zeiss proposition.

Now imagine, as a customer, you walk into an optician's shop. The optician points to this hightech column and offers to have your own personal vision process filmed, measured and the conditions of your 'living' eyes ground into your new eye glasses. Who wouldn't be tempted to experience that relieving comfort of 'relaxed vision'?

This is introducing a thoroughly fascinating and emotional event at the point-of-sale of Zeiss partner opticians. Customers who had always limited their decision making to picking the right 'branded' frames, suddenly become highly emotionally involved with choosing the right 'brand' of glasses, too. All those millions of customers who actually suffer from eye fatigue should naturally be inclined to find out how 'relaxed vision' can help them, too.

How Did the Competitive Game Change?

With the introduction of the 'relaxed vision' criterion Zeiss (as well as their partner opticians) was able to stand out from the mass market and, with its highly refined lenses, force aggressive price suppliers into a second league. 'Relaxed vision' had the potential to rise above the mass of competitors and establish itself on a higher level with new freedom for growth and value creation.

The Relaxed Vision Tower, by measuring sight, provided substance and credibility to the new strategy. In a sense, it served as the 'material' evidence for the 'immaterial' Zeiss competence, making 150 years of research experience in the 'art of vision' suddenly visible and tangible. In addition, the Tower created an exciting and involving customer experience at the point-of-sale, one with the power to leave the customer deeply impressed and catapult Zeiss back into a class of its own.

For so many years before, the sales talk had revolved around the rather technical question: 'So you want antireflective glasses, antiscratch and super thin? Do you prefer the economic version from our standard "partner" manufacturer or would you like the premium version from Zeiss?' It is easy to predict who would be the logical loser in that competition.

Now, imagine how the Competitive Game at the point of sale gets an entirely new twist when the optician introduces that hightech 'relaxed vision' to his customer, redefining his options much like this: 'So, you still have trouble with strained and tired eyes. Now, we can film and measure your individual "vision process" and get you some tailor-made "relaxed vision" glasses, or you could choose just to go ahead with "standard" eyeglasses.'

Quite obviously, the Game is changing here. Instead of revolving around technical 'glass' characeristics, we are now dealing with a new and highly aspirational gold standard. Everything is in place for Zeiss to de-class their mass-market competitors. The game is about to be taken to a higher level of sophistication – and Zeiss is in a perfect position to become the 'logical' winner.

Importantly, 'relaxed vision' turned out to be much more than a catchy buzzword for brand communication. It represented a value shift, both in the market and in the company itself. The new 'measure of all things' had to penetrate the entire organization and plant itself firmly in the consciousness of every employee. In the 'optical' business group, a complete reorganization of the product line-up and price strategy was necessary. There are different levels of 'relaxed vision' in different price categories and for different wallets. Equally important was the 'staging' of the new dimension of sight in the opticians' stores. An optician who serves his customers on this high-tech level can easily distinguish himself from his competitor around the corner, who in most cases concentrates on offering an extensive assortment of fashionable eyeglass frames. This turned out to be a highly fascinating proposition to recruit opticians nationwide as dedicated Zeiss partners. In a sense, Zeiss sales partners were upgraded to 'high-tech' opticians, easily recognizable through the illuminated frontdoor advertising flashing 'Zeiss Relaxed Vision Center.'

Zeiss partners receive a 'relaxed vision' tower at no charge, and in return designate Zeiss their Number One supplier for several years. For Zeiss this became a powerful lever for growth.

HOW GLOBAL POWER PLAYERS RULE THE GAME

Game Strategy deals with deliberately steering events in the market and competition by convincing and engaging other players, who sign up to your game *voluntarily*. Our next case study provides an intriguing view of how this works.

We are talking about diamonds. There's hardly another market in the world where value standards are as unified, clear and differentiating. The entire world revolves around the famous four 'Cs': Carat, Clarity, Color and Cut. The four 'Cs' are the measure of all things: for dealers, for customers, for scientists and for the media. Most people are unaware of the fact that this standard was 'officially introduced' just after 1945. Before that time, the value of diamonds was largely based on carat weight alone. The driving force behind the introduction of the four 'Cs' was the DeBeers firm.

The old quality measure for diamonds (before the 1940s): carat weight.
The new quality measures, as pushed by DeBeers ever since: the four 'Cs'.

We are going to show how DeBeers were also acting in their own self-interest by campaigning for the quite complex four 'Cs' standard. The goal was to steer and control pricing and value perception over the long term, in a market – as we shall see – especially subject to inflation and price declines.

Diamonds: Girl's Best Friend or a Perfectly Staged Value Illusion?

The fundamental conflict in the sector rests on the fact that diamonds are composed of nothing more than pure carbon. Carbon is the fourth most common element found on Earth, as abundant as water in the oceans. Pencil lead consists of the same basic substance as diamonds and so do charcoal briquettes. The raw material is extraordinarily 'common' – in contrast to rare materials such as gold, silver or uranium. On top of it all is the further *harmful* fact (for the industry in any case) that diamonds are for all intents and purposes imperishable. Ever see anyone throw away a diamond? Around 1870 massive diamond mines were discovered in South Africa, resulting in a huge supply increase. In the shortest of times, mining investments exploded, and along with them the stock of diamonds. In brief, the common raw material was not even in short supply and an accelerated price decline threatened the entire market. In the 1930s DeBeers founded the Central Selling Organization (CSO) as a global marketing cartel. They were able to achieve an almost perfect balance in supply and demand around the globe. Even the apparently impossible was achieved. Despite a massive increase in supply, the value of diamonds rose with astonishing constancy, except for some brief turbulence in the 1980s. This price and value stability benefited not only the diamond producing industry but also customers and diamond owners. So much for history.

There was, however, a considerable weak point in the power game: control was exercised only over the relatively small quantity of *newly mined* diamonds. This comparatively small quantity of diamonds faced a veritable Mount Everest of 'old diamonds' and 'used diamonds,' collected and stored over the years, decades and centuries in the jewelry boxes and safes of hundreds of millions of people across the entire globe, and that naturally are 'imperishable', rust-free and never lose their value over the years. This massive second market for 'used' diamonds represented a constant, sleeping threat of existential dimensions. Imagine what would happen if because of economic recession, war or natural catastrophe, the diamond markets were to be flooded with 'old diamonds.' Prices would drop through the floor and a tidal wave of diamonds would inundate the market, shaking the DeBeers empire to its foundations – a secret nightmare for the firm's management. How can the company protect itself against an uncontrollable collapse in the market?

How the Four 'Cs' Enabled DeBeers to Exert Market Control

At this point the introduction of the famous four 'Cs' enters the picture. When these new criteria were introduced in the 1940s, there were suddenly thousands of possible classifications for the value of a diamond. The way in which diamonds had previously been valued was a kind of secret science, impenetrable to lay people. This absolute lack of transparency served the valuable purpose of hindering the development of a secondary market. The previously unorganized and uncontrollable market for used diamonds was now channeled through the qualified network of the DeBeers dealer organization. In order to sell diamonds, owners were forced to turn to the experts in jewelry stores, who valued the diamonds according to the rules of the Game set down by DeBeers. Through this complicated set of classification standards, the previously uncontrollable secondary market was channeled into the expert network of the CSO. So round one goes to the diamond clan!

But the Next 'Sword of Damocles' Is Already Hanging over the Diamond Market

Now the bell rings for round two, because today DeBeers must face its next strategic challenge. In the meanwhile, it is possible to 'breed' diamonds in the laboratory for a relatively modest cost. Over the course of centuries, alchemists attempted to produce pure gold from common raw materials. In vain, as we know now, and nor will it ever be possible in the future. However, it is a different thing with diamonds. Today it is possible to manufacture artificial diamonds that from a chemical perspective are practically identical to natural diamonds, at a fraction of the cost. Now there is the very real danger of a massive collapse in prices. Importantly, there is no 'natural law', no scientifically mandated reason why diamonds produced in the laboratory should be any less valuable than natural diamonds.

The German newspaper *Süddeutsche Zeitung* reported the following test. Two diamond 'breeders' from the firm Apollo presented one of their do-it-yourself diamonds to a jeweler in New York City by the name of Shenoa & Company. The salesperson examined and checked the jewel carefully and said: 'Beautiful diamond. How much do you want for it?' The US firm Gemeis today produces diamonds for decorative purposes. A diamond produced in Gemeis laboratories at a cost of $4,000 is entirely comparable to a natural diamond costing $20,000 or more. From an objective, scientific perspective, the two are identical.

Now imagine the nightmare scenario from DeBeers' point of view. For millions of diamond purchasers, there is no aesthetic or optical possibility to differentiate between a natural diamond and a man-made diamond. Even professional jewelers are often unable to see a difference with conventional instruments. Not even scientists see differences that they would call 'relevant.' In other words, at the beginning of the 21st century the emergence of man-made diamonds threatens to cause nothing less than an earthquake in the value perception of a multibillion dollar market. The price and value surge that had been going on over centuries was facing the threat of collapse.

What should a global player like DeBeers do in such a situation? First of all, DeBeers has no way to influence the scientific facts, but they can influence the Game in the market and the rules according to which it is played. At the end of the day, that is what counts for market success.

In the spirit of Game Strategy, DeBeers must define a new criterion that can separate 'valuable' natural diamonds from 'inferior' artificial diamonds. Scientists began the search for such a criterion and finally came up with this. Natural stones consist of layers of carbon atoms in the form of clumps, while the atoms in man-made diamonds are distributed far more evenly. As a consequence, the two types of diamonds absorb light differently. Looking at it soberly and seriously, this value criterion is entirely random. Why should the value of a diamond depend in any way on the distribution of carbon atoms? We are dealing with the deliberately calculated establishment of a rule of the Game and not a natural, scientific or logical fact.

Facing the challenge of man-made diamonds: the order of the carbon atoms is deliberately and arbitrarily introduced as a 'disqualification criterion' for man-made diamonds.

Today the race is on to develop highly sensitive, high-tech measurement devices to permit experts to measure the light refraction of a diamond. In the logic of the Game, these devices are able to distinguish between 'artificial' and 'natural' diamonds. Looked at from the perspective of the Game Changer, these devices actually have the function of separating 'desirable' from 'undesirable' diamonds. By ennobling those carbon atoms, DeBeers took on the role of a Game Changer, able to define a new standard, precisely designed to defeat the enemy – artificial diamonds. To put it in the terms of Game Strategy:

An unwanted opponent in the market was disqualified by a new and deliberately selected quality criterion!

The new measurement devices would be able to fulfill a nearly existential purpose. They should be able to hinder inflation by maintaining the value illusion and, in so doing, protect the interests of the diamond cartel and diamond owners.

Why You Need to Win 'Allies' Who Start Playing by *Your* Rules

Admittedly, DeBeers is a hugely powerful company that enjoyed favorable pre-conditions, permitting it to intervene in the market. However, you have to hand it to DeBeers: they could not simply *impose* their Game Changing Idea – they needed to *recruit and win over allies* in order to introduce the new criterion, including scientists, experts and opinion leaders. We anticipate that this new criterion, based on the layering of carbon atoms, will in all probability attract a swarm of committed fellow players. In the final analysis, it is in almost nobody's interest that the value illusion of diamonds collapses because of 'man-made' production. Certainly that applies to the hundreds of millions of customers who own valuable diamond jewelry. In a nutshell, the market is a game and the winner doesn't just follow the rules, but knows how to control them.

THE ESSENTIALS IN OVERVIEW

In the billion dollar advertising market, RTL set a new measure of performance. In the market for antiparasite products, Bayer established a new measure of all things, as did Zeiss in the market for eyeglasses and DeBeers in the diamond market. In each of these case studies, an individual firm defined a new standard for the market. They changed the definition of quality and performance. They influenced the valuation standards according to which not only they but also their competitors would be measured in the future.

The performance measures that decide a competition are among the most powerful instruments in a game. The typical player views them as part of the general conditions. The Game Master starts from the viewpoint that measures and standards in principle are subject to change. Because clients want to maximize their utility, they are willing to learn and accept new – qualified – criteria for quality and performance.

Quality and Performance Standards Can Be Changed

Consumers enter hundreds or even thousands of markets as purchasers. The Federal Office of Statistics in Germany recognizes 1853 market classifications.

Going further to the level of individual product categories and subcategories produces a five-figure number – *tens of thousands of market categories*. Each of them has a different standard for quality and performance. The average consumer has an active vocabulary of about 3000 words, but he can buy products from far more than 3000 categories, from toothpicks to Didgeridoos. No one is an expert in all markets; no one knows how to recognize superlative performance in each and every purchase decision. Herein lies the opportunity for the Game Master to actively intervene in the competition and educate customers about new quality measures.

You Can Influence Competitive Power Relationships

A qualified standard gives consumers what they need to compare and evaluate different sellers in the market and to select the 'best.' Change the standard and you also change the relative strengths of the different sellers. In this chapter, we looked at three examples:

1. *In the competition among TV channels.* According to the original measure of 'reach to the total population' RTL would today be at about the same level as the state-owned broadcasters. By applying the standard of 'reach to ad receptive target audiences' RTL has double (!) the market share of ARD or ZDF. This gives RTL the lion's share of advertising spend and a massive power shift.

2. *Pharmaceutical products for pets.* If antiparasite products are measured solely by their 'killing power', then the market leader Frontline appears to be unbeatable. However, by applying the new performance measure of '100% infection protection' Advantix can suddenly use its own strengths and demonstrate a considerable quality advantage over Frontline.

3. *The diamond market.* Natural and artificial diamonds are chemically identical. The sector is in the process of establishing the special layering of carbon atoms as a 'disqualification criterion' for artificial diamonds, in order to eliminate this existentially threatening competitor from the market definition of 'true' gemstones. Here, too, it is a question of controlling the market's power relationships.

Move the Market in a 'Premium' Direction Through a New Standard

New standards can raise upward the market's perception of value. The measures of performance and quality are also the drivers of value creation. Previously, the value of diamonds was measured solely by carat weight. Through the four 'Cs' over a thousand upward value gradations are possible. The price of a one-carat stone can be multiplied tenfold when it reaches top scores in each of the four 'Cs' categories. This demonstrates how the Game Master can influence the behavior and price sensitivity of his customers.

To open the market for eyeglasses required the rejection of common glass-oriented standards and the introduction of a new value scale that raised natural, relaxed vision to the measure of all things. With 'relaxed vision', Zeiss rose above the price-driven mass market and created new freedom to grow in the premium segment.

You Need Allies to Establish New Standards

The standards for quality and performance do not rest on scientific facts, but rather on an informal consensus among the players in the market. Even a global syndicate like DeBeers did not use its power openly to convince the world to accept the four 'Cs' value scale. New rules of the Game have to be inherently sensible and convincing if they are to be accepted by the market. RTL initially was not in a position of power to force its new standard on the advertising industry, which had several billion euros to divide. Naturally, media managers let themselves be convinced of the 'advertising relevant target audience' idea, because it appeared both reasonable and qualified.

In the same manner, Bayer was able to convince rational thinking and scientifically trained veterinarians of the validity of their new standard, as did Zeiss within the broad-based network of opticians.

Second Game Strategy: reshaping the market landscape

Today, all players engage in 'segmenting' the marketplace – much like slicing a pie. Most players do this with the objective of identifying a 'niche' where they enjoy relative liberty from competitive pressure. Segmentation is all about dividing the market into smaller and smaller units, until it falls apart into mere 'fragments.' 'Positioning,' as it is most commonly understood, is about finding the optimum 'position' within the complex market environment.

The Game Master thinks and acts differently. He seeks to change the face of the market landscape with an entirely different objective: he wants to redirect the fundamental dynamics of the Competitive Game. Our case studies will show how, in this manner, he can avoid negative market trends; he can create booming new categories and he can build structural barriers able to defend against his most dangerous competitors. He can achieve all this without major product innovations or massive financial resources.

The game is played in the context of an *established market landscape* that can be broken down into submarkets, segments, classes, levels, camps, categories and fragments. Take the automobile market for instance: this enormous market has evolved into an elaborate structure over the course of the past century. On some fronts of this structure a mighty battle rages, while on others there is an uneasy ceasefire. Each segment represents a unique culture or subculture. While one automobile segment booms, a neighboring one might find itself in the midst of decline. Life pulses within these market structures, while tectonic shifts gradually move the market's general conditions. Some categories and segments will thrive, while others – even new ones that only sprang up yesterday

– by tomorrow will be little more than history in the *design of the market landscape.*

> The 'structure of the marketplace' is the overriding framework comprising all categories, segments, leagues or classes, sectors, levels and generations.

HOW MARKET STRUCTURES 'REGULATE' THE COMPETITIVE GAME

It is commonly believed that the market landscape has 'grown organically,' as if it were following some preordained blueprint. However, the reality is different: market structures are conceived, created or 'made' by human beings, more specifically by all the companies that offer products and services. These companies 'establish' new categories, segments or niche markets, attract new generations of consumers and drive forward the structural process of change. Statisticians and market researchers live from and with these structures. They subdivide markets in order to make them measurable and break down cultural diversity into countable units fit for their databanks.

This arrangement naturally benefits the firms participating in the market game. Structures provide an overall 'big picture' and sense of orientation. Often, market participants informally agree on a simple model of the complex and differentiated market reality according to which they align their behavior. A particularly simple example of such a 'market model' can be found in the complex *political landscape.* At some point in the past, a 'two-wing' model was conceived, separating a left wing from a right wing. Looking a bit closer, you find an 'axis model' of the political landscape, moving from a political far left extreme to a far right one.

For decades, almost all participants on the political scene oriented themselves to this axis: some parties positioned themselves to the left and some to the right, while others struggled to hold the 'middle.' In exactly the same manner, the media and electorate argue and debate according to the 'logic of the axis.' This kind of simple model makes life easier for all the players. In the World Wide Web, we are currently witnessing a two-generation model: Web 2.0 splits off from Web 1.0, and there is now even a Web 3.0 looming on the horizon. However, even this structural categorization is nothing more than a deliberately simplified image of a far more complex marketplace reality.

When 'Positioning' themselves, the players in the market usually refer to a generally accepted and highly simplified 'model of the market.'

Touching on the Phenomenon of 'Structural Effects'

When the structures of the market evolve and a structural shift occurs, the Game in the market also changes. With the division of the World Wide Web into two generations, two opposing camps suddenly emerged: Web 2.0 with a 'positive charge' and Web 1.0 with a 'negative charge.' Internet companies were assigned to one of the two camps by the media, investors and opinion leaders, like it or not. The members of the camp Web 2.0 profit from a positive trend, because they represent the future. At the same time, the market punishes members of the camp Web 1.0, irrespective of their solid business results. They are abruptly dismissed as representing 'the past.' In a sense, they became victims of newly emerging market structures – and even the healthiest business performance couldn't help them. This type of powerful impact on your business – resulting exclusively from newly emerging structures – is called 'structural effects' in the terminology of Game Strategy. Depending on which category, segment or class a product or company is assigned to, structural effects can generate positive or negative 'leverage,' with significant bearing on their marketplace success.

In an extreme case, such structural effects can lead to massive marketplace distortions. When in the 1990s the global economy split into the New Economy and the Old Economy, quite a few small operations that had been 'founded in a garage' were highly praised, for no other reason than they had been assigned to the 'New Economy.' On the other hand, a number of healthy but traditional firms bursting with profits suffered from an 'Old Economy' label. This demonstrates something that is true for all markets: structures 'regulate' who wins and who loses in the market, because the market participants shape their behavior according to market structures and models. This holds for the companies themselves, but also for consumers, dealers, investors, opinion leaders and journalists. Everyone understands: *the simpler the model, the more marked the resulting behavior pattern of the players.* That brings us to the central thesis of this chapter:

By influencing market structures, it is possible to deliberately influence or change the normal behavior pattern of your customers or trade partners – and hence the dynamics of the Game.

What Distinguishes 'Game Changers' from Ordinary Players?

Most companies simply accept the existing structures of the marketplace as part of the general conditions, without spending a lot of time thinking about them – just like the rest of us when we accept the tried and tested 'axis' of the political landscape. Most of the time, good, ordinary players search for their own unique Positioning in an existing market landscape, or search for and occupy 'gaps' and 'niches' in the market model. At the same time, every ordinary player is on the lookout for major structural shifts. The instant a new category booms anywhere in the market, as soon as a trend wave appears, the good ordinary player will try to surf it. For example, as soon as the category Web 2.0 came into being, there were a lot of surfers on the move: investors, the media and consultants, and, naturally, the Internet companies themselves. Nobody wants to miss a trend shift when it could offer the promise of a competitive edge in the market.

> **Ordinary players in the market think like this: 'We must position ourselves within the given market landscape and we must follow and surf the trend when certain segments boom.'**

Anyone who has tried it knows that surfing is an art unto itself, but the Game Master isn't satisfied with just surfing. He demands more. He strives for outstanding growth and knows how to intervene in a precise manner in the very internal workings of the market in order to give himself a competitive advantage.

Ryanair showed what this can mean. On the one hand, a new market was conceived and born, but at the same time the new low-cost airlines opened up a 'second front', throwing down the gauntlet to national flag carriers. Over 50 low-cost airlines are now assembled along this front. Together, they constitute an informal alliance, strong enough to fight a massive battle and revolutionize the market. Ryanair not only established a new category, but laid the structural foundation for the two-tier structure of the air travel sector. The result is a fundamentally changed market dynamic and the creation of a new model that has changed the very nature of the competition. The conclusion is clear: directly intervening in the structures of the market constitutes a powerful competitive tool – and it doesn't require too much to make it work for you.

> **The Game Master thinks: 'All of the market structures in place today were defined at some point in the past and put into place**

> by people. That means I, too, have every right and opportunity
> to actively shape these structures, and in this way change the
> competitive situation to my advantage.'

Admittedly, this claim might seem a bit bold at first glance, but Game Strategy means deliberately ignoring any and all taboos when it comes to thinking about new ways to achieve growth. Right now, we are talking about taking on an entirely new role in the market: as a maker of structures, the one who establishes the frontlines, builds the bridges and fixes the road signs – ultimately, as *the designer of the market's landscape.*

This image may make some readers a bit uneasy and others will skeptically wrinkle their brows. If you belong to the latter category, consider for a moment that 'changing structures' doesn't always mean fomenting a revolution in the sector (as Ryanair did). Something that works on a large scale can often be equally effective on a smaller one. Our case studies will prove that there are also minute, delicate interventions in market structures that can result in exceptional growth. Specialized and niche markets, too, offer opportunities for Game Changers to use structures to their own advantage.

BALANCING ACT BETWEEN FLOP AND GLOBAL SUCCESS

The simplest way and means to intervene in the structure of the market consists of establishing a new segment or subsegment, a new 'class' or even a new market itself. Wherever there is innovation – new products, new services, new concepts – companies have always been creating new segments.

The added value of Game Strategy starts one step further. Game Strategy explores how the Game in the market, the behavior of the players (including dealers and customers) and the dynamics of the market changes when new categories or structures come into being. Ultimately, we want to understand more exactly how Game Changers can use this knowledge, how they can intentionally change structures in order to give a new twist to the Game in the market, create new frontlines, block off powerful competitors, avoid negative trends or even create a totally new growth dynamic. This is the focus of the next case histories.

The Game Master changes structures in the market landscape because he wants to 'manage' market dynamics or change current competitive power relationships in his own favor.

Red Bull: Born to Fail?

Most of our readers will have heard or read a lot about the global success story of Red Bull. Here, we will zero-in on one aspect that is particularly relevant from a Game Strategy point of view: how Red Bull strategically 'managed' potentially disastrous market dynamics, even before the product was launched.

The Red Bull story begins in 1984. During a trip to Asia, the Austrian Dietrich Mateschitz (40 years old at the time) was introduced to a drink called 'Krating Daeng – Red Water Buffalo,' sold in brown medicinal bottles and offering a miraculous cure for jet lag. Excited by his discovery, Mateschitz made the dramatic career move of resigning his position as a successful manager at Blendax (now an oral care division of Procter & Gamble) and acquiring rights to the original formula for this magic elixir from its Japanese owners. Making a bet with his personal savings equivalent to about $500,000, he founded his own company. For three years he struggled with the 'Red Bull' concept – product, name, packaging – but ended up bitterly disappointed. The new soft drink was a spectacular failure in all product and taste tests. The sweet, syrupy flavor was just plain disliked by the tasters. 'Like melted jelly beans,' complained one, 'like cough syrup,' mocked another. Mateschitz later recalled this moment as 'the bitterest defeat in my entire career.'

Here's where the story should have ended. When a new product fails all the tests after three years of product development, then the ordinary market player knows what he has to do: pull the plug. You can lead a horse to water, but you can't make him drink. A flop is a flop, assuming there were no dramatic technical testing errors. However, that would have been too easy: modern market research isn't like reading tea leaves.

The Game Strategy View

Imagine yourself for a moment in the market landscape at that time. The category 'energy drinks' doesn't exist yet, but of course there were lots of soft drinks and other sodas. Product taste testers were given a new drink that looked like a soda.

It had bubbles like a soda. It contained water, sugar, flavorings and was carbonated – just like a soda. It is easy to imagine what the testers thought: 'Sure, right, a new kind of soda.'

Naturally, the market researchers drew the testers' attention to the effects of the drink: the 'energy boost' it gave. What was so special about that? Didn't colas contain caffeine? Simple Game Strategy analysis highlights three points:

1. The new product was 'classified' by the product testers as a new type of soda. There was quite simply no alternative at that time, since 'energy drinks' as a defined category didn't exist back then.
2. In this way, that classification turned the new beverage into an unwilling player in the Game of soft drinks and sodas. Red Bull had to stand up to a direct comparison with other soft drinks and sodas, without much chance of success. Here's an exotic bubbly beverage from the Austrian hinterland climbing into the ring with the glamorous soft drink brand leaders like Coke, Sprite and others.
3. As a supposed player in the soft drink market Red Bull was subject to be measured by the rules of the Game that applied to sodas and soft drinks. However, the 'measure of all things' for soft drinks is 'taste.' There was no escape from this premier quality criterion for Red Bull. The testers probably said to themselves: 'First and foremost soft drinks are supposed to be fun and taste good, not have some kind of effect. Red Bull doesn't taste good. Ergo, it's not much of a soft drink.'

Red Bull was signed up involuntarily as a player in a game for which it was entirely unqualified, and was forced to confront vastly superior competitors and be measured against quality criteria it never had a chance of meeting. In the logic of this game, Red Bull was a *born loser.*

This simple Game Strategy analysis casts a new light on the test results at that time. Red Bull didn't fare poorly because it was a lousy product. It fared poorly because the new drink was mistakenly classified as a soft drink, and accordingly measured against the 'wrong' expectations, criteria and quality standards.

If you had overlooked or not understood this fine analytical distinction, then based on the original test results, you would never have launched Red Bull – and lost out on a global success and a billion dollar brand. As an experienced marketing man, Mateschitz recognized his opportunity to create his own game, instead of playing an old game that he could never win against vastly superior opponents.

What Happens When You Are Able to Establish a New Category?

With the establishment of 'energy drinks' we witnessed a market discontinuity in the truest sense of the word. To put it in the words of Game Strategy, *Red Bull started its own game, playing by its own rules.*

Red Bull deliberately abandoned the Game of soft drinks and sodas on its own volition. In so doing, the brand maker achieved two goals:

1. Red Bull avoided comparison with the bigger and vastly superior soft brands, according to the motto: 'We aren't anything like soft drinks! Those are nothing more than inexpensive fun soda pops. Red Bull is the Father of a new class of high-quality performance beverages!'
2. Simultaneously, the inventors of Red Bull freed their new beverage from the pressure of being measured against that criterion according to which soft drinks are the 'measure of all things', namely 'taste.' In your own category, it is possible to establish other, different quality standards, which to a certain degree you can define according to your own terms.

The Red Bull team profited from the advantage that we call the 'founder's privilege'. In a very real way, Red Bull became king in a realm it had established on its own. Here the brand makers can set standards, define yardsticks and introduce new rules of the Game. The premier rule of the Game in the category of energy drinks is: 'Hey guys, having an effect is what it's all about!' Good taste was downgraded to a secondary characteristic and relegated to the background. Bad taste has traditionally been a confirmation (!) of effectiveness. We can all remember Grandmother chiding us: 'If it's going to work, it's got to taste horrible'. From necessity a virtue is born: as an 'efficacy' drink, Red Bull was able to capitalize fully on its poor taste.

With the establishment of energy drinks, another tectonic shift in the competitive frame occurred. When Coca-Cola and Pepisco finally decided to launch their own energy drinks, they had to orient themselves to the standards, yardsticks and rules of the Game laid down by Red Bull – the energy original! Coke's energy drink is called 'Full Throttle' in the USA. It looks suspiciously like Red Bull –

similar taste, similar packaging, similar price. The almighty Coca-Cola bows to the unwritten doctrine of the original, in order to be perceived as an authentic member of the new class of products. The same is true for 'Adrenaline Rush' from Pepsico, and for over a hundred other competitors. Ironically, all of them even attempt to duplicate the syrupy, melted jellybean taste that was almost the downfall of Red Bull in the original taste tests – *simply to be accepted as an 'authentic' energy drink.* It is hard to imagine a more effective way to demonstrate that, by founding his own category, the inventor of Red Bull intervened directly in the very internal workings of marketplace competition.

Red Bull was doomed to be a 'logical' loser in the 'soft drink game'. Only by starting their own new game (the 'energy drinks' game) and establishing their own new rules did they create the conditions needed to become the actual winners of global success.

An Idea Morphs into a Marketplace Reality
In the beginning, the invention of 'energy drinks' as an independent category was just an idea that the makers of Red Bull considered 'useful.' There was no scientific necessity to classify Red Bull as a new category. A chemicals laboratory could just as easily have classified Red Bull as a 'soda' or a 'soft drink' – albeit with a higher percentage of caffeine.

The manager of Red Bull, behaving as a Game Master, did have an interest in seeing that his idea ('Red Bull is its own category') was transformed into a marketplace reality. Said another way, he wanted to succeed in having their new segment of energy drinks 'officially' recognized in the market landscape. In other words, the Game Master had to achieve an *informal consensus* with the other market players: consumers had to believe in it, and so did the retail trade, gastronomy and the media. Only when everyone by and large agrees does the new category take life and become part of the marketplace reality. Only then does a new structure take shape and have a long-lasting effect on the dynamics of the market. Only at that point do the 'structural effects' begin to function in the manner described above.

For the inventors of Red Bull, the challenge lay in declaring as clearly as possible the independence of the new category, especially when compared to soft drinks. They decided to separate themselves from the soft drink and soda categories on four levels:

1. *A different 'category benefit' from soft drinks.* The idea of a soft drink could
    be summarized as 'fun and taste,' whereas 'energy drinks' stand for a higher
    and more qualified purpose. Having a concrete effect is a serious promise that
    must be delivered. Remember that the Asian ancestors of Red Bull were sold
    by pharmacies in brown medicinal bottles. If Red Bull were to be mistaken
    for a soda with a kick, then this same kick slips into the ranks of secondary
    qualities, subordinated to the core idea of a soft drink: 'fun and taste.'

2. *A different packaging from soft drinks.* Mateschitz insisted on a characteristi-
    cally slim cylindrical can, a shape that had never before been seen in a soft
    drink. The trade in the original German and Austrian markets reacted sur-
    prised, even angrily. They demanded a broader range of containers, *just like
    with other soft drinks.* In this situation, giving in to the demands of the trade
    would have been extremely dangerous, since it would have hindered differ-
    entiation from normal sodas.

3. *A different pricing from soft drinks.* Early on, the retail trade and gastronomy
    thought the Red Bull inventor was out of his mind. Why should this strange
    new drink be two to three times more expensive than Coca-Cola, the biggest
    and most famous soft drink brand in the world? *This is because it is a per-
    formance drink, and not just any other soft drink.* Serious performance can,
    should, perhaps even must be more expensive. A price per can in line with
    that of Coca-Cola and other sodas would have put Red Bull back on the wrong
    track – just another fun drink like all other sodas! The makers of Red Bull
    had to break free decisively of all pricing guidelines that applied to normal
    soft drinks.

4. *A different style of communication from soft drinks.* In order to separate itself
    from the soft drink universe, Red Bull had to break out of all 'expected' soft
    drink communication formats. There were no lifestyle ads; that, too, would
    have risked the credibility of the new category and put Red Bull right back
    in the territory of soft drinks.

A new category needs to be obviously independent if it is to be recognized
and respected as such. The founders need to create category signals that can be
distinguished from the 'badges' of neighboring categories and markets.

Lessons from Red Bull

Many believe that a new category definition (such as 'energy drinks') is no more
than a slogan in the market, a new generic name, a new label for a new product.

Some people may be reminded of a librarian expanding the classification system in the archives by establishing a new category.

Game Strategy sharpens our consciousness that the creation of a category can fundamentally influence the surrounding market landscape. New camps, front-lines and barriers are created. A new dynamic is unleashed. The founder of a category has the unique opportunity to intervene directly in the events of the market and to steer the Competitive Game according to his own interests.

Just like the makers of Red Bull:

1. They withdrew their new entry from an 'unwinnable' competition, namely against soft drink brands.
2. They opened a new game, establishing their own rules and conventions, which had to be accepted by their competitors.
3. They neutralized, or better said, transformed the biggest presumed product disadvantage (namely its terrible taste), not merely into an insignificant secondary problem but actually the fundamental characteristic or 'emblem' of the new category, that every competitor had to imitate if it wanted to be accepted as a credible energy drink.

In the truest sense of the word, the makers of Red Bull emerged as 'Game Changers.' They played with the structures of the market landscape in order to 'manage' market dynamics, to block off powerful competitors (namely soft drink brands) and create the market environment required for dramatic und sustainable global growth. Today, just short of 20 years later, Red Bull has annual sales of about three billion euros ($4 billion) across 130 countries around the globe. In most regions, its market share is between 70 and 90% of the energy drink market! Mateschitz is a billionaire, owns more than a dozen private jets, a Formula 1 racing team and most recently his own television channel. All thanks to a product that initially flunked all the tests.

OUTFOXING A NEGATIVE TREND IN THE MARKET

Markets can be as moody and unpredictable as a film star. There may have been an economic boom lasting several years and all of a sudden, the wave dies down, stagnation starts or the market may even contract. All of this is part of a structural shift. Companies have to adjust to this and recognize the trends early on in order to respond as quickly as possible. In a positive case this means: 'My market is booming, I can surf on the trend wave and let the internal dynamics of the market work for me.' What happens in bad times, when suddenly a negative trend wave sweeps over the market? A lot of people would say: 'There's nothing anyone can do. No one can resist the market's dynamics on their own, turn or even reverse them. A negative trend looks like an unlucky shift in fate that one simply has to accept.'

The Game Changer thinks differently. He doesn't let himself become a pawn, subject to natural market forces. He understands how to transform a negative trend into an opportunity for exceptional growth by taking control of the market's structures. Do you believe that extraordinary marketing or sales offensives are the only answer? Our next example shows how small, but astonishingly precise, interventions in the design of the market landscape can be enough to generate remarkable results.

A Boom Market Suddenly Goes into a Tailspin

You would be hard pressed to find a more competitive or price-driven market than the North American automobile sector, which enjoyed a marvelous stroke of luck during the boom of the so-called SUVs (sport utility vehicles), those high-priced off-road vehicles that actually end up getting used primarily for city driving. In the course of just a few years, those models became the 'motors' of the entire industry. At their peak, every fourth car on American highways was an SUV. The entire nation was swept by SUV fever, to the joy of American auto manufacturers. That is because SUVs were playing on their home court. The Mother of all off-road vehicles was the American Jeep, and US models dominated with a market share often in excess of 85%. In the home of the cowboy and real men, Japanese, Korean and German manufacturers hardly stood a chance of breaking into this fortress.

Then at some point, the whole mood shifted. Around the turn of this century a new trend wave took the market by surprise and shook it to its very foundations. When oil prices rose dramatically, SUVs were suddenly slammed with a gas-guzzling reputation. The media stoked this anti-SUV mood. A dark shadow fell across the market, the negative image first slowed what had seemed like irresistible growth and then sales declined precipitously. The party, as they say, was over.

In the boom years at the end of the 1980s the Japanese automobile manufacturer Toyota decided to develop its own SUV. In their home market, off-road vehicles were minor factors, but the global market was so promising that the Japanese introduced their first SUV in the middle of the 1990s.

Since 98% of SUV owners never actually drive the vehicles off-road, the Japanese simply put the large body of an SUV on the chassis of a standard sedan. In this manner, a 'pseudo' off-road car was created, which actually was better suited to the urban jungle – while it was totally inappropriate for off-road use. What a paradox: an off-roader that can't go off-road! A classic 'wannabe' product with a built-in inferiority complex, and launched at precisely that moment when the SUV market had collapsed. Is it conceivable that the new vehicle's better handling (more like that of a sedan) and superior fuel economy would be enough to save the day? After all, there were dozens of other vehicle categories that were smaller, handled better and were more economical than an SUV.

With the abrupt trend change, the Japanese found themselves confronted with a triple challenge:

1. They were late. The boom was over. Buyers had become cautious. The media was spreading an anti-SUV mood. The market melted away. How could Toyota create a success and growth story in a shrinking market?
2. In America the Japanese were not seen as having any core competence as far as off-road vehicles were concerned. Toyota may have been the most success-ful automobile manufacturer in the world, but the SUV sector demanded an authentic outdoor image, which is about the last thing Americans associated with Japan.
3. For true off-road vehicle enthusiasts, they were nothing more than 'wannabe' SUVs with a huge inferiority complex. If this stigma were allowed to persist, long-term image damage would be the result. Which driver wants to risk being laughed at behind the wheel of a 'phony' SUV?

What were Toyota, Honda and the others to do? The negative trend in the SUV market couldn't be reversed by a couple of foreign manufacturers of 'pseudo' SUVs. 'Bad luck,' some would have thought. 'Sorry, but that's a structural shift. You've got to accept it fast. As has been said in the past, Those who are late will be punished by life.'

The Game Master's Point of View

The Game Changers in the market look at hopeless situations such as the one described above from an open and free perspective. Their attitude goes: 'Basically,

I always have a choice about which game I want to play in the market!' Or, from the viewpoint of Toyota and its followers: 'We can either do the logical thing and play the Game of the SUV market with our new models or we can just as well start a completely new game – and establish our own rules.'

The Game Master recognizes *he has options*, something the mere player overlooks. No one forces him to participate in the SUV game, especially not now that the boom has died out and there are no realistic chances of success. The Game Master focuses on the alternative: establish his own category, separating himself from classical SUVs. This option exists because the new models are in fact different and distinctive, with distinguishing characteristics, qualities and attributes compared to classical SUVs.

Toyota Invents a New Category and Escapes a Negative Trend

Therefore the Japanese decided to invent their own class for their new models, christening it the 'Crossover SUV', aka the CUV or XUV. In so doing, they simply walked away from the classical SUV category. They cut the cord from the mother category in order to start life on their own. This is absolutely critical to understand. In order to survive, a new category needs its own idea, able to justify its right to exist. Such a new idea is already visible in the designation 'Crossover.' Here comes the perfect 'cross-breeding' of an 'off-road vehicle' with a 'sedan'. The credo is: 'Crossovers offer the roominess and attractive outdoor image of an off-road vehicle, together with the fuel economy and handling of a family sedan – the best of both worlds.'

Unleashing Powerful New Market Dynamics

The new game idea quickly proved to be extraordinarily successful. From a Game Strategy perspective, not only is the idea key but also those 'structural effects' arising from the establishment of a new category and resulting in a fundamental change in the market and competitive situation.

1. The new vehicles uncoupled themselves from the negative dynamics that had come to dominate the SUV market. They withdrew from comparisons with other SUVs, escaping the negative category image that had been stirred up by the media.

2. 'Pseudo'-ness was no longer a problem. The fact that Crossover vehicles were built on the chassis of a normal sedan was no longer a disadvantage, but actually part and parcel of the original Crossover idea. It is the sedan chassis that makes the new category the 'best of both worlds.' Crossovers couldn't be compared to classical SUVs, and so were able to avoid the kind of off-road showdowns where they almost certainly would have lost.

3. As a new, independent class of vehicle, the opportunity arose to create a positive, independent aura. Crossovers increasingly moved toward the 'premium' end of the spectrum, attracting new target customers, the well-heeled and cosseted Baby-boomer generation. These people love Crossovers, because alongside the raw, off-road image they also offer the comfort of a luxury sedan.

In the new game new rules and laws were introduced. Again, they helped those who invented the Game. Economical luxury became the driver leading further development of the Crossovers. New gas-saving models were launched, and some of them were even equipped with a hybrid engine system. At the same time, manufacturers built ever-more comfortable interiors that especially appeal to women.

The SUV Is Dead; Long Live the Crossover!

While the SUV market finds itself in what some observers call 'free fall,' the Crossover class's growth motor is humming. Today there are already 43 different CUV models on the road and by 2009 that number is projected to grow to over 70. Market researchers predict that by 2009, CUVs will have advanced from fifth place to first as the fastest growing vehicle class. CUVs were the true heroes of this year's Detroit Autoshow. Between 2000 and 2006 they registered a growth of 500% and the trend continues unabated.

This example shows that it is entirely possible to escape a negative trend in the market. Mere players would most probably have tried to position the new vehicles as 'smaller, more economical and comfortable SUVs.' This was the case with Ford's launch of the Escape model in 1999. From a Game Strategy perspective, the attempt was doomed from the start, since it implicitly acknowledged membership in the SUV category and had to suffer along with that category's negative image. In order to create a positive, independent dynamic, you had to first create the new category.

The Japanese auto manufacturers established their own category for their new models in order to uncouple the connection with classical SUVs. In that way they laid the structural groundwork for their own remarkable growth and market success.

What We Can Learn from This Case Study

In the offices of the statistics authorities (such as the National Bureau of Statistics) or large market research organizations (such as Nielsen) there are hundreds of employees whose primary function consists of classifying, categorizing and to a certain degree mapping markets. The actions of these organizations nurture the misperception that the market landscape is growing according to its own dynamics.

The Crossover example illustrates how the establishment of new categories or subcategories can contain a 'higher' strategic intention, which is the real goal behind the creation of categories and structures: namely intervening intentionally in the events of the market in order to generate a new competitive situation, to avoid a negative dynamic or to unleash a new positive dynamic force in the market. You can do that with products that initially seem to be just the opposite of groundbreaking innovations. Many people believe success depends on the quality or fascination of your product. Game Strategy makes us conscious of the fact that market success and growth first and foremost depend on which game we are playing and according to whose rules.

HOW TO CONQUER 'IMPOSSIBLE' MARKET POTENTIAL

What was possible in the automobile industry can also be transferred to specialized markets in the business-to-business sector. The following case study demonstrates how a small intervention in the structure of the market, executed with nearly surgical precision, was able to bring about a dramatic shift in competitive dynamics.

We would expect that most of our readers are not specialist experts in the field of diabetic therapy – and you may not be too excited about delving deeper into that rather 'dry' academic matter. However, from a Game Strategy perspective it is important to realize that even in the world of health and pharmaceuticals, where doctors and scientists are among the key players, Game Masters can change the rules, win allies and turn the Game and the competitive power relationships. This, of course, is only legitimate if it is in the best interests of their patients, too.

A few years ago, we received a call from the pharmaceutical firm Aventis (today known as Sanofi-Aventis). They were searching for a sustainable growth strategy for an insulin product called Lantus. The sales of that product had peaked two years after launch and now the marketing team was setting out to capture a business potential that industry insiders called 'unconquerable' in the truest sense of the word.

Facing the Insurmountable 'Insulin Barrier'

In the market for diabetes medication (more precisely for Type 2 diabetics who are still able to produce some of their own insulin) a distinction is made between 'tablet patients' in the early stages of the illness and more advanced 'insulin patients' who need to take daily injections of their medicine. The sector talks about a kind of natural 'diabetic career.' You start with one tablet a day, then two, then three, and at some point there is the major and irrevocable 'camp transition.' After several years the typical patient finally moves forever from the 'tablet camp' to the 'insulin camp.' And therein lies the problem. The tablet patients experience massive emotional resistance during the transition to the negatively charged insulin camp, even though they accept intellectually the need from a medical perspective. This so-called 'insulin barrier' creates huge headaches for insulin manufacturers. Patients behave as if on the other side of that barrier they were entering a prison from which there was no release. It is a life sentence in the 'insulin camp' and is not much of an exaggeration to say this is how many patients feel.

The Goal: Unlocking a Major but 'Impossible' Market Potential

For insulin manufacturers like Aventis there is an extraordinarily attractive market and growth opportunity: A *million tablet patients* in Germany alone receive insufficient therapy, and really should have made the transition to insulin injections a long time ago, *and for the rest of their lives.* From a medical standpoint, every attempt to move insufficiently medicated tablet patients over to insulin was not only clinically legitimate, but urgently needed, because otherwise more serious consequences threatened, among them dialysis, blindness and amputation of limbs.

Now the strategic thinking task was how to convince a million undermedicated patients to move to the 'correct' insulin camp. How can you help them to break through this massive invisible barrier? And finally, how can the insulin preparation Lantus capture a large share of this 'impossible' potential?

Getting a Deeper Understanding of the 'Insulin Barrier'

Let's take a deeper look at the issue. What is the 'insulin barrier' ultimately about? What is it really that makes the 'insulin camp' so scary? There is a lot more to it than just the fear patients have about giving themselves shots. Today's modern 'pens' take most of the pain and complexity out of injections. What the patient really fears is a radical change in lifestyle, and one that he will have to live with for the rest of his days. He experiences the move from the tablet camp to the insulin camp as an irrevocable change in *personal status,* a final, definitive alteration in his own *self-image.* The thinking of the typical tablet patient runs something like this: 'When I'm finally over there, in the insulin camp, my life will change radically and forever. I've got to give myself insulin injections up to four times a day. I've got to plan all of those injections according to meal times, which means I've got to plan my meal times down to the half-hour exactly, and figure out in advance how much I can eat. I've got to take blood sugar measurements every day and count every slice of bread I eat. There's no getting around it: my whole future routine will revolve around my illness and the treatment. From the day I start those insulin injections, my whole life hangs from the end of the needle.'

It's natural to recognize and respect major status changes in life, especially the positive ones. Think about your bachelor's party before getting married or those herds of chain-smoking men walking around in circles in the waiting room, getting ready to evolve from mere 'husbands' into 'fathers' with everything that brings with it. Even in these generally *positive* instances the 'status shift' is charged with fear and anxiety. However, in the case of diabetes we are dealing with a *negative* status shift: from 'normal person' to an 'insulin patient' forever dependent on that needle.

The Classic Marketing Approach Turns out to be a Dead End

Aventis was not the only company looking for a solution: so was the entire market of insulin manufacturers. How do we surmount this barrier? How can we succeed in converting insufficiently medicated tablet patients to insulin?

The market had developed and implicitly agreed on a very simple 'model' of the market landscape which guided the thinking of the pharmaceutical managers. They imagined two camps – a tablet camp and an insulin camp – separated by an emotional insulin barrier that they had to overcome. This view became part of the structure of the market and it doesn't require much effort to see how it could be interpreted to be part of the fixed general conditions.

With this two-camp model of the market in mind, there was an obvious (apparently!) solution that the industry discovered in fairly short order. It consisted of creating a new *transitional therapy*, designed to be an *entry-level insulin therapy*. It sounds logical enough: if making a 'hard' switch to insulin doesn't work, then the entry-level therapy builds a bridge the patients can more easily cross over to insulin. Unfortunately, if this entry-level therapy was such an obvious correct solution, how come every attempt to use it failed? What went wrong?

The Game Changer's Different Perspective

The Game Master always starts with the question, 'How do the market's structures influence what happens' or 'How do structural effects influence the Game?' In the foregoing example, he is not content to accept the idea of a transitional therapy, but rather wants to understand how this new class of therapy fits into the surrounding market landscape and which consequences – which 'structural effects' – result from that position.

One thing is fairly clear about the entry-level insulin position. The entry into the insulin market is logically on the other side of the barrier, where the rest of the market is located. As a result, the patient views this kind of transitional therapy as the first step into the negatively charged insulin camp, which represents a major status change in life and a negative self-perception. He has no choice but to internalize this status change completely and emotionally before he will accept an entry-level insulin therapy.

This explains why an entry-level insulin therapy has no hope of solving the problem. It may promise a soft landing after the jump over the barrier, but the barrier still exists and still has to be surmounted.

A Strategic Sleight of Hand

When dealing with this type of subtle mind game, we like to convene a 'Game Changer's Workshop.' That may sound a bit pompous, but it serves the purpose of reminding the participants of one iron rule: 'No thought is taboo to the Game

Changer. He elevates himself to the second level of the Game in order to restructure it to his purposes.' This simple thought process usually is sufficient to free-up everyone's thinking.

On this basis we proposed the following line of thought to the Lantus team. Transitional therapy is a pretty good idea in principle, but who says it has to be on the *other side* of the barrier, in the negative camp? Why do we have to define it as an entry-level insulin therapy? Wouldn't it be far better to conceive of a transitional therapy as the *last stage of tablet therapy*, which would keep it on *this* side of the barrier, still in the positive tablet camp?

What we were doing, in the truest sense of the word, was nothing less than intervening in the design of the market, integrating the new class of therapy not behind the wall, but *in front of it*. This seemed like a pretty clever and provocative idea: a final stage of tablet therapy, which just happens to include the first daily insulin injection. It might seem a bit contradictory at first, but on closer examination everything becomes clear. It isn't the injections that constitute the shift in camp, but rather the expected life change resulting from them. If you can avoid the latter, then the patient is logically and emotionally able to remain in the positive tablet camp.

In order for the new class of therapy to be a success there was one inviolable rule. *The final stage of the tablet therapy must be designed in a manner that does not require a dramatic change in quality of life.* The Lantus product itself was ideal for this purpose, thanks to its regular and long-lasting effectiveness profile. In this new stage of tablet therapy, everything stays the same (well, almost everything!). There was no complicated planning of mealtimes. In general the injection didn't have to be timed with a meal, and just one lasted the entire day. The new class of therapy had to be designed so that the patient could keep his personal status and self-perception ('I am still a tablet patient!'). The early stage diabetic receives first one tablet, then two, then three, and from there it is just one *small step* to a complete tablet therapy, which happens to include a single daily injection. The patient stays happily in the tablet camp and simply changes to a new subsegment. Tablets continue to be the mainstay of the therapy, just as they were before.

A Nice Kind of Trojan Horse

At this point, some of you may be wrinkling your brows and asking: 'The patient still has to take an injection, even if it is only one a day. How can this mean he is still in the tablet camp? Doesn't that automatically make him an insulin patient?'

Here's where you have to pay very close attention, because a single injection every day does not imply a status change or a new self-image. Someone who eats vegetables once a day is not in the 'camp' of vegetarians. Someone who drinks one glass of wine a day doesn't consider himself in the 'camp' of alcoholics. Therefore a diabetic whose basic medication consists of tablets, but who also receives one injection a day, does not consider himself to be a member of the camp of 'insulin patients.' He continues to be a 'member' of the tablet camp, because he continues to have a relatively uncomplicated life, which insulin patients no longer enjoy.

It's not much of an exaggeration to say: 'We transferred an insulin product to the positively charged tablet camp.' Dressed in the clothes of tablet therapy, insulin is no longer terrifying. That's why we compare this strategy to a 'Trojan horse.' A strategic sleight of hand, legitimated by the fact that the 'camp shift' results from a medical necessity.

Playing Strategically with Structural Effects

To translate this case into the formal language of Game Strategy, in the market of diabetes therapy two camps oppose each other: one positively charged and one negatively. In the natural dynamics of the Game, things always flow from the negative pole to the positive pole. However, the entry-level insulin Positioning tried to force tablet patients to switch from the plus camp to the minus camp. This explains in Game Strategy terms the fatal flaw in the entry-level insulin therapy.

Aventis' strategic sleight of hand consisted in establishing the new transitional therapy not as a segment of the minus camp, but as still part of the plus camp. To a certain degree, Lantus was trying to establish a positive link with tablet therapy. The strategic goal was to let the structural effects of the plus camp work for the product. The 'small step' toward a final stage of tablet therapy no longer represented a significant problem for the majority of undermedicated diabetics.

Aventis established new structures in the market landscape, creating the preconditions for sustainable growth and unlocking an 'impossible' market potential.

Launch and Success

After final testing and confirmation by the company's team of medical experts, Lantus was launched in the market as 'basal-supported oral therapy,' or BOT for short. The name itself indicates that we are talking about an oral therapy, which means a tablet therapy. Basal-supported means simply a harmless, tiny injection of basal insulin, which only needed to be administered once a day, thereby playing a supporting role to the tablets.

The BOT idea caught on immediately with the entire scientific community. The BOT principle was the subject of reams of medical literature, and today is on the curriculum at all universities. Meanwhile, Lantus has gone on to become the leading insulin in Europe. It is the first product that broke through the billion euro annual turnover threshold.

A decisive factor in the success of BOT – as the final stage of tablet therapy – is that it *opened the doors to a new, nearly exclusive distribution channel, namely general practitioners and family physicians.* Because it involves an extension of tablet therapy, general practitioners are the first to presume that they are responsible for BOT. Aventis was able to free itself of the constraints of a limited circle of 1200 diabetes specialists and enlist the support of a large part of the 45 000-strong force of general practitioners. In this new market, Lantus was a pioneer, a first mover, and therefore able to stake out its territory months before the competition could respond.

What We Can Learn from This Case History

Many managers have difficulty accepting the notion that an individual company can intervene in the structures and dynamics of the market, or actually behave as 'designer of the market landscape.' The 'Lantus' example shows that this is in fact entirely possible. The new transitional therapy unleashed a new dynamic that affected millions of undermedicated patients. They opened the door to a new distribution channel, namely general practitioners. So now the question is, how could Aventis achieve this? How can an individual firm use such a powerful lever in the market and bring forth a totally new dynamic force?

To understand this, we must remember that at one point in time, the new therapy 'BOT' was nothing more than an idea – in fact an idea that did not involve any kind of a new product, but rather those that had been on the market for many years. For this idea of a new class of therapy to fundamentally change the 'model of the market landscape' only one condition had to be met: allies had to be recruited for the idea, in particular, doctors, scientists, specialized journalists and opinion leaders. The more these allies accept the new model of the market landscape, the more surely the new model could emerge as the accepted market reality.

THE LAW OF THE SELF-FULFILLING PROPHECY

Market structures are movable primarily because they are 'virtual.' They are based on ideas, preconceptions, pictures or models of the market that have been generally agreed upon by the marketplace participants.

If you want to introduce new market structures, you need a convincing or, better still, 'highly infectious' *Game Changing Idea*, able to recruit and win over the other players in the market. The market has got to 'want' the new structure. The American automobile market 'wanted' the Crossover category once things started going downhill for classical off-road vehicles. Sanofi-Aventis was able to introduce the new BOT therapy class only because doctors 'wanted' it. The expert community believed the idea made medical and therapeutic sense.

Strictly speaking, the Game Master cannot 'introduce' new market structures, but he can 'propose' his idea to the market. If the market finds it convincing, then other players begin to orient themselves accordingly. In this manner, an abstract idea is gradually transformed into part of the market reality. So in a way, you could say the mechanism is modeled closely on the law of the self-fulfilling prophecy.

You don't need exceptional market clout or enormous capital to change the market structures. Either the 'big idea' finds fellow players or the Game remains unchanged. No one can extort or impose new structures. The invention of Web 2.0 is an exceptionally convincing idea that unleashed a structural change. This case shows how the law of self-fulfilling prophecies functions and what astonishing effects it can produce.

An Idea Splits the Market

It happened sometime during 2004. A new category was born: Web 2.0. This is a lot more than just a 'buzzword'; behind it stands a Game Changing Idea that literally divided the market into two generations.

Sketching the 'Web 2.0' idea, in the world of the Internet, the interactive age had dawned. A hundred million users gradually evolved from more or less passive consumers of the World Wide Web to active creators. The future of the Internet belongs to those companies who understand how to capitalize on the knowledge, creativity and intelligence of their users. Google was one of the standard bearers of Web 2.0, because the ratings of websites by their users influenced how well they did in the market. This part of the Google search engine algorithm is the basis of its superiority vis à vis competitors. Those Internet companies who are able to use the magic of the networking effect will rank among the winners tomorrow. The Internet has become the first truly interactive medium in history.

This idea excites a large part of the world. Many already speak of a *cultural revolution*. For centuries, the mass media were basically one-way streets: books, print media, radio or television. Suddenly in the Internet, *interactive* services boomed, services that were created by the users themselves, with their own content. It is important to recognize that Web 2.0 rests 'only' on an idea. There is *no* new IT platform behind it, *no* new programming language and *no* new system of rights management. There is 'only' a new idea, but one believed by millions of people around the globe.

The Market Adjusts to the Structural Change

The Web 2.0 idea heralded the beginning of a structural change. All of the sudden, a new 'model of market landscape' emerged. Two camps popped up on the surface of that model, one labeled 'Web 1.0 generation,' the other labeled 'Web 2.0 generation.'

The market participants made it real, behaving as they always do. Sooner rather than later they embraced the new trend and oriented their behavior according to the new model of the market.

The media in particular 'loved' the idea of the interactive cultural revolution and ensured that the new idea virus was spread around the entire world. Investors were the first players in the market, swarming like bees around those young Internet companies perceived as belonging to the ideal types of the Web 2.0 age. For example, My Space, a user generated platform on the Internet, enabled several dozen million users to establish their own personal virtual presence; on YouTube, the Internet's video channel, users could post their own video clips; or Xing, the contact network for business people. This kind of virtual exchange platform, also called 'online communities,' boomed everywhere.

It wasn't long before the Web 2.0 virus started infecting the Internet companies themselves. They, too, altered their behavior. New business concepts and IT platforms were developed in order to prove that they belonged to the class Web 2.0, as if it were a seal of guarantee for their future potential. Everyone wanted to surf the Web 2.0 megawave.

Actually, they didn't have much of a choice. Suddenly a curse was cast upon all of those firms unlucky enough to be suspected of belonging to the Web 1.0 generation. They came under enormous pressure, even when their core businesses were perfectly healthy.

The Structural Effect: 'Losers' Suddenly Become 'Winners'

The new winners in the Internet are called My Space, YouTube, Facebook or Xing. They have one thing in common: they all belong to the category of 'on-line communities.' This is an amazing phenomenon, considering that in the first ten years of the World Wide Web on-line communities were not much more than sideshows, totally off investors' radar screens. Now all of a sudden they were heralded as the new heroes.

With the invention of Web 2.0 on-line communities were transformed from neglected 'nobodys' to leading actors on the Internet stage.

Don't forget, nothing had actually happened to the concepts of the online communities. To this day, many still lack a convincing business model, but simply by incorporating the interactive idea of Web 2.0, they came to be seen as the big winners of tomorrow, profiting from positive structural effects. In 2005, the Australian media mogul Rupert Murdoch paid a spectacular $580 million for My Space. One year later, Google swallowed the video platform YouTube for $1.6 billion. The predominantly German business club Xing cashed in on a remarkable 150 million euros at its public offering, based on a relatively modest annual turnover of only 10 million euros during 2006.

There's no doubt that we are talking real money with the investors' billions. At the same time it is clear that Web 2.0 is actually just a virtual category that exists only because millions of people believe in it.

Even 'virtual' new structures can unleash a 'real' marketplace dynamic.

The Brain Behind the Cultural Revolution

The man who invented Web 2.0 is an American of Irish ancestry by the name of Tim O'Reilly. O'Reilly is not a powerful tycoon and nor did he invest billions to incite this web revolution. The circumstances surrounding the birth of Web 2.0 were actually quite modest. O'Reilly is the owner of a computer-specialist publishing firm in California, and a well-known personality on the Internet scene: an expert in ancient languages, Harvard graduate, amateur farmer and Internet mastermind. In 2004 he wanted to organize a conference on the future of the Internet. He assigned a colleague the task of coming up with a powerful slogan, and along came the idea of Web 2.0. That's all. To hatch a revolution, sometimes all you need is a single *Game Changing Idea.*

'By helping people understand the Web 2.0 phenomenon, we can set something in motion,' said O'Reilly. 'We can actually make this future vision a reality.' O'Reilly understands how the world – or the marketplace reality – changes. He designated Web 2.0 a self-fulfilling prophecy. In so doing, he helped shape the future of the Internet.

It is entirely possible that if you are reading this book a few years after it was published, you may smile at the fact that the category Web 2.0 has long since disappeared from the market landscape. That is entirely conceivable. New markets can persist for an eternity, but they don't have to. Some games last decades or even centuries; others disappear after just a few years.

> **The 'Web 2.0' idea changed the market reality much like a self-fulfilling prophecy: the Cultural Revolution actually happened, merely because it was predicted.**

What We Can Learn from 'Web 2.0'

Many people believe 'Web 2.0' is just a modern slogan or buzzword, suitable only for media hype. Game Strategy realizes that there is a lot more behind it, namely a new perception of a changed model of the marketplace reality or, more precisely, a Game Changing Idea, according to which the players orient themselves. It results in the creation of totally new behavior patterns, new dynamic tendencies. The 'old' game in the market starts a new round. These very real consequences should reveal the true identity of the 'Web 2.0' idea.

Individual players almost always revolutionize their markets with a highly infectious idea. Tim O'Reilly did not need a new technological platform, no new software, no global organization, no millions in the bank to revolutionize a market. It was sufficient for him to employ a single, highly effective idea to put in motion the powerful mechanisms of the market. It may surprise you to know that Tim O'Reilly never realized any economic benefit himself from the Cultural Revolution he started, but rather acted out of pure idealism. He wanted to help shape the future of the Internet. There is nothing wrong with that. Nowhere is it carved in stone that a Game Changer has to act out of a capitalistic motivation.

CHANGE THE WORLD WITH A RADICAL IDEA

As the Web 2.0 example shows, market participants like simple models of the marketplace landscape. Old web generations, new web generations: for many, that's how simply the market is structured. The underlying reality is naturally far more complex and multilayered. No doubt a lot of first class and sustainable companies are unjustly branded as Web 1.0. At the same time, a lot of other companies successfully surf the Web 2.0 wave, despite having little real substance and even less of a future. But the market participants love simple market models, according to which they can orient themselves. Even the hoary Axis model structuring the political landscape makes life easier, despite it being 'just' a model.

Now let's take a look at another example of how a single player sets out to push through an entirely new 'model of the market reality' – with the aim in mind to achieve a fundamental behavior change among the global players.

> **The players in most markets informally agree on a highly simplified 'model' of the complex market reality. By successfully propagating a new model, which seems to mirror the current market reality in a more convincing way, you can trigger a fundamental rethinking and behavioral change in the Competitive Game.**

An Economics Professor's View of a Better World

Coimbatore Krishnarao Prahalad is among the most influential economics professors and business masterminds of our time. This native of India teaches at the University of Michigan and advises multinational companies as well as global organizations such as the United Nations. Presumably because of his Indian origins Prahalad began in the winter of 1995 to think about the poorest people in the world. He calculated that four to five billion people around the globe subsist on less than two dollars a day. He posed himself the question of how poverty could be abolished once and for all during the 21st century.

As a world economist he formulated the provocative theory that what we consider today the 'global economy' actually affects only about 20 of the world's population – *80% of humanity is excluded from the globalization game.* Prahalad is convinced – and many famous economists share this view – that the only sustainable way to solve the problem of poverty lies in integrating the Third World into the global economy. He coined the concept of *integrative capitalism.* This concept aims at defeating the corrupt shadow economies of the Third World, raising standards of human rights and using environmental protection to generate positive effects on climate change.

Prahalad is a man of deeds, not just another professor in an ivory tower. To improve the world, he had to change the globalization game – to create a new thinking and behavioral standard among the global players. So he started with the 'model' of the global market.

Analysis: A Traditional Model of the World

Prahalad observed that economic analysis historically viewed the world in a two-camp structure: here are the rich industrial nations, there the poor of the Third World. Between the two is an enormous gap that is growing ever wider and deeper. Rich and poor drift further apart, instead of coming closer to one another. Prahalad determined that this view of the world had become firmly entrenched.

Now Prahalad proceeded to analyze in the spirit of Game Strategy. The two-camp model is highly emotionally charged. What has historically occurred between the 'rich' and the 'poor' camps can best be characterized as either 'fighting poverty' or 'exploitation.' Fighting poverty means: the rich give donations and loans to the poor, and expect little if anything in exchange. A pretty uneconomical concept. Exploitation means: those who do business with the Third World are, or are suspected of being, blatant exploiters.

Prahalad decided that the traditional two-camp model of the market – here the rich industrial nations, there the poor developing countries – is unsuitable to realize the vision of integrative capitalism.

The two-camp model is chock full of old prejudices, provokes negative thinking and prejudices the emotions of the global manager. Old thought templates become rusted and hinder the kind of paradigm shift, the rethinking, the kind of behavioral change that Prahalad had in mind.

To establish a new Game, under the banner of 'integrative capitalism', Prahalad needed a new model for the world. In a very real sense, Prahalad had to do *nothing less than re-order the world.*

A Pyramid-Shaped Model of the World

So Prahalad set to work and conceived a new model of the global economy: in the form of a pyramid, whose peak ('TOP' or 'top of pyramid') represented the industrial nations and whose base ('BOP' or 'bottom of pyramid') represented the broad mass of four billion people in the Third World. In this new design it should be noted:

1. There is no two-camp order anymore. The new pyramid model is a single, unified framework. The gap between rich and poor has disappeared. The Third World is already an integral part of the new whole.
2. The Third World now enjoys a significant enhancement in status. In the pyramid model, the base – and along with it the four billion people in the Third World – clearly occupy the *more important* position. *The base bears the weight of the pyramid. At the same time, the base comprises most of the volume of the pyramid. Long term growth in a global economy therefore must come from the base of the pyramid!*

How Prahalad Justifies His New Model

By re-ordering the world market, Prahalad established the structural foundation needed to root out old thought patterns and create a behavioral change among the global players. He had to give the Game a new dynamic and a new direction in order for the Third World to become an integral part of the Game in the future.

The new model of the pyramid suits these purposes perfectly. Any global player who accepts the idea of the pyramid will in all probability redirect his thinking, opinions and actions according to the inherent 'logic of the pyramid.'

That is why we call it a Game Changing Idea or, a bit more modestly, an idea with the inherent potential to change the Game.

Prahalad introduced three fundamental reasons why his new pyramid model was a better reflection of reality than the old two-camp model:

1. In the markets of the poorest of the poor a significant capital power lay slumbering. Taking together eight countries – China, India, Brazil, Russia, Indonesia, Turkey, South Africa and Thailand – gives a total of 3 billion people or 70% of the world population. Calculated at purchasing price parity (PPP) they constitute a collective 'gross national product' of 12.5 trillion dollars. That is more than the GNP of Japan, Germany, France, Great Britain and Italy together. A market of these dimensions, argued Prahalad, simply cannot be ignored. These countries fully deserve their role as the base of the pyramid.

2. Already today it is evident that the Third World is the decisive driver for future global growth. For example, 50% of the increase in the cell phone market comes from poor countries such as India, South Africa or Latin America. In China alone there are today 373 million cell phone connections, in India there are 83 million and in Brazil 65 million. Market size and market growth also support the argument that the BOP has the dominant role in the expansion of wireless technologies across the globe. For example, Fishermen in India's coastal state of Kerala after a long day at sea will call a number of possible docks along the coast. They then decide where to bring their catch according to the highest bidder. Their simple catamarans haven't changed for centuries, but the new process of determining prices on the basis of reliable information has revolutionized life in Kerala. In the Third World a business model for entrepreneurs could be based on providing one PC for four users or renting a single cell phone and charging according to minutes used. The Indian conglomerate ITC decided to connect farmers in India's rural regions with PCs. To do this ITC conceived an electronic town market, giving soyabean producers the opportunity to access prices not only from local auction houses, called Mandis, but also from the Chicago Board of Trade. That enabled farmers to improve margins on their products, by more accurately matching supply and the timing of sales according to current market conditions. Prior to the introduction of computers, small-time criminals had ruthlessly exploited ignorant farmers.

3. The base of the pyramid already houses today the motor for technological innovations and revolutions for the next years and decades. At this very moment, innovations are being pursued with the potential to produce a 30 to 100 times cost effectiveness ratio and is able to change the global market fundamentally. The innovations that will put a decisive stamp on the 21st century no longer originate in the industrialized countries, but at the BOP. For example, the Tata Company in India is developing a car that will cost no more than $2000. This requires radical innovations in all areas: in the materials used, in production, in design, but also in durability, since the roads in India are so poor. Don't forget that Ford was once the largest company in the world, because it was the first to be able to produce automobiles for simple farmers. A similar effect of scale can be envisaged if someone is able to offer a car costing $2000 to the vast middle class of the Third World. If you need a cataract operation in the United States, you can count on a bill somewhere between $2500 and $3000, but in India they have developed a procedure for the same operation that can be performed for between $30 and $50. This cannot be explained by lower personnel costs alone. We are talking about a process revolution. Comparable examples, we learn from Prahalad, exist in huge numbers. They all demonstrate that *the globalization revolution will come from below, from the base of the pyramid.*

What Managers Can Learn from Prahalad

Prahalad has been lobbying around the world for his new model of the globalization game. Without question he finds a receptive audience among the global players: multinational concerns are beginning to rethink their expansion strategies. Scientists and politicians are starting to think in a new way. Senior representatives at the United Nations are working directly together with Prahalad. *Business Week* named his bestseller, *The Fortune at the Bottom of the Pyramid,* Book of the Year. This case demonstrates the following:

> **By developing and forcing through a new 'model' of the market, you have a very real opportunity to create a breakthrough change in thinking and behavior.**

In this spirit, renowned economics professors such as Prahalad are engaging themselves as passionate Game Changers. The 'global players' pay them the highest compliment of all by beginning a new round in the Game based on their new game ideas – even when it comes to deadly serious subjects such as Third World poverty or globalization. The game is played everywhere by a vast range of parties with differing or even competing interests.

THE ESSENTIALS IN OVERVIEW

Now you know about the second variant of Game Strategy, namely the art of changing market structures as a precondition for significant growth or – as is the case with Prahalad – to force through certain idealistic views.

Most players look at the 'established' structures of the market landscape as if they were part of the untouchable framework conditions in the Competitive Game. The Game Master knows that, on the contrary, these structures can be powerful forces that he can use to intervene in the competitive events of the market.

How Market Structures 'Regulate' Competition
New Economy, Old Economy, Web 1.0, Web 2.0, the Crossover category, energy drinks, BOT – all are examples of relatively new categories that changed the design of the market with far-reaching effects on the competitive events of the marketplace.

• Red Bull transformed itself from a predicted flop into a global success. The brand maker withdrew his new beverage from an unwinnable fight against sodas and started his own game with his own rules. Today the Coca-Cola Company and Pepsico have entered the new category; however, by and large they have no choice but to play by the rules established by Red Bull.
• The 'pseudo' SUV overcame the negative market mood for classic off-road vehicles by founding a new category: 'Crossovers.' As a clever blend of off-road and sedan ('the best of both worlds') they broke free of a negative market trend and created their own boom.
• The insulin treatment Lantus saw that its greatest chance was to free itself from the negatively charged insulin camp by creating a new subcategory in the

positive tablet camp. With this move, Lantus conquered an 'impossible' market potential.

The strength of a company or a product is not always found in its 'inner' values or qualities. By knowing how to create and exploit structural effects in the surrounding market landscape, you can achieve extraordinary growth.

No License Needed to Change Market Structures

Normally, the structures of the market are viewed as part of the fixed general conditions. Most players far too seldom realize that these structures are not 'given,' but rather are 'made,' and that they, too, can contribute to the design of the market landscape.

As a reminder, here are three of the most important theses in this section:

Thesis 1. *Many structures are purely virtual, depending 'only' on an informal consensus in the market.* This holds for the category 'energy drinks,' for the category 'Web 2.0,' even for the 'New Economy' and 'Crossover SUVs.' New market structures are not founded on logical or scientific necessity, but often on strategic expediency.

Thesis 2. *Nevertheless, they can unleash or facilitate real, new dynamic forces.* A new category or structure transforms itself from an 'idea' into an irrevocable market reality as soon as enough players consent to conform to it. It is totally irrelevant that the web 2.0 generation was built 'solely' on an idea. For the Game Changer O'Reilly, what counted was the reality of the resulting dynamic force. He wanted to change the Internet and help shape the future.

Thesis 3. *Sometimes only a minimal impetus is needed to force through new structures.* Because new structures require a consensus in the market, first and foremost they must contain a convincing idea if they are to be successfully introduced. The new diabetes therapy BOT very quickly developed its own momentum like an avalanche, because it resolved a serious therapeutical problem and was welcomed by doctors and opinion leaders. A 'highly infectious' idea is able to unleash powerful forces in the market and can achieve far more than conventional marketing or sales offensives.

Think Again about the Model of *Your* Market!

The participants in the marketplace readily agree on a simple model of reality: for example a two-camp order, a pyramid or an axis. Because most of the players orient themselves according to such simple models, behavior patterns can quickly become solidified. If the Game Master succeeds in propagating a new model of market reality, he has a chance of breaking through this stultified thinking and behavior routines, and achieving a complete re-thinking. This was what Professor Prahalad was able to do on a global scale. We often recommend that managers reconsider the model that prevails in their market, why it prevails and, above all, how it affects the competitive outcome.

Third Game Strategy: restaging the competitive confrontation

Today, 'Positioning' yourself usually involves defining your own role in the market game. Typical game players define their role, for instance, as the 'innovation leader' or as 'the original' or 'the price breaker' – or they may slip into the 'challenger' role in a rather conservative competitive environment. This fairly straightforward approach is part of how most ordinary players understand the term 'Positioning'.

The Game Master looks far beyond his own role. He wants to 'stage' the entire competitive confrontation, the big 'Who versus Who.' He employs one of the most archetypal staging techniques used over the past thousand years – ever since biblical writers staged the legendary conflict 'David versus Goliath.' The oversimplified 'black and white' Role Pattern behind this competitive confrontation is 'small and good versus big and evil.' Our case studies will show how Game Changers in today's markets use similarly powerful role plays to shift power relationships radically among competitors by focusing the attention of the entire market (including the media) on the big competitive showdown.

Competition rules everywhere in life and in the foreground are always the big confrontations: 'Who versus Who,' David versus Goliath, James Bond versus Goldfinger (or currently against Dominic Greene), bosses versus workers, low-cost airlines versus flag carriers, the superpowers of the East versus those of the West, perpetrators versus victims, the rebel versus the system, citizens versus foreigners, Coke versus Pepsi, Champion of the poor Robin Hood versus the rich, copy versus original, black versus white, natural pharmaceuticals versus chemical ones – the list goes on endlessly.

One thing that characterizes all of these big match-ups is that, in each, the opposing parties are reduced to stereotypes. Take 'David versus Goliath' for example: a simple, black and white allocation of the roles. *David plays the little, good (future) King and Goliath comes on as the big, evil Philistine.* The authors of the Bible made no attempt to represent the conflict between the two in a subtle, nuanced manner. David does not appear as a true individual, with all his strengths and weaknesses, emotions and passions, talents and characteristics, but rather simply someone who stands for 'Good.' Conversely, Goliath's human reality is obscured by the stereotype of 'Evil.' In this Role Game, David is 100% good and Goliath 100% evil. Does that sound a little bit like Hollywood? The result of this simple role allocation is that, 2000 years later, everyone who reads the Bible finds himself instinctively sympathizing with David. Ever heard of anyone feeling sympathy for or compassion with Goliath?

The simplistic Role Game 'David versus Goliath' (little good man versus big evil one) comes with 'built-in' emotions: you invariably feel *with* David and *against* Goliath.

Whenever two players or parties in a competition are reduced to simplistic roles, we refer to a 'Role Pattern' or a 'Game Pattern.' A pattern serves the purpose of dramatizing a conflict or a competition, rendering it more emotional or ideological. We encounter role and Game Patterns everyday in real life. Think of the 'War against Terror.' Here the superpower USA plays 'Protector of World Peace' against a somewhat arbitrarily designated 'Axis of Evil.' Once again, this is a 'good versus evil' pattern, expressed in a way that seeks solidarity from the World on the side of America.

Lawyers earn their keep by reducing the role of the opposing sides to a black and white role stereotype. Take the recent divorce proceedings between Paul McCartney and Heather Mills, where the attorney for the amputee ex-model tried to characterize the conflict as 'heartless husband versus crippled wife.' He was using a Role Pattern to try to gain public sympathy for his client.

The media in particular like simple Role Patterns. They use them to shape public opinion and sell more newspapers. One example is the conflict of 'bosses versus employees,' an all-time favorite. 'The powerful versus the powerless: the bosses stuff their pockets while the employees have to tighten their belts.' Even if there quite a bit of truth to this pattern, it remains a simplification that conceals the nuances and complexities of real life.

When Karl Marx cried out for the class struggle, he, too, was using a Game Pattern: *the oppressed proletariat versus capitalistic exploiters.* Of course there was more than an element of truth here as well, but it remained focused exclusively on the 'good versus evil' aspect. Marx was clearly intent on arousing the workers of the world and inciting revolution.

Role and Game Patterns are usually used by power players as a favorite instrument to awaken emotions and fuel the fires.

By 'Role Pattern' or 'Game Pattern' we mean reducing a conflict or a competition to a simplistic role stereotype, and often one that is highly emotionally or ideologically charged.

WHAT ARE 'GAME PATTERNS' AND HOW CAN YOU USE THEM?

Competitions in the marketplace are often decided by direct confrontations: Airbus versus Boeing, Coke versus Pepsi, butter versus margarine, natural gas versus heating oil, digital cameras versus analogue cameras, Wikipedia versus the *Encyclopedia Britannica.* In the final analysis, these kinds of competitions are nothing more than Role Games. The opposing parties are reduced to highly simplified role stereotypes on the basis of which the outcome is decided.

1. Custom-Built Homes versus Mass-Produced Houses

In Germany, as in many other countries, home-buyers (looking for a newly built house) have to make a complex principal decision: do they want to go for a custom-built home, individually designed for them by an architect and built by masons brick by brick, or would they rather have a mass-produced house, which is produced at a much faster pace in a factory? A very careful decision needs to be taken, because we are dealing with a major investment. For most people, building a new house is a once-in-a-lifetime occurrence. If you want to make a fair and proper decision, there are at least nine criteria involved in the choice between an architect-designed house and one that is mass produced. Which of the two offer (1) the more 'solid' quality of the house, (2) the better price to start with, (3) a more reliable upper limit or 'price cap', (4) the shorter time involved in construction, (5) the higher flexibility or individuality of the design, (6) the better guarantees and warranties, (7) the lower energy costs, (8) the better chances of future resale and (9) the superior image?

No doubt, some customers are willing and able to conduct a complex comparative analysis, to evaluate all of the criteria, to weigh those criteria and in the end even develop a kind of point-based system on the basis of which they reach a thoroughly rational decision. However, if you look at the vast majority of target prospects and how they make their purchase decision, a simple 'black and white' Game Pattern emerges that dominates the entire competitive confrontation and – even more importantly – the purchase decision of the customers.

Game Pattern: 'A real house versus an inexpensive substitute'

In Germany, only a house designed by an architect is regarded as a 'real house' while the industrially built models have emerged historically as a cheaper substitute. Today, this stereotypical role allocation has little to do with the facts.

According to expert opinion, mass-produced homes are often every bit as solid, flexible in design and as high value as custom-built homes. It is quite surprising how the pattern shrinks nine comparative dimensions to just a simplistic 'black and white' format. This particular Game Pattern emerged from historical prejudice. The fact that it may be false and unjustified doesn't change the fact that the pattern 'rules' and 'regulates' the Game. Assuming the majority of customers have already bought into the pattern at an early stage in their purchase decision, then the custom-built home is the 'logical winner.' How decisively such 'Game Patterns' can influence and distort the competition can be seen in a single number. Architect-designed houses have an 85% market share in Germany, while mass-produced houses end up with nothing more than 15%. It doesn't matter how solidly they are built or how individually they are designed. They are trapped in a 'Game Pattern' that severely limits their success and chances for growth in the long term. Very few customers are willing to pay a fortune for what is perceived to be an 'inexpensive substitute.' Mass-produced houses are doomed to stay inexpensive.

Interestingly, in other countries, England for example, this competiton between architect-designed houses and mass-produced houses never existed. As a result, no negative Game Pattern ever had a chance to arise. It is not surprising that there are quite a few German mass-produced housing firms that have discovered the British market and are able to sell houses at prices in excess of a million euros. In the UK, there is simply no prevailing pattern that limits their chances in the market. On the contrary, a very different pattern has emerged, and one from which German mass-produced housing firms actually profit enormously:

Game Pattern in the UK: 'Made in Germany' versus 'Made in Great Britain'

This pattern conceals the fact that German mass-produced houses are manufactured on an industrial scale. Instead, the image of outstanding German engineering excellence takes a leading role. German mass-produced houses are enjoying a fantastic boom in England. The *Sunday Times* writes of an 'invasion of Great Britain', this time in a positive sense. The CEO of a German mass-produced housing firm recently rhapsodized: 'It's positively delightful: in England we can command the prices we want.'

This observation can be generalized. Whenever customers must make decisions in complicated competitions, they ultimately tend to rely on simplified 'Game Patterns' to orient their thinking and behavior. Such patterns work to the advantage of some players in the market while putting others at a real disadvantage.

Game Patterns 'regulate' the Competitive Game, especially in complex markets.

2. 'Flying Horse' versus 'Red Bull'

In several European markets, two energy drinks run up against each other. They have a similar effect, similar taste, similar price; so many similarities make it tough for consumers to make a decision. They therefore go out and seek a pattern that simplifies their decision, and one appears immediately:

Game Pattern: 'The copy versus the original'

A single aspect dominates the thinking, judgment and decision of the majority of target prospects. The imitator may be qualitatively similar or even equivalent. Nevertheless, the one-dimensional Role Pattern 'regulates' the purchase decision for the majority. 'Flying Horse' is trapped in a classical negative Role Pattern.

Once again, we can see how a role or Game Pattern can favor or limit the potential of individual players in the market.

3. Natural Gas versus Heating Oil

For most of us, it is a difficult comparison. Heating oil installations are more expensive but easier to maintain than natural gas. Both systems have differing running and maintenance costs. Even political considerations make the comparison difficult. Which form of energy is more environmentally sustainable in the future?

Most individuals shy away from complicated decisions. The majority of customers tend to base their choice on a simplified pattern, and that holds true in this case as well:

Game Pattern: 'Modern, clean energy' versus 'traditional, dirty energy'

The pattern shifts the decision from a complicated factual analysis and puts it on an entirely emotional level. If you buy into this pattern, then you end up preferring natural gas over heating oil. This pattern did not just happen historically. It was forced through by none other than the natural gas industry. *Role or Game Patterns are without question powerful strategic instruments!*

What Makes Game Masters Different from the Rest?

The mass-produced house as an 'inexpensive substitute', Flying Horse as 'the copy' and heating oil as 'traditional, dirty energy' are all kinds of role stereotypes that establish themselves over years and decades, and become deeply engrained in the consciousness of the customer.

To a very real extent, Game Patterns can 'program' the thinking and behavior of the customer. It should come as no surprise that the typical player ends up believing these patterns are part of the fixed general conditions of the market. Trying to change deeply entrenched thinking and behavioral patterns is judged very difficult indeed.

Most ordinary players in the market believe the following: *If there are firmly entrenched role stereotypes or Role Games in the marketplace (such as 'copy' versus 'original'), there is not much*

we can do about it as an individual company. We have to live with it, defend ourselves and make the best of it.

The Game Master is, as usual, far more demanding. He understands that role and Game Patterns in the market have the potential to be important steering, control and power factors. For that reason, he is simply not prepared to accept them as part of the fixed general conditions of the competition.

The Game Master thinks differently. *Game Patterns regulate the competition. If I want to win big time, I've got to be the one who redefines the Game Pattern to my own advantage and force it through. In that way I can take control in the Competitive Game, ideally at the expense of my opponents.*

A classical example is the legendary Cola Wars between Coke and Pepsi. The further you go back in time, the more dominant was the pattern 'original versus copy.' Coke profited from this original pattern and did everything it could to reinforce it. 'The real thing' was its slogan for years on end. It reminded people that Pepsi was stuck in the imitator's role. For a long time, this pattern 'regulated' the competition, making Coke the logical winner.

In the 1980s and 1990s, the makers of Pepsi acknowledged that they had to break out of this disadvantageous Game Pattern. So they developed a new counter-pattern, running something like this: 'The new generation (Pepsi) takes over from the old generation (Coke).' Pepsi became trendy, the choice of pop Superstars, and supported by the slogan, 'The choice of a new generation.' Along with this new pattern comes by logical extension the perception that Coke-buyers belonged to the 'old generation.' At the height of its success, Pepsi was briefly able to dethrone 'the original' as market leader. In the context of the previously prevailing pattern, this would in all probability have been unachievable.

The Game Pattern as an Instrument of Power

Rethinking is needed as Game Patterns cannot be viewed as things that have automatically risen in the market over years or decades. The Game Master wants to gain control and wants to use Game Patterns as instruments, precisely because they are so powerful. The following case histories demonstrate how in this manner a Game Changer can improve his status in a competition – how he emotionalizes, idealizes and politicizes the competition to his own advantage; how he pushes back his opponents and limits their chances of success; how he turns the Game in the market in order to achieve a new level of growth.

> **Game Patterns are among the most important instruments a Game Maker has at his disposal, and through them he gains influence and control in a conflict or competition.**

'STAGING' THE COMPETITIVE CONFRONTATION – HOLLYWOOD-STYLE

The game in the market is decided where frontlines are drawn, where a direct 'con-front-ation' takes place. This is where it is important to properly stage a major 'Who versus Who'. The Game Master, in a manner of speaking, assumes the role of a Hollywood director, dramatically shaping the competition according to his own conception.

The following examples from a variety of different markets have been selected because they illustrate the functions and effects the Game Changer employs in order to influence competitive events in his favor.

1. Dove's Campaign for 'True Beauty'

Dove, Unilever's brand of soaps and body care products, started a new advertising campaign in the fall of 2004 under the banner 'Campaign for True Beauty.' Dove managers had observed that while there were about 12 supermodels in the world, there were some three billion women who didn't meet the exacting standards of this ideal of physical beauty. That ideal, propagated by the media and fashion industries, put normal women under enormous pressure, and sometimes actually made them ill. In a ten-country study of 3200 women, the producers of Dove confirmed that only 2% felt themselves to be really beautiful and 47 to 67% – depending on the region – thought they were overweight. In Brazil, every second woman had considered having cosmetic surgery. In England – according to another study – 60% of women look in the mirror and find their personal appearance 'scarcely bearable.' The Dove team decided to use this situation for a global production: 'one against all!'

Launching an intriguing new Game Pattern: 'True beauty versus today's prevailing false beauty ideals'

The new Game Pattern was chock full of aggressiveness, emotions, ideology and politics. From a Game Strategy perspective, the question arises: What is the point of the pattern? How does it change competition? What good does it do the producers of Dove? Three fundamental functions become clear:

1. *The activation function.* The Game Pattern puts the competitive confrontation into the spotlight, at the center of the stage. All the public attention suddenly focuses on the big match-up. Consumers were as startled as the media. Dove had opened an international dialogue about beauty ideals. Which other brand in this category had ever succeeded in attracting the same kind of attention? The brand makers were playing on the stage of society at large, founding partnerships with schools, social clubs and governments. The campaign for true beauty generated media attention for Dove unattainable with normal marketing budgets.

2. *The solidarity function.* All of a sudden, the choice of a soap or body care product is more than just a casual selection from the store shelf. Exaggerating slightly, it is elevated to an ideological matter of principle. By introducing ideology into the competition, pressure is put on the players (in this case consumers) to take a position, to choose sides. The consumer is encouraged to think: 'If I buy Dove, I am supporting the political campaign for natural beauty. If I buy a competitive product, I am supporting the one-sided, dogmatic and unfair beauty ideal that has caused women so much suffering.'

   In a way, the customer is encouraged to *elect* Dove, just as she elects a political party. Specific product or quality differences relative to other body care products become secondary when the competition has been raised to a higher, ideological level. On that level, Dove can win more easily than on the product or quality level. Dove managers were assured the passionate solidarity of a huge feminine fan club: 75% of women interviewed by Unilever said they wanted the media to portray a more realistic and open beauty ideal. Three out of four members of the target group are therefore potential members of the 'Dove party'. Why bother about the remaining 25%? A market leader like Dove can live without them.

3. *The profiling and status function.* The new Game Pattern gives Dove a new strength and a clear brand profile. Interestingly, Dove's unique position had less to do with its 'inner' product strengths, values or qualities, but more with its *role as an ambassador* against the false beauty ideals of our time. Dove takes on the role as a figurehead for an ideological movement, becomes a player on the political stage in the struggle against anorexia, bulimia and eating disorders, helping young women to develop healthy self-confidence. It would be impossible today to develop such an honorable and distinctive status solely on the basis of technical performance and product quality. The result is clear for all to see. Dove accelerated the annual growth rate for its 2.5 billion euro turnover from one digit to two. The launch campaign alone achieved growth of up to 600% for the promoted product lines. Across Europe, sales of the core product line, Dove body lotions, tripled. Dove has become one of Unilever's growth locomotives.

2. Staging Conflict in a Political Campaign

Political campaign strategists are among the most eager users of Role Patterns. Not only do they create a profile for their own party but they also try to assign roles to opponents. A few years ago, California was mired in a political crisis, and the media consultants for ex-bodybuilder and Hollywood star Arnold Schwarzenegger staged a game in classic Hollywood style.

> **Reducing the complex political situation to a highly simplified 'black and white' Game Pattern: 'The *Governator* versus an outmoded and corrupt system'.**

While his political opponents attempted to disqualify Schwarzenegger as nothing more than an inexperienced bodybuilder and actor, the glamorous Austrian immigrant Governator mocked his rivals as 'Girlie Men'.

Yes, of course, this battle takes it a bit far, and the tactic might have boomeranged. Nevertheless, the Game Pattern worked for Schwarzenegger in two ways:

1. *The profiling and status function.* Schwarzenegger draws on a kind of 'heroic' status according to a Hollywood-style Role Pattern. You need a 'Governator' when you want to change an outmoded and corrupt system. The hero 'needs'

a powerful and dangerous opponent in order to bring his own strengths into relief. Schwarzenegger defined his role less on the basis of his own 'inner' strengths, values or qualities, and more according to his own Game Pattern.

2. *The solidarity function.* In this pattern, 'good' and 'evil' are clearly identified. If you buy into the pattern, it is quite likely you will choose the Governator's Party. The political advisors surrounding the incumbent Gray Davis failed to establish a stronger counter-pattern and, as a result, Schwarzenegger succeeded with an overwhelming majority as the logical and actual winner. In a similar way – and especially in the USA – many campaigns are staged. The presidential candidate John Kerry managed to go quite a distance by forcing through a one-dimensional pattern:

Game Pattern: 'War hero Kerry versus shirker George W. Bush'

Kerry assumed the role of a highly decorated Vietnam hero and attempted to force Bush into the role of an unpatriotic draft dodger. Perhaps it was a bit transparent and clumsy, but Kerry tried to force the entire contest into a black and white Game Pattern. All that notwithstanding, at the end of the day, George W. Bush was at his peak in the war on terror, and won the election easily.

3. 'Hightech' versus 'Nature' – The Eternal Battle of Faith

For most customers, the choice of the right sports shoe is nothing more than a common, everyday decision. You compare quality, comfort and design. You try on a couple of pairs, walk around a bit in front of a mirror, and the purchase decision is then often a matter of superior fit and comfort.

For some time, Adidas created a name for itself on the basis of its innovative and almost futuristic sports shoes. The most extreme example was a model called 'Adidas_1, intelligence level 1.1.' A shoe that could 'think for itself' was a provocative novelty in the market and, for competitors like Asics, a real challenge. How to respond? The first reflex might have been to start a technological 'arms race,' which ran the risk of not being able to beat Adidas at its own game.

The managers at Asics had a better idea. Instead, they opened a front where they defined an opposing 'counter-ideology.' Their ideal is the natural shoe, promising a 'barefoot-feeling.' The makers of Asics argued that evolution did a real favor to the human foot. Biomechanics and sports physicians regard the foot as something beyond improving; 26 bones, 33 joints, 20 muscles, over 100 ligaments and 30,000 nerve endings work closely together whenever someone takes a walk. The individual parts are so intimately connected to each other that shock absorption, stress transfer and surface feeling all blend into one harmonious whole. So the Asics managers declared battle with the following classic Game Pattern:

Game Pattern: 'Nature versus Hightech'

The activation function plays the key role
The product competition abandons simplistic quality criteria and takes on the appearance of an *ideological decision*. The media love these kinds of classic marketplace confrontations. The magazine *Spiegel* raved about an 'ideological religious war' and a 'bitter cultural battle' in the sports shoe market. The real, objective differences between sports shoes are perhaps quite small, but the ideological polarization makes them seem larger than life. Moreover, the Adidas versus Asics competition also portrays the same kind of archetypical pattern used by Hollywood. Take the boxing epic *Rocky*: the hero Rocky Balboa (Sylvester Stallone) gets himself into shape *naturally*, jogging on the beach and sparring with sides of beef hanging in a meat locker. His Russian challenger Ivan Drago, on the other hand, trains with futuristic high-tech fitness machines. No question who wins. Natural once again defeats Technical. That's what Hollywood wants.

4. A Truly Surprising Confrontation: Europe versus Google
If you employ a Game Pattern as an instrument, then your goal is to shake up a market, spark a public debate, make influential partners your allies, all in order to start a major offensive to defeat your opponents. Sometimes those opponents can be taken completely by surprise.

Everything started when Google management formulated a new Mission Statement in 2005. The search machine no longer was supposed to plow through the collected wisdom of the World Wide Web but rather 'organize the world's information and make it universally accessible and useful.' From this came the idea to scan all of the libraries of the world and make them available fully unabridged and on-line. In the first ten years no fewer than 15 million books – mostly from the English speaking world – were to be stored in the global memory of the Web.

When this plan became public knowledge, European politicians gathered around Jacques Chirac to discuss how to respond. Above all, they feared that

Google's initiative would result in American hegemony of the Internet, 'Americanizing' world culture and causing European heritage to fade away in the global memory of the World Wide Web. European politicians started a game that certain media provocatively called 'Europe versus Google.'

Game Pattern: 'American Culture threatens European Culture'

If you accept this highly emotional and politicized pattern, sooner or later you conclude that Europe must save its own culture. *Something has to be done!* Chirac relies on the 'activation' function of the Game Pattern.

The President of the French National Library, Jean-Noel Jeanneney, explicitly called Google's initiative a 'Declaration of War' against Europe. 'If we accept this and do nothing to oppose it, then we inevitably end up being dominated by Anglo-Saxon actors: not because these actors have something against us or are consciously behaving in an imperialistic fashion. This company is driven by profits. Something that is already apparent in commercial orientation at Google today between content and advertising.'

Jacques Chirac quickly forged the plan for a gigaproject in the shape of a megasearch engine by the name of 'Quaero' (Latin for 'I seek') – in a way, Europe's answer to Google. His simplistic Game Pattern aimed at helping him find partners and financial contributors, not only in France, but also all across Europe.

The solidarity function behind the Game Pattern

Chirac wanted to put his Game Pattern high on the public agenda, in order to win over companies as partners for Quaero, including France Telecom, SAP, Siemens, Deutsche Telekom, the Fraunhofer Institute and Bertelsmann. A research fund of over a quarter million euros was established, with 19 national and university libraries signed up in order to prevent the threat of American cultural hegemony.

This example shows how politics and ideology can overwhelm economic issues, how frontlines of emotional solidarity can be drawn and how even exemplary companies like Google can be forced to take on the role of a dangerous global power. It shows how rational decision makers, managers, ministers and heads of state can take part in emotional games – and sometimes even stage them.

The Three Most Important Functions of Game Patterns in Review

Game Patterns have significant influence on how the public (or customers) view a competition, how they assess it emotionally, which side they take and which party they select. The power of a pattern resides above all in its three strategic core functions:

1. *The activation function.* This involves getting the conflict into the center of the public stage and on to the agenda of the media. Conflicts and competitions acquire drama, controversy, emotional involvement and media attention when someone reduces them to a simplistic Game Pattern. Karl Marx wanted to shake up the masses, activate them and mobilize them for a great revolution. To do so he created the simplistic pattern 'Oppressed proletariat versus capitalistic exploiters.' Even when the Game has no comparable social or political relevance in the markets, we are still dealing with activating customers or the public at large. Think how Dove invoked rebellion against false beauty ideals.

2. *The solidarity function.* In Game Patterns, the roles are not only clearly assigned, but they often (not always!) take the conflict on to an emotional or ideological level: *for* good and *against* evil, *for* the Governator and *against* the corrupt system, *for* 'true' beauty and against the 'false' ideal, *for* the original and *against* the copy, *for* the oppressed proletariat and *against* the capitalistic exploiters, *for* the US Superpower and *against* the 'Axis of Evil'. The pattern 'programs' emotions in the conflict or the parties involved. The Game Master employs this function in order, for instance, to win a customer or dealer over to his side.

3. *The profiling or status function.* In Hollywood, an interesting and universal truth prevails. It takes a powerful opponent to turn a film character into a true hero! The stronger the opponent, the stronger the hero. An intriguing thought is that the hero 'needs' his adversary! James Bond 'needs' Goldfinger to prove himself a hero. In the same logic, the US government 'needs' the 'Axis of Evil' in order to take on a positive global leadership role in the 'War on Terror.' The natural gas industry 'needs' heating oil as the 'dirty, old fashioned' opponent in order to profile itself as clean and modern. Schwarzenegger 'needs' the corrupt system in order to introduce himself on the political stage as the Governator. Dove 'needs' the false beauty ideal in order to fashion itself as

the ambassador for true beauty. The Game Changer defines his own status not only on the basis of his 'inner' strengths and qualities but also by creating a unique profile through a Role Pattern.

LESSONS LEARNED FROM POLITICAL CAMPAIGNS

Up to now we have been dealing with what Game Patterns are, what functions they fulfill, how they can regulate competition and how individual companies can profit from them.

Now we are going to put the spotlight on the Game Pattern as a practical strategic instrument. How do you use Game Patterns? What steps must be taken to develop one? Do they also work in a serious competition or are they better suited to 'stagings' in lifestyle markets? How can you impose a new pattern on the market and how do you recruit allies to help you?

Learning from the Practice of Campaign Strategists

A political campaign is a perfect way to study Role Games and patterns. The very first thing you notice about a political campaign is the simple picture, 'Who versus who?' Two opposing parties clash in a direct confrontation. Millions of people are forced into making an either/or decision in just a few weeks or months. A campaign isn't just about the relative number of votes or seats in parliament, but winning or losing – 'all or nothing.' The winner ends up as chancellor or president, while 'the loser' returns to the backbenches, or just fades away altogether. It is precisely because this direct confrontation is so conspicuous that it is worth the effort to study exactly how political campaign strategists attempt to sway voters in favor of their party.

Unlike most managers in the business world, campaign managers aren't satisfied with 'Positioning' their own party. Their strategic thinking about the confrontation includes the opponent as well. Each party naturally defines its own role ('What do we stand for?'), but the strategist also wants to assign a role to the adversary ('What do we want him or her to stand for?'). This is nothing more or less than a classic Role Game. In the following example, we will reconstruct the 2008 US presidential primary campaign for the Democratic Party, *Hillary Clinton versus Barack Obama*.

Electoral Choices Are Just too Complicated!

If you look at it analytically, the campaign 'Clinton versus Obama' is not dramatically different from lots of other decisions that consumers make in complicated markets. The important thing is to understand the broad range of different dimensions that distinguish the 'Who versus Who?'

First, the voter is facing two opposing political agendas and programs that make things complicated for him. How exactly are Hillary's ideas different from Obama's? What are their respective positions regarding dozens of domestic or foreign issues? It is pretty safe to say that not too many of the hundreds of millions of voters in the US would be able to make sense of all that.

Second, you've got two candidates facing off, two human personalities, each with their individual profile, strengths and weaknesses. The man and politician 'Obama' with all his multifaceted capabilities, experience and characteristics meets the 'Hillary person,' who is no less complex.

Wouldn't it be wonderful if the entire electorate would approach this multifaceted 'either/or' decision by considering the matter in great depth? That, unfortunately, is a bit Utopian, to put it mildly. Only a dwindling minority of voters approach the complex matter with this kind of diligence. As a consequence, the first challenge facing campaign strategists is to break down the roles of the adversaries into a simple pattern that can make the voters' decision easier.

The First Step: Distilling the Distinguishing Factors

The 'Who versus Who?' consists of countless dimensions and aspects. In the first step, a compact list of distinguishing factors must be condensed from all this, a process that is every bit as creative as it is analytical. In the contest 'Hillary versus Obama' several one-dimensional patterns emerged in the media, many of which are extremely ideological:

- Mature political veteran (Hillary) versus fresh and young newcomer (Obama)
- Female ('female politics') versus male ('male politics')
- White ('white politics') versus black ('black politics')
- The continuity of the past (Hillary as the 'next Clinton') versus the prospect of fundamental change (Obama)
- The charismatic (Obama) versus the knowledgeably competent (Clinton)

- Global political experience (Clinton) versus global political inexperience (Obama)
- Safe bet (we know what we are getting, Clinton) versus risk (the unknown new, Obama)

Each of these pairs of opposites is a bit like a snapshot of 'Who versus Who?', albeit from a completely different perspective. Obviously, some of the snapshots favor Hillary, while others favor Obama. Most of them point to a clear winner and a clear loser.

Here, it is already obvious that under no circumstances can *all* these aspects dominate the competitive confrontation in the nationwide public arena to the same extent. Some will prevail, and one is likely to dominate the Game and 'regulate' to a certain extent who ends up the winner or the loser. Let's say, for example, the media would have propagated a 'black politics versus white politics' pattern, simply because Obama is the first black contender for the presidency. With this pattern, Obama wouldn't have stood a chance, simply because the majority of the US population is white and unlikely to vote in favour of 'black politics'.

Once again, it is a Game Pattern that will govern the public opinion. Therefore, the challenge of the two opposing parties now is to define and push through their own Game Pattern and stage the competitive confrontation to their own advantage.

The Second Step: Qualify a Preferred Role Pattern

Once the spectrum of possibilities has been distilled and clarified in the first step, experienced campaign strategists try to create that one- or two-dimensional Role Pattern that simultaneously favors their own party while putting the opposing party at a disadvantage.

The following pattern dominated the early stages of Hillary Clinton's campaign: 'Hillary, the experienced politician continuing the strong course of the previous Clinton era versus a comparatively inexperienced junior Senator from Chicago without much of a political track record (especially in foreign affairs).' In this pattern, Hillary attempts to draw on the significant positive halo of her ex-President husband, Bill Clinton, and her many years of subsequent political experience as the junior Senator from the State of New York.

The opposing pattern behind Obama's campaign can be reduced to the formula 'Change (we can believe in) versus stagnation (in the face of an economic crisis).' On an emotional level, this pattern plays to the general mood of dissatisfaction in the country, after eight years of an unpopular Republican administration under George W. Bush. Even though Hillary is a leading Democrat, she is tainted by being part of the overall status quo and political establishment.

Each party tried to dominate the Role Game and stage it according to their own conception. The decisive question boiled down to, which of the two parties would succeed in making their pattern dominate public opinion?

The Big Question: Which Pattern Wins?

A large part of the electorate knows long before an election which of the two parties they prefer. As a result, the outcome of an election is often decided by 'swing voters' who make their decision during the campaign itself. They are the ones that are likely to adopt one of the patterns offered by the media or the competing campaign teams.

In complex competitions, a 'dominant pattern' usually crystallizes, according to which a majority of the deciders orient themselves. Each campaign team lobbies for its pattern in order to recruit as many voters and supporters as possible. In a way, you could say that the dominant pattern 'programs' the thinking, feeling, decisions and finally the voting of broad sections of the population.

A player who successfully imposes his pattern on the public wins emotional power over his opponent and advances to become the likely winner.

Why a 'Battle' in the Market Works in the Same Way

Let us look at Airbus versus Boeing, AMD versus Intel processors, on-line banks versus bank branches, Schick (Wilkinson) razors versus Gillette and Linux 'open source' software versus Microsoft Windows. With all respect for the seriousness of politics, on a strategic level it is not much different from 'Hillary versus Obama.'

Confrontation situations in the marketplace are equally complex. They, too, can be 'sliced' into X different dimensions. Different opposing pairs can be identified, some casting one party in a favorable light, some the other. A worthwhile exercise is to examine these different aspects of the Role Pattern in a structured manner and – just like the campaign strategists – design a favorable Role Pattern in the marketplace in order to generate a competitive advantage.

BREAKING FREE FROM A NEGATIVE ROLE PATTERN

In many markets, you can detect underlying Game Patterns that have emerged over time and that guide the customer's thinking, decision making and behavior much like an invisible hand. Certain brands, companies or even whole sectors can find themselves 'trapped' in such a pattern, as we saw was the case for mass-produced houses ('cheap substitute' versus 'real houses'). These patterns can significantly limit the growth potential of individual players in the market.

Now we are going to examine the art of breaking free of this kind of captivity. To do so requires first recognizing, describing and analyzing a disadvantageous pattern as the core problem. Subsequently, the negative pattern needs to be rooted out and replaced by a dominant counter-pattern that a Game Changer can design to his own advantage.

The following case history concerns Balaxan (name changed upon request), a well-known medication for schizophrenia. Schizophrenia is a life-long illness that changes forever the life of the affected individual and those around him. The illness typically manifests itself in a series of major incidents, in which the patient often attracts attention and shocks his or her environment by confused, erratic and aggressive behavior. In such cases, the patient is treated for three to six weeks in a special clinic. For his entire life, the patient is destined to take medication to help maintain him in a stable condition.

Some readers rightfully might find it cynical to compare the dynamics of a pharmaceutical market like schizophrenia with a 'game' in the first place. Even more disturbing might be the idea that such a thing as 'role plays' and 'Game Patterns' regulate the competition in a market where doctors seem to make only rational choices based on science, studies and medical expertise – in the best interests of their patients and according to the Hippocratic Oath. Would you expect that in such a market environment one individual player could be able to restage the competitive confrontation and destabilize the previously prevailing power balance?

Surprisingly, the answer is, yes! The pharmaceutical market works just like a 'game' in any other market, whether we like it or not. The pharmaceutical companies, the doctors, the patients, the opinion leaders and the media all engage in a game; they are acting on simplistic Game Patterns and sometimes a Game Changer turns up and modifies the rules. Is that an ethical issue? No, it isn't if it happens to be the best for the patients.

The Balaxan Dilemma

Historically, all *new* schizophrenia medications have to survive an 'acid test': only when they demonstrate in clinical tests to be superior to tried and trusted standard medications will they be used in life-long extended therapy, which is called in medical jargon the 'maintenance phase.' The 'winners' of this 'acid test' are usually those 'acute' medications that have an additional calming (more accurately, 'sedating') effect. Because they are able to bring back under control quickly and safely a patient suffering from an acute incident, doctors are willing to accept certain side effects of sedation: patient drowsiness, a light stupor, some disturbances in concentration or their ability to express themselves. These kinds of attendant symptoms are considered 'minor' and therefore tolerable.

At its introduction, Balaxan was recognized as highly effective, but without any of the sedative ingredients. On the one hand, this meant that it was going to be difficult for Balaxan to win against the tried and trusted 'acute' medications in clinics. On the other hand, this also meant that in the life-long maintenance phase, patients treated with Balaxan were largely free of the troublesome side effects of sedation.

This is where 'the dog bites its own tail:' Balaxan's biggest advantage ('no sedation') was at the same time the greatest barrier to a breakthrough market entry.

The Balaxan Dilemma: Balaxan's nonsedative properties make it a *superior* choice for the post-clinical 'maintenance' therapy and an *inferior* choice for the clinical phase. Ironically, the product's biggest, unique and most desirable strength turns into the biggest barrier to a successful market entry at the clinical level.

How would you approach that kind of dilemma with classic marketing wisdom? What is different about the Game Strategy approach to detect the right way out of the dilemma? Let's take a closer look.

The Conventional Marketing Approach Doesn't Solve the Issue

Classical brand management has worked for decades with clear and proven recommendations: 'Define your Positioning!', 'Clarify your USP!', 'Find your unique benefits!', 'Differentiate yourself from the competitors,' 'Identify a niche.' Balaxan easily met all of these requirements. The medication was differentiated because of its nonsedating effect and as such was ideal as the 'first choice' for long-term therapy. The main features of this Positioning were relatively clear. Yet, at the end of the day, it was not enough to generate an attitude shift or even behavior change among physicians, who argued: 'In my clinic, I prefer to use the tried and trusted standards. Why should I encourage a patient to switch during the "time after an event" when the patient is dismissed from the clinic to a new medication with which I have little experience? That's asking the patient to take an avoidable risk.'

Indeed, every change in the medication of a patient comes with certain risks for which the physician must bear full responsibility.

The Game Strategy View of the Problem

The purpose of Game Strategy analysis is to set aside all of the complexities of the marketing situation and to reduce the competition to a classic confrontation: *Balaxan versus tried and tested acute medications.* Two parties with different characteristics, qualities and advantages encounter one another. For the acute medications, it is straightforward. Their role consists in stabilizing and normalizing the condition of the patient, something they are able to do to the full satisfaction of physicians. They stand for a *safe decision.*

Balaxan, on the other hand, is a new medication, for which no long term experience exists and which has yet to prove itself in the 'acid test' versus tried and trusted standards. As a consequence, choosing Balaxan represents a certain degree of risk. Therefore, a very simple pattern emerges that 'regulates' to a certain degree the doctor's decision making:

> **The initially prevailing Game Pattern: 'Tried and tested standards' versus 'unproven new alternative' (... facing a patient that has just been delivered to the clinic with an acute incident of schizophrenia).**

Consider the hectic business in today's clinics. Physicians must be able to decide and act quickly and efficiently each and every day. It is understandable that they reduce the roles of Balaxan and the acute preparations to a simple 'decision' pattern, and one that works to the disadvantage of Balaxan. So long as this pattern exists and dominates their thinking, it will be difficult for Balaxan to win, totally irrespective of any qualitative benefits the medication may have.

From a Game Strategy point of view, the challenge now is to demolish the disadvantageous pattern and replace it with a counter-pattern that permits Balaxan to reveal its true strengths.

The Game Changer's Approach: Introducing a Powerful Counter-Pattern

The contest 'Balaxan versus acute medications' consists of a variety of dimensions, and not only the unfavorable comparison 'the unproven alternative versus the tried and tested standards.' The first step is to evaluate closely these further dimensions. A connection is easily found. The acute medications are more appropriate for a clinic, whereas Balaxan has better chances in the maintenance phase, that is when *the patient returns home*. Getting to the heart of the matter, the following picture emerges:

*   In the three-week clinical phase after an acute incident, the patient is removed from society, which cannot tolerate him in this condition. The patient finds himself 'in isolation' in order to restore stability and normality.
*   After the stay in the clinic, the patient must be returned to society. Upon release, he is confronted with a completely new challenge, 'reintegration.' Viewed in this way, the therapy after the clinical stay is much more than a 'maintenance phase.' It is actually *the integration phase*.

Thus the following new pattern crystallizes:

The new Game Pattern that can change the nature of the competitive confrontation: 'Integration Therapy versus Isolation Therapy'

What Is the New Opportunity Afforded by the New Pattern?

The long term therapy after a clinical stay is now redefined as the 'integration phase,' which has its own challenge, namely *the successful resocialization of the patient*. It is not enough to speak of a 'maintenance phase,' since we are dealing with a lot more than 'maintaining' a stable medical condition. After returning to everyday life, *a new therapeutic goal* appears, which is better addressed by a different type of medication. How can the best therapy for the 'isolation phase' be the best therapy for the 'integration phase' at the same time? Quite logically, diverging and to a certain degree even contradictory therapeutic goals require different kinds of drugs.

It is easy to imagine that immediately prior to his clinical stay, the patient has deeply shocked and unsettled those around him due to his schizophrenic behavior: his family, friends, neighbors and colleagues at work. After three to six weeks in a clinic, the patient returns to the same people in real life, but his environment is now highly sensitive to his presence. Every conspicuous behavioral signal from the patient is likely to make people around him feel uncomfortable, nervous or alienated. Some are likely to avoid the patient or withdraw altogether. 'Uh oh … my neighbour is a psycho … and still acting and talking kind of strange …' That kind of response is happening at a point in his life when the patient most needs the understanding, care and support of others.

Quite understandably, the sedating effect of the acute preparation with its side effects of drowsiness, stupor or problems in oral expression can result in a very real *barrier to resocialization.* Of course, from a purely medical point of view, the illness may be perfectly under control, but from a human, social or ethical standpoint that is just not enough. Emotional health and social well-being are things the physician simply cannot afford to ignore. Putting the patient's interests *as a person* first means addressing the question of whether the sedative acute medications are in fact appropriate in the time after a clinical stay.

The integration phase demands a different kind of therapy, one for which Balaxan is the 'logical' first choice.

In summary, the new Game Pattern cannot make Balaxan the preferred choice at the clinical level either. However, it comes with the power to change the doctor's therapeutic direction at the point when the patient returns back home.

Balaxan as the Expert for 'Patient Integration'

Here's the new strategic thinking. The ideal medications for the clinical phase are – precisely because of their sedating effects – only the second-best solution for the integration phase. Balaxan is the ideal first choice for the integration phase, because (1) it contains no significant sedative and (2) its excellent tolerability and minimal side effects significantly increase the chances of successful resocialization.

The new Game Pattern 'integration versus isolation' serves several purposes at the same time:

1. *The activation function: taking the decision to a higher level.* For entirely
   legitimate reasons the competitive confrontation goes far beyond a mere
   product choice. It has moved on to a 'higher' ideological level. Physicians
   must deal with a fundamental question: 'Am I "only" concerned with therapeutic success in a purely medical sense or to what extent do I see my patient
   as a human being in a highly vulnerable emotional condition, so that I need
   to take care of his emotional and social needs as well?'

2. *The 'solidarity' function.* There is a certain pressure to take sides. It is hard
   to remain 'neutral' in an emotionally charged question of principle. Can physicians simply withdraw from the Balaxan message and refuse to talk to
   Balaxan sales representatives? Can they really argue openly against the
   Balaxan case or wouldn't they be suspected of disregarding or denying the
   patient's right to smooth reintegration? What kind of image does a doctor
   portray of himself if he doesn't want to get involved?

   Traditionally, many physicians, driven by everyday stress, have paid
   too little attention to the ethical challenges of resocialization. As an 'ambassador for integration' Balaxan becomes a fighter for a more modern attitude,
   able to recruit doctors, opinion leaders and medical journalists to this new
   theme.

3. *The profiling and status function.* Balaxan takes on a clear role, namely as the
   first choice for the integration phase. The brand emerges as the 'integration
   expert' or even as the 'ambassador for the emotional and social needs' of
   schizophrenia patients. The new Game Pattern has created the conditions
   required to upgrade from 'unproven alternative' to a true 'challenger,' leader
   and protagonist in the market.

   In addition, the pattern serves a function that was previously not apparent, but which is actually critical to a complete understanding of the Balaxan
   strategy:

4. *The repositioning function.* Once doctors have intellectually approved and
   'bought into' the new Game Pattern, in the future they are less likely to use
   acute sedative preparations during the integration phase. In the logic of the
   new pattern, the acute medications are limited to the role of clinical medications. Put more concisely, Balaxan's new Game Pattern encourages doctors

to limit the usage of competitive products to the rather short clinical phase. In the logic of the Game, Balaxan is now exerting a certain degree of control over its seemingly superior competitors.

What the Balaxan Example Shows

When in complex markets simple patterns emerge, according to which customers (in this case physicians) orient themselves, certain one-sided distortions occur in the Competitive Game. As long as the pattern 'unproven alternative versus tried and tested standards' dominates, the pendulum will always swing in favor of the acute preparations.

Game Strategy thinking means recognizing that such disadvantageous Game Patterns are actually the core problem limiting the growth potential of your own brand and having the courage to search for a solution in a dominant counter-pattern.

MOVING OUT OF THE SHADOWS INTO THE LIMELIGHT

The previous case histories reveal something that merits thinking about. In a Role Pattern, *the relative status* of the competing parties is often predetermined. In the classical pattern 'original versus copy' this is particularly evident. Players with an inferior status (like the 'copy') have relatively little chance of winning the competition, except of course through price. In other words, if your company or your brand is held captive in that kind of unfavorable Game Pattern your challenge is to push through a dominant counter-pattern that allows you to redefine your own status.

This is what Balaxan achieved when it was transformed from the 'unsafe alternative' into the 'ambassador of reintegration.' The following example from the telecommunications sector provides a further dramatization of the strategic art of using a new Role Pattern as a springboard to a higher status level. Here, too, we are dealing with a company suffering from a major 'status problem.'

It all began a few years ago when we received a call from an investment banker friend of ours. He had just taken a stake in a promising telecommunications firm in England called QIKTEL (name changed by request), which had somehow run into serious business problems. 'We've got a fantastic product with a virtually unlimited market potential,' he said, 'but somehow our business partners have abandoned us.' We were soon to find out that QIKTEL faced an existential crisis.

Stuck with a Sales Process That Was out of Control

QIKTEL specialized in the delivery of premium services in the telecommunications sector. Their target prospect consisted of small and medium sized companies throughout the country. Since QIKTEL could not afford its own national sales force, the young company was obliged to cooperate with about 100 leading telecommunications retailers, the majority of whom were owned by independent entrepreneurs. Their core business consisted of a very simple model. They offered medium sized customers more favorable telephone rates from one of the major telco providers and kept a share of the monthly savings as their commission.

QIKTEL relied on the support of these retailers to sell a relatively complex product, called an electronic 'communications manager,' able to distribute and manage a firm's incoming calls optimally. The telecommunications retailers unfortunately viewed this as a marginal add-on business, because it was difficult to explain and from their perspective a relatively 'small' product. Compared to the 'standard' telephony products of the major telco providers, QIKTEL's 'communication manager' was only a 'sideline,' but not a priority. The bleak assessment of QIKTEL management was that despite having 100 retailers under contract, only five of them actively promoted the QIKTEL product. None of the others could be persuaded to support the brand, even when offered generous sales commissions.

A First-Class Product That Can't Be Sold

The frustration of the QIKTEL managers was understandable, particularly in light of the very considerable market potential indicated by the firm's market research team.

QIKTEL's 'communication manager' addressed an ubiquitous issue indeed. In England, several hundred thousand (!) small and medium sized firms had acquired a toll-free telephone number with the prefix 0800. Recent studies indicated, however, that these numbers were no guarantee of good customer service, because between 15 and 20% of all incoming calls *never reached the person desired*. Either the caller 'starved to death' in the waiting queue or he tried to call during the lunch break, or after office hours, or during the weekend, or ended up connected to an answering machine, but didn't leave a message; or worse, he sent a fax that the right recipient in the company never received or received too late. As a result, between 15 and 20% of all customers calling were frustrated and possibly subsequently switched to a competitor. How's that for 'customer service'?

This is where QIKTEL's 'communications manager' came in (or better, *could have come in*) as an effective solution. Market researchers confirmed that the product generated considerable interest among small and medium sized firms. The growth potential seemed unlimited, and yet unattainable as long as there was a decisive barrier in the sales channel.

The telecom dealers preferred to concentrate on their much simpler core business – selling low-cost telephony – and saw no persuasive reason to bother with understanding and promoting the complex new QIKTEL product.

The quality and effectiveness of QIKTEL's 'communications manager' was undisputed. The software distributed incoming calls within the firm according to an intelligent algorithm – always searching for the next available human respondent. It gave the caller an opportunity to be connected directly to the appropriate department (the so-called IVR function: 'push "two" for sales, "three" for customer service, …'). It played soothing music during the waiting period and even consoled patient callers ('You are already the second caller in line and should be connected in about 30 seconds'). It automatically tested all available human respondents, before directing the call to an answering machine. The stated goal is to actually save up to 100% of all incoming calls, thereby guaranteeing perfect customer service.

However, what is the use of a relevant and qualitatively first-class product when in the sales process it suffers from the lowly status of a 'sideline'?

The Situation Goes Critical

With each 'lost' month, QIKTEL's management became more frustrated. The problem seemed crystal clear. Now they faced several important decisions that had to be taken in order to start a turnaround and lead the company to a successful future. Various proposals were circulated internally to determine how best to proceed:

'We've got to simplify our product.'
'We should create and train teams better able to inform the dealers.'
'We should lower our prices.'
'The dealers only care about money. We should raise their commissions.'
'We need a comprehensive partnership program with the dealers.'

'We should start selling directly over the Internet.'

'We need our own sales force able to cover all of our customers.'

The last proposal, establishing their own sales force, was rejected for financial reasons and direct selling over the Internet seemed the wrong approach for such a complicated and innovative product.

Now what? No feasible solution got around the problem of the telecom dealers. QIKTEL stood at a critical crossroads in its history. One manager said: 'We've got one last shot. If that doesn't work we can kiss our flotation plans goodbye.' Management was ready to consider a fundamentally new direction for the future.

The Game Strategy View of the Problem

Game Strategy thinking forgets about the internal company perspective and focuses exclusively on what is happening in the market, in this case the sales channel. QIKTEL's 'communications manager' was competing directly with much more easily sold and profitable low-cost telephony products offered by the major telcos. Every telecom dealer blessed with an ounce of common sense considered his options in the following manner: 'Either I sell another quick and uncomplicated fixed line telephony product or I start a long sales discussion regarding these complicated QIKTEL products that I don't know too much about.' It was no surprise that the dealers preferred to sell the low-cost telephony products. It was entirely logical that they would rather do business with the major telcos. From a Game Strategy point of view, the core of the problem could be reduced to a simplified pattern, according to which the dealers oriented their thinking and actions:

The problematic Game Pattern that stands in the way of QIK-TEL's market success: 'Complicated sideline product (from QIKTEL) competes against a simple mainstream product (from the big telcos).'

In this Role Pattern, QIKTEL is assigned an inferior status and simply cannot win. In addition, the company had to face the further difficulty that things were not going well in the telecom dealer's sector. Competition was tougher than ever. More and more dealers had to share an ever-shrinking pie. Margins were driven down. Customer loyalty was a thing of the past. Every year telecom dealers lost 20% of their customers. In this difficult business situation they fell back on their proven mainstream business with low-cost telephony ('at least you know what you've got'), rather than moving to new, uncertain territory with QIKTEL products – with no clear prospects.

The moment you understand that the core problem lies in the unfavourable Game Pattern, it is clear why the solutions proposed by QIKTEL management had no chance of turning the company around. The power of the Game Pattern cannot be neutralized by additional sales effort or price reductions, or through increases in sales commissions. It would be premature to reject the independent dealers as sales partners. Their uncooperative behavior is entirely understandable in the framework of the pattern. As long as this pattern dominates the thinking and decisions of the partners, QIKTEL is doomed to being the 'logical' loser.

The strategic conclusion from a Game Strategy point of view is that *the only chance for a turnaround is to break free of this unfavorable pattern and replace it with a dominant counter-pattern*. Break free of a Game Pattern? Establish a 'counter-pattern'? QIKTEL's managers had never thought like this before. However, as the example of the political campaign strategists (Obama versus Hillary) demonstrated, this way of thinking is perfectly normal in other paths of life, such as politics, and it works just as well in the marketplace.

How Game Changers Craft a New Game Pattern

Now it is time to put on your Game Changer hat and reassign the roles in the competition. It is time for a 'Game Changer's Workshop' to rethink the competition in a free, radical and totally unrestricted way.

The battle 'QIKTEL versus the Telco Giants' had countless dimensions. The two aspects 'sideline and complicated' product versus 'mainstream and simple' ones may have been part of the competitive reality, but at the same time they conceal untold other equally relevant points of view.

In the experimental creative phase, we played through as many variations as possible of how to break down the competition between QIKTEL products and the telco's low-cost telephony products and create a new counter-pattern. The first step consisted of making an inventory of the points of difference between the two parties. This produced a simple observation that later proved to be especially significant. Each telephone call has two 'ends:' one participant calls ('outbound') and one receives the call ('inbound').

This emerged as one possible alternative to define the competitive confrontation: The fixed line telephony products that constituted the core business of the telecom dealers are ultimately 'outbound' products. The perspective of the *caller* dominates: he just wants to save money with low-cost tariffs. QIKTEL's strengths are exactly the opposite, namely 'inbound' products. These concern the perspective of the *receiver*, who wants to make sure that all callers, but especially customers, receive the best possible treatment.

Thus a new counter-pattern crystallizes, which will reveal during further analysis that it bears a surprising turnaround potential for QIKTEL:

The new Counter-Pattern that can dramatically uplift QIKTEL's status in the Game: 'Inbound versus Outbound.'

The Strengths of the New Counter-Pattern

The counter-pattern contains a fascinating new thought: Every year in England, billions of business phone calls are made. In the past, telecom dealers only made money on the 'outbound' end, which is to say with outgoing phone calls. Who says you cannot make just as much money (or even more!) with the 'inbound' end of the phone call? The question is entirely justified, because now more than ever 'inbound' means in business: 'My customer is calling! Somebody wants to do business. Every customer who doesn't get through means a potentially lost sale.'

Remember that a high percentage of small and medium sized firms use 0800 service numbers and that nonetheless between 15 and 20% of all incoming calls disappear 'into the void.' A British company that invests, for example, £10,000 a month to promote its 0800 number is not only wasting between 15 and 20% of its promotional budget, but also risking between 15 and 20% of possible sales. In a time when 'customer service' is ever more important, QIKTEL's 'inbound' software could make a significant contribution.

Therefore, in theory at least, the new pattern looks like a worthwhile way to build on the strengths of QIKTEL. The potential of the pattern becomes clear when we see how it was deployed.

Unleashing the Power of the 'Inbound/Outbound' Game Pattern

In our new 'Inbound versus Outbound' pattern, low-cost telephony products offered by the telco giants stand for the 'outbound' half of the business, burdened with all of the problems and tribulations that telecom dealers have to confront everyday:

1. The outbound business is going nowhere. In the years to come it will probably go into decline. However, the number of telecom dealers continues to grow, with the result that each of them will get a smaller piece of a smaller pie.
2. Outbound margins for telecom dealers are low and under increasing pressure.
3. Outbound is plagued with an extremely high level of 'customer churn.' Each telecom dealer loses about 20% of their customer base to competitors every year.

It is no exaggeration to say: 'The outbound business is broken and has been reduced to little more than a price-driven commodity market.'

Now let's look at the flip side of the pattern: QIKTEL stands for the future-oriented *inbound* business. While still in its infancy, this new business opportunity comes with a very promising future:

1. Inbound is a *young market*, just getting started. While the outbound market has largely exhausted its growth, the inbound business still has significant, sustainable potential. One indicator of this is the large number of British firms that have recently acquired 0800 service numbers. Each and every one of these firms is a potential QIKTEL customer.
2. Inbound services are billed by the minute. However, the *margins* in the inbound market are *three times higher* than in the outbound business, where they are under pressure and are starting to shrink. These higher margins are also sustainable over the long term because inbound competition is limited and inbound stands for a premium service offering ('there could be a customer trying to call me'). This can be seen as an investment in future success. For that reason, premium prices are viewed as entirely justified.
3. Inbound is an instrument to *build customer loyalty*, because inbound solutions tend to be firmly anchored in the IT infrastructure of the customer. That means higher barriers to switching and fewer reasons to change suppliers. In the outbound business, telecom dealers lose 20% of their customer base each year. By tying QIKTEL's inbound solutions to classical outbound contracts, telecom dealers have a further means to secure client loyalty. That saves the effort and costs of acquiring new customers.

The new Game Pattern can be summarized in the following formula: 'Outbound is stagnation. Inbound is the growth opportunity for the future. Discover the inbound opportunity!'

Now the challenge is to tap this future potential and develop it to the fullest. QIKTEL's financial director estimated that in principle every dealer has a realistic chance of doubling the revenue from each customer through inbound products. This estimate is based on those few customers who have already purchased QIKTEL in the past.

What is the Function of the New Game Pattern?

If you buy into the original Game Pattern, then a sensible telecom dealer's only rational choice was *against* QIKTEL. However, the new 'inbound versus outbound' pattern works with a completely different logic: 'When the outbound business potential is exhausted, then the logical move ahead is the inbound opportunity.'

A healthy strategic platform is created, able to change the Game, and perhaps even launch a sustainable turnaround. Admittedly, expectations should be realistic. The telecom dealers will continue to purchase low-cost telephony products from the major telcos. That notwithstanding, QIKTEL now has a unique opportunity to raise dramatically its own status and secure higher priority in the dealers' day-to-day business. How exactly does the new pattern achieve this?

1. *The activation function.* Previously, the telecom dealers had to decide whether or not to take on a relatively small sideline with QIKTEL's 'communications manager.' Under the new pattern, all of a sudden a new fundamental decision must be made, with far-reaching consequences: 'Today's outbound business is getting ever more difficult. Can I really afford to ignore the inbound opportunity?' Provided that you 'buy into' the Game Changing Idea, QIKTEL now represents a business decision of considerable magnitude.

2. *The profiling and status function.* In the new 'inbound versus outbound' pattern, QIKTEL stands eye to eye with the major telcos. The previous difference in status (sideline versus mainstream business) has been erased, at least according to the logic of the pattern. QIKTEL can establish a profile as the inbound expert, which represents the growth opportunity of the future.

3. *The repositioning function.* 'Inbound' stands for a rather sophisticated and demanding new core competence in the telco sector. An inbound expert has to be knowledgeable about the organizational structure and internal processes of its medium size clients, as well as their demands for premium customer service. Many customers would agree that this kind of expertise is nothing they are used to getting from the major telcos – quite the contrary. The inbound sector clearly offers a chance to defend QIKTEL against a possible counterattack from the larger telco firms. The desired customer conclusion is: 'You don't buy premium inbound services from the engineers of one of the major telcos, but rather from QIKTEL, the inbound experts.'

So much for the strategic underpinning. The game has been redefined and a new Game Pattern put in place, according to which QIKTEL becomes the logical choice. The next step consists of recruiting some committed allies from among the telecom dealers, in order to transform the new game idea as quickly as possible into the actual market reality and a genuine business success.

What All This Means in Terms of Operational Strategy

The new strategy required far-reaching changes in the entire company. The *product portfolio* had to be adapted and extended in order to encompass all aspects of the inbound business. This resulted in *new pricing models*. The *sales system* had to be modified completely to accommodate the theme of inbound partnerships. The 'big bang' launch of 'the inbound opportunity' culminated in a major event for independent retail dealers across the entire country. Finally, the new Game Changing Idea served as the inspiration for the company's ambitious international expansion plans.

TURNING THE TIDE OF AN ALMOST-LOST BATTLE

Role and Game Patterns can be extraordinarily powerful emotional and psychological instruments. If one of two opposing parties is able to force through its Game Pattern (for example, to the public, the media, the customers or a jury), that can often constitute a decisive advantage.

Leading attorneys are masters of using such Game Patterns or counter-patterns as strategic tools to take control or turn the tide in seemingly hopeless cases. How they do this can be seen in the following example of a legendary US murder trial. We have selected this example deliberately, in order to show that even in a murder trial, where the death penalty is at stake, 'Game Patterns' can play a decisive role in steering the course of the trial and its ultimate outcome.

The Trial That Was Almost Lost
The murder trial of the black Californian football star Orenthal James Simpson came to be known as the 'trial of the century.' In 1984, O. J. Simpson was accused of brutally stabbing to death his ex-wife Nicole Brown Simpson and her friend Ronald Goldman in front of their Los Angeles bungalow. From the beginning, all signs pointed to Simpson. There were fresh blood stains – from himself and the two victims – at the scene of the crime, in the escape vehicle and in the home of the ex-football star.

The prosecuting attorneys opened the Game in court by trying to cast Simpson in the role of a well-known chauvinist and wife-beater.

The prosecutors tried to impose this Game Pattern: 'Brutal macho perpetrator versus helpless female victim.'

The pattern established the framework within which the prosecuting attorneys placed the clues and evidence. They defined the murder case as a typical example of the larger historical pattern of conflict, 'Men oppress women,' using all of its emotional power to support their case. In order to convince the jury of their pattern, the prosecutors revealed Simpson to be a man prone to violence, who time and again had stood out by his aggressive behavior toward women. Their thinking ran like this: 'If we can convince the jury of our pattern, they are much more likely to accept our factual arguments and in all likelihood convict O. J.' The logic of the foregoing pattern only had room for a *guilty* O. J. Simpson. In this manner, the prosecutors used a pattern powerful enough to fuel negative emotions toward Simpson.

The case seemed airtight: At the beginning of the trial 88% of Americans thought O. J. was guilty.

The Defense Introduces a Baffling Game Changing Twist
Then came the surprise. Despite everything against him, nine and a half months later Simpson was acquitted by a 12-man jury. Sensational! How was it possible?

How were the star defenders Shapiro and Cochran able to turn the trial around? As Game Masters, they knew better than to let themselves be snowed by the Game Pattern of the public prosecutors. Possibly their only chance lay in establishing a *dominant counter-pattern*. During their investigation, the defenders noted that one of the police officers who had arrested O. J., Mark Fuhrmann, was a well-known racist. This track led the Simpson defenders to the following counter-pattern:

The Defense succeeded by pushing through an even stronger Counter-Pattern: 'White racists against black minority.'

In the logic of the new Role Game, Officer Fuhrmann, acting out of racial hate, falsely accused Simpson on the night in question. Based on this counter-pattern, the defense attorneys invoked the entire history of racial conflict in the United States and tailored their case accordingly. They quoted Officer Fuhrmann's statements such as, 'The only good nigger is a dead nigger.' Tape recordings with over 60 similar proclamations were played to the media and presented to an outraged American public. A cry rose from the entire Afro-American community, and the American people and media gave vent to their fury. The Simpson defense team became stage directors of public emotions. The new Game Pattern suddenly dominated the entire case. 'A murder case (man against woman) is transformed into a racism case (white against black),' wrote the newspapers. The Simpson defenders suddenly took the lead, turned the trial around completely, winning the solidarity and emotions of the jury, the media and the public. In the new 'white versus black' Game Pattern, O. J. is redefined from a 'perpetrator' to a 'victim,' and the following calculated effect is achieved: *a guilty Simpson no longer fits in the logic of the new pattern*. The incriminating facts against Simpson were reduced to 'disruptive factors' because they didn't fit the 'Simpson as victim' pattern. The jury simply ignored them and acquitted Simpson. Before the trial 88% of the public believed O. J. was guilty; afterward, 75% were convinced of his innocence.

This trial shows how effective Game Patterns can be in shifting the conflict to an emotional level, thereby changing it fundamentally and turning 'safe' winners into losers (here the prosecution) and preordained losers into winners (here the defense and – foremost – O. J. Simpson himself).

Nonetheless, this example concerns a murder. Judge and jury must decide the future – the life or death – of the accused. It is about freedom, life imprisonment or the death penalty. The jury was obliged to reach a decision on the basis of the facts and yet, the evidence and facts were not decisive in this trial, but rather the emotions that resulted from a Game Pattern.

What's Different about Game Strategy Thinking?
Wait a minute, a murder trial that is largely governed and controlled by simplistic 'Role Games?' This runs against conventional thinking. It is also quite a disturbing idea, no doubt. However, at the same time, it is part of today's reality whether we like it or not. Therefore, we need to face it and deal with it instead of simply 'rejecting' something that is simply a fact of life.

First, using Game Strategy is different from what we expect lawyers to do. It is far more customary (and feels a lot more comfortable) to evaluate a trial and build a defense case on *solid facts* only. An average lawyer in the foregoing case would in all likelihood have concentrated on rebutting the arguments, facts and serious evidence of the prosecutors. Simpson's star attorneys certainly did all of that, but they went far beyond, placing themselves on the second game level, recognizing here the core problem. The Simpson case was supposed to be cast in an historical Role Pattern ('men oppress women') in which their client was preassigned the role of the 'loser.' Instead of accepting the pattern as part of the presumably fixed natural conditions and putting themselves on the defensive, Simpson's legal team saw their chance to turn the Game around by establishing a dominant counter-pattern and imposing it on the case. In America, the Simpson verdict remains controversial. The purpose of this book is not to question or complain about legal verdicts, but rather to understand the strategies through which master players can reverse a foregone competition – against all odds. This is because this art is equally relevant in the marketplace.

THE ESSENTIALS IN OVERVIEW

Role Games or Game Patterns 'regulate' competition. In many markets, over years or decades, such patterns become crystallized and customers orient their behavior accordingly, just like in the pattern 'original versus copy' as the simplest example. While many marketplace participants tend to accept this kind of historical pattern as a preordained reality, and therefore part of the fixed general conditions, the Game Changer focuses on the question of how he can use the Game Pattern as a strategic instrument. The power of a Game Pattern is derived from its four primary functions:

1. The activation function
2. The solidarity function
3. The profiling and status function
4. The repositioning function

The Activation Function

Shift the competitive confrontation into the spotlight of public attention, center of the stage. How many markets are there that have become 'un'-exciting? – 'low involvement' in the words of marketing people. Customers make decisions with a degree of indifference, without an increase in pulse rate, without any emotional commitment. Brand loyalty is rarely a factor in these markets. A Game Pattern can increase the emotional involvement, the heart throb and the excitement among customers and dealers. Dove staged the pattern 'true beauty versus superficial beauty ideals' and raised the emotional temperature in the market. The comparatively banal decision in a competition among soaps was supercharged to a matter of principle.

The Solidarity Function

Game Patterns can emotionalize a competition and imbue it with ideology and politics. They can serve the purpose of forcing other parties in the market (customers, dealers, opinion leaders or the media) to take a stand on the issue or to mobilize attitudes against an opponent. Barack Obama's Role Game 'change we can believe in' versus 'stagnation' (in the face of economic crisis) struck a chord with millions of people around the world, and fueled a kind of public solidarity, which has often been referred as 'Obamania.'

The Profiling and Status Function

A Game Pattern offers new opportunities to develop a unique profile. The telecom midget QIKTEL was able to solve the problem of its sales channel by establishing the pattern 'inbound versus outbound' and claiming for itself the role of 'inbound expert.' In a way, it became the counterweight to the horde of telco giants whose low-cost telephony products represented the 'outbound' side of the business. In this manner, not only did QIKTEL raise its status in the Game, it catapulted itself to the top of the priority list of the telecom dealers, who had previously barely been aware of the company.

The Repositioning Function

The core principle here rests in assigning to your opponent a role that only has very limited development chances. The Balaxan Game Pattern, 'integration versus isolation,' contained the logical seed that acute medications were only the second-best alternative for the 'reintegration' phase, because their side effects created a resocialization barrier for the patient. In this pattern, the previously invincible adversary was assigned a very limited role: as first choice for the relatively brief clinical stay.

Role Play or 'Positioning'?

It is common practice for companies to seek their own 'Positioning' in the market, which in essence means defining *their own role* in the Game. The fact is, however, that competition in the market is often decided on the front – that is in direct confrontations – very much like political campaigns or courts of law. In these walks of life, strategists are not content to 'Position' their own party or client, but attempt to shape a Role Pattern that also includes their opponent. That these patterns have proven to be powerful emotional instruments speaks volumes for their use in the marketplace as a means of turning the Game to your own advantage.

Fourth Game Strategy: taking the Game to the next level

Today, even the best player is at his wit's end when the market game loses some of its original energy, when the market is declining or the Game gets stuck in a routine. Some categories just become a bit dusty over the years and decades, others are 'ailing,' tumbling or even dying out. In all these cases, even the best 'positioning' doesn't stand a chance. What good would it do to position yourself successfully as the uncontested Number One ... in a market that is falling to pieces?

The Game Master takes the market game back to the drawing board. There, he attempts to analyze and define the 'Original Idea' of his category. He then proceeds to reinvent that idea without respect for any sacrosanct beliefs, traditions or conventions. In this manner, the Game Master can take the market game to the next level, infusing it with an entirely new and fresh dynamic. As a result, he is able to dethrone the previous market leaders and assume that role himself. The following case studies will demonstrate that doing so does not necessarily require technological product innovations or huge financial investments in order to succeed.

You know the Swatch of course: you may even be wearing one right now. A lot of people look at the Swatch as a kind of typical *trendy product innovation* that started to conquer the world about 20 to 25 years ago. Actually, there is a lot more to it than that, as we are about to see. Commentators have often said about the Swatch makers: 'They reinvented the watch.' This is because the Swatch is much more than just a stylish variation of the good old wristwatch. The real breakthrough from a Game Strategy point of view is that the Swatch makers invented *an entirely new and highly profitable business model* – one that was totally different from the business model that had been in place for almost 500 years in the watch business.

Let's take a brief look at the origins. The portable clock was invented around 1510. During the following 470 years, up until the arrival of the Swatch, a lot happened. Countless watchmakers introduced new brands and models, year in and year out, decade after decade. The watchmaker's craft was refined to the highest level of delicate art and the Mecca of watch making was Switzerland.

At the end of the 1970s a structural change swept the marketplace. The Japanese flooded the globe with modern, ultra-precise but at the same time inexpensive quartz watches. An earthquake hit the Swiss watch market. Switzerland's share of worldwide watch production had sunk to just 9% by 1983. In the mid-1970s it had been over 30%. Nothing less than an existential crisis threatened the sector.

At its absolute nadir, in March 1983, a Swiss entrepreneur of Lebanese extraction by the name of Nicolas Hayek introduced in Zürich the first 'Swatch': *a wristwatch that looked just like a fashion accessory, thriving on the twice-yearly introduction of completely new and highly attractive design collections.*

How the 'Original Idea' of the Market Can Limit Its Growth

Many would say that the Swatch story is about 'the right idea coming at the right time' – not much about it that I can learn for my own business. In Game Strategy, we take a slightly different view of the Swatch case. One thing that catches our attention is that the Swatch idea was born in a moment of severe market pressure – in fact, the Swiss market was on the verge of collapsing. Under that enormous pressure, some masterminds of the industry broke through to a different level of innovation, liberating themselves from some of the most deeply engraved thinking patterns.

True, there had always been innovations in the watch market, but no one had ever questioned what we call the 'Original Idea' of the category:

Attempt to capture the 'Original Idea' of wristwatches: a watch goes beyond timekeeping to be an 'artistic work of lasting value.'

… or even a piece of jewelry that in the best of cases would be passed on from generation to generation. This idea had been the reigning philosophy behind the tradition and heritage of the entire watch making industry and it was also the guiding thought driving innovation.

In the midst of the deepest crisis Hayek and his team recognized the fundamental limitation imposed by this idea: *every person needs only one single watch* – with the exception of a small number of dedicated collectors. This casts an entirely new light on the situation:

The Original Idea of the watch market came with inherent limitations that worked as the main growth barrier for the entire market over the course of several centuries.

Hayek took on the role of a Game Changer and attacked this limitation head-on – a new collection for every season. Customers purchased a Swatch for every occasion, every outfit and every mood. They craved a Play-Swatch, a Party-Swatch, an Office-Swatch, a Flirt-Swatch and a Sport-Swatch. Collecting Swatches became a popular pastime. In a centuries-old market steeped in tradition, a totally new behavioral pattern emerged in less than a single year.

Hayek liberated the 'Original Idea' of the market from its inherent limitations. As a result, two unknown medium sized firms called ASUAG and SSIH merged into the largest watch manufacturer in the world: the Swatch Group – a true *Game Changer*. Unit sales have grown in the meanwhile to hundreds of millions. Swatch captured 25% of the global market. Hayek became known as the 'Saviour of the Swiss Watch Industry.' His highly profitable plastic watches have made him so wealthy that he was able to buy up a long list of traditional Swiss luxury brands one after another, including Bréguet, Blancpain, Glashütte and many more.

To generalize: any market, any product or service category comes with an underlying *Original Idea* which is important to question because it can contain limitations that constitute major hindrances to the sector's growth and vitality.

The evolution of an entire product or service category can wander aimlessly down certain thinking corridors, leading in the worst case to a dead end. The Swiss watch industry had been driven for centuries by the demand for artistic perfection, and continued to make elegant pieces of jewelry with lasting value. No one had ever broken free of this thought prison or sought to take a completely new route to innovation – until Hayek came on the scene.

How a Game Changer Approaches Innovation

In Game Strategy we distinguish between two kinds of innovation. On the one hand, the 'usual' routine innovations are practiced by almost every company, such as changing the product, while the overall game in the market remains the same and continues to be played according to the same rules. On the other hand, there are those radical kinds of innovations that result *in a new business model*, and with it a new game that functions according to very different rules. To achieve that kind of innovation, you first need to break free of conventional thought patterns and restrictions.

The 'usual' innovation routine is of course part of the on-going survival system of every company and usually offers (almost) limitless freedom of movement and creativity. Even the Original Idea of the traditional watch category (as a piece of jewelry with lasting value) had given the watchmakers ample leeway to bring forth a vast range of brands and models: from solid diving or aeronautical watches to the aristocratic timepieces of Patek Philippe.

> **A good, ordinary player thinks like this: 'Product innovations are part of daily business. To win in the market, you've got to have regular technical improvements, new products and variations. You must extend your product range and constantly renew it.'**

Game Changers also employ that kind of 'on-going' innovations. They, too, run ceaselessly on the same treadmill in order not to fall off. Innovation cycles become ever shorter and the competitors ever faster. Whoever is able to gain a slight advantage cannot hold on to it for very long. Everybody has got to keep their eye on the ball.

That is why the Game Master sometimes demands a lot more. He places himself on the second game level, observing and questioning the evolution of the sector. He challenges the 'Original Idea' of the product category and discovers the unwritten definition of the business model of the market in order to discover its hidden limitations.

> **How Game Masters think: 'In everyday business, innovations are usually developed within the framework of certain conven-**

tions, traditions or thought paths. If I want a greater measure of growth, then I must unearth these limitations, challenge them and – if possible – break free of them. As a result, I get a chance to revitalize, accelerate or reinvent the entire business model of my product or service category.'

It is through this more radical way of thinking, as in the case of the Swatch, that a new business model can come into being, one that can break through into an entirely new dimension of growth.

This chapter will show that by modifying or reinventing the Original Idea of a market, segment or category, by liberating it from its inherent limitations, you can shake the very foundations of established power structures. You can dethrone old kings and place yourself in a position of dominance. You can unleash a new dynamic: dying traditional markets can experience a tremendous renaissance and some niche categories can be transformed into mass markets. Strangely enough, you often don't need a technological innovation in order to truly revolutionize an established market. What *is* needed once again is a powerful and 'highly infectious' game changing idea.

TAKING THE GAME TO THE NEXT LEVEL ... WHAT DOES THAT MEAN?

Each and every market came into being at some time in the past, and the world often looked different than it does today: trade fairs, circuses, clocks, coffee and fashion have existed for centuries. The markets for televisions, computers, packaged tours, lawn mowers, cameras and motorcycles have also been around for several decades. Yet, despite the best efforts of an army of marketers in each of these categories, all attempting to adapt their products to changing tastes and fashions, they gradually accumulate a bit of the dust, convention and tradition from the past. Taking the Game to the next level means first recognizing the unwritten definition of a category, testing that definition and exploring the opportunities to set it free.

The 'Drawing Board' Experiment

Consider *any* market, industry or business sector. What would it be like to reinvent it, independent of any requirements, conditions and rules of the present, which really means totally unencumbered by any of the traditions of the past? Wouldn't most markets, segments, sectors appear even just a little bit different? Isn't there always a gap between the market as it is ideally conceived on the drawing board and the way it has actually evolved? Systematically analyzing this gap is the first step toward taking the Game to the next level.

Let's take the example of motorcycles. Originally they were conceived as a means of transport for less prosperous people who couldn't afford an automobile. Then the world changed: cars became accessible to the masses and everybody was better off thanks to the post-war economic boom. Out of necessity, the motorcycle was reborn, returning as a second vehicle for more prosperous individuals who were looking to experience a bit of that Easy-Rider feeling during their free time. This is another business model, one that appeals to a different target prospect and permits a luxury price level. Funnily enough, this change in direction resulting in a different business model (different target groups, different purchase, usage and behavior patterns – in short, a different game altogether) also presented the manufacturers with an entirely different set of challenges. At Harley Davidson, so-called 'sound designers' played with (and in fact ended up patenting!) that throaty roar so loved by Harley enthusiasts. At the same time, Harley Davidson is famous – and loved for – its somewhat antiquated drive engineering. With the advent of a new Original Idea, the engineers and designers had to shift their focus.

The Drawing Board Experiment:

1. **Describe the Original Idea or formulate the unwritten definition of your product category. Which conventions and traditions constitute the cornerstones of today's business model?**

2. **Consider what the category would look like if it were to be invented today. How would it be defined if only the demands, conditions, opportunities, needs and possibilities of the present were taken into consideration, regardless of any past conventions and traditions?**

The office of national statistics in the Republic of Germany has identified over 1800 product or market categories. Each of these has developed its own business model that is by and large respected by all current market participants. Imagine for a moment, however, that you could examine each of these business models on the drawing board. How many of them would appear in need of major renovation? How many would benefit in a similar dimension like the watch industry or the motorbike industry? How many of these markets need a pioneer like Hayek with the smarts and the guts to liberate his market from conventional thinking patterns?

The 'Old Hand's' Blind Spot

If you want to succeed in the market, you might be tempted to heed the advice of the 'old hands.' They understand how the market 'ticks' or 'works.' They can explain the precise mechanisms of the business sector. They know how the Game is played at its best. Markets are complex, difficult and have become extremely differentiated: the IT sector, the trade fair business, the pharmaceutical sector, financial services, logistics. If you want to win, your first move might be to enlist an 'old hand' as a manager, consultant or board advisor. Or shouldn't you?

The irony of business history is that the old hands are rarely dethroned by other old hands, but rather by newcomers and outsiders, that is by people who aren't too deeply entrenched in the traditional game, but are able to recognize its limitations and throw them overboard. This is actually an exercise in Game Strategy and is superbly illustrated by the story of the founding of the logistics concern Fedex.

Around 1965 an American student at the Ivy League's Yale University by the name of Frederick W. Smith came to the realization that the logistic sector at the time wasn't up to satisfying and supporting the demands of ever-more automated industries. With the benefit of a totally fresh perspective, Smith's thoughts ran something like this: 'Industrial progress and the capacity of logistical processes go hand in hand. As industry and business have become increasingly dependent on new technologies, so has human labor been replaced by machines. This in turn demands logistical processes that are faster, more reliable and more precise. How, for example, could a New York medical clinic rely on instruments made in Los Angeles and for which emergency replacement parts could be delivered only several days later?' The same kind of question was posed to a greater or lesser degree in just about every sector. Smith concluded that traditional means of transport represented a significant hindrance to industrial progress.

Approaching the matter as the enthusiastic and freethinking student he was, Smith developed for a college project a rough outline of a modern, highly efficient logistic process. Back then, to connect 100 destinations with one another you had to have an incredible 100×99 or 9900 individual connections. In his passionate essay, Smith proposed a central hub, through which 100 axes would connect all of the destinations. Therefore, instead of 9900 air routes, he needed only 100, a dramatic increase in efficiency. Once underway, he also wanted to connect all of the diverse transport systems – air, sea and overland – with each other in order to improve the control, coordination and speed of freight expedition. Eight years later the fearless Smith founded the Fedex Company, and introduced its revolutionary 'overnight' service. In order to prove that the new system could function, he started from the very first day with a network of 25 destinations. The young entrepreneur raised $90 million in capital, enough to purchase a brand new fleet. Today, Fedex has an annual turnover in excess of $30 billion and Smith is universally recognized as one of the pioneers and revolutionaries of the 20th century in America. (By the way, his college paper didn't do better than a 'C.')

The Fedex story showcases the Game Strategy principle of the drawing board in an ideal fashion: reinvent the business model of the sector exclusively on the basis of the *needs and requirements of the present*. It is less about a clever, creative stroke of genius – like the discovery of the light bulb – and more about employing cold, analytical thinking, free of limitations. Even the 'hub' idea was actually something borrowed. Other sectors had been using it for years. Smith did nothing more than adapt it to the logistics sector.

Today it is easy to ask: 'Where was the global market leader UPS at the time, with its 64 years of experience as a logistics company?' The experienced experts and managers – the 'old hands' – were apparently too wrapped up in the old game to recognize that the original model of the market was long overdue for a change.

Why Wait for a *Technological* Breakthrough?

A lot of people believe that a technological breakthrough is the necessary precondition to reinvent a market. The light bulb replaced oil lamps, the automobile the horse and carriage, the personal computer the typewriter, and on and on. However, the disappointing thing about technological breakthroughs is that they rarely occur according to a timetable. You cannot force one with either the best of intentions or diligence or capital.

If you are responsible for the success of your company, then you know you cannot delegate responsibility for growth to the head of the research and development department. 'Dear board members and investors, just bear with me a bit longer, but as soon as our research department is ready with their next breakthrough product, we will be able to really get going in the marketplace.' Talk like that as a CEO and, well, enjoy the rest of the meeting.

It is also no excuse for smaller companies to complain that while their big competitors have billions for research and development, they have to make do with tiny budgets. If you really want a breakthrough market success, you would be ill advised to hope that a technological innovation will miraculously land on your doorstep.

Let's talk about how Game Strategy can reveal *other* ways and means of revolutionizing a market: namely on the drawing board, with radical thinking. At the drawing board, the rule is to forget entirely how the market evolved. Here the only question worth asking is how the market would be invented today, if there had never been a past. The drawing board experiment is something you can do at any time, using a flip chart or white board if you prefer. The time to get started is now, today – there is no reason to wait until the entire category is on the brink of disaster, as was the case for the motorcycle or the Swiss watch industry.

OLD 'TOP DOGS' CAN BECOME TERRIBLY SHORT SIGHTED ...

In established markets, the prevailing power relationships have become entrenched over years and decades. The market is shared among a number of old dogs who won't give up their positions easily. The old dogs know how to protect their own territories. However, the world moves on, and old market leaders can get lost in their routines and often risk becoming slow and short sighted. Therefore they miss the right moment to ring in the next round of the Game and to adapt the market to a new age. In these moments the old top dogs can be ousted from their positions, and more often than not by newcomers or outsiders. Taking the Game to the next level is perhaps no better illustrated than by the case of Apple's launch of the iPod. Yes, of course everyone knows the iPod success story: you very possibly have one yourself and know how it changed your way of 'consuming' music. However, we are going to look at this well-known success story from a different perspective: the Game Strategy point of view.

The Origin of the Mobile Music Player

1979 was an historic year for Sony. The Walkman had just been invented. The idea has been attributed to Sony's co-founder Masaru Ibuka. He loved Bach and Beethoven, and wanted to relax on long plane trips with the music of his favorite composers. Corporate lore has it that the technical team came up with the first prototype in just four days – by reengineering a Sony dictating machine first designed for journalists. The Original Idea for the new device can be summarized as follows:

> **Attempt to capture the Original Idea of the 'Walkman' category: a mobile music player is a portable music-playing device for people on the go, with which you can play a limited inventory of your 'own' music. In a way, it is rather like a smaller *mobile substitute for the 'real' thing*, which is your home stereo.**

Sony and its imitators implicitly accepted this Original Idea for over two decades. Starting from nothing, a new billion dollar market emerged, dominated and controlled by Sony. True, dozens of competitors forced their way into the market, but Sony remained the unquestioned Game Master. In the course of 25 years, over 335 million Walkmen walked out the doors of electronics stores. At some point, old-fashioned audiocassettes were replaced by CDs. The Walkman changed into the Discman. So what? Technology changed, but the business model remained the same. Then in the 1990s the compressed MP-3 format took over from CD disks. The old hands in the market thought this was just another form of storage memory and so continued to play the Game as if nothing had happened. This was a mistake of historic dimensions, as soon became apparent.

The Walkman, Reinvented for the Internet Age

In 2001, Apple reinvented the music player and called it the iPod. A truly astonishing accomplishment for a computer company that at that time was a total newcomer to the music business. At the time, there were dozens of other MP3 players, but the iPod contained the seed of a brand new idea. It was this new Original Idea that enabled Apple to take the Game to the next level with new rules of its own making.

Apple's chief, Steve Jobs, was the first to recognize the new role in people's lives that portable music devices could play in the MP3 age:

> **Reinventing the Original Idea of the category: with the iPod, the mobile music player is pretty much your complete music collection in the palm of your hand – fully accessible with the tips of your fingers – for mobile use as much as at home.**

Users instantly understood and loved this new idea. Many of them stored their entire CD collection on the new devices and used their home PC to make up special playback lists for different moods, occasions and situations. With the opening of the iTunes MusicStore in April 2003, customers could download 'fresh' music over the Internet whenever they pleased from a selection of over a million songs. As the successor to the Walkman, the iPod represented a totally new business model that unleashed a boom never seen before.

In major European countries, the market for MP3 players grew by a factor of 150 (!) following the introduction of the iPod. Customers were happy to pay between 5 and 20 times the price of a traditional player. Worldwide this year the 100-millionth iPod will be sold and, on top of that, 2 billion songs will be downloaded over the Internet at a price of 99 cents each. Apple's stock price is up more than eightfold. The iPod dominates the global market with a share of between 70 and 80% in the main regions. The device is praised as a societal and cultural phenomenon. The popular press has called it the first icon of the 21st century and in England the police force has cautioned iPod owners to beware of thieves attempting to steal their devices. What a flattering sign of success!

How Apple Built a Fortress Around Its Business

In the seventh year since introduction, the iPod stays serenely above the fray, able to keep global power players like Sony and Microsoft at bay, despite their attacks with fully loaded war chests. All indications point to the iPod being able to maintain its advantage over the long haul. After all, customers have already spent billions on music from iTunes, which can only be played on the iPod. *Switching to the competition would mean throwing away everything that you have invested up to now in the 'iPod system.'* With each new song downloaded from iTunes that becomes a little less likely. With every dollar or euro that customers spend on iPod accessories or music, the walls of Apple's fortress grow stronger and taller. This is despite competitive assaults with devices that are technically or qualitatively superior.

Apple created a new business model that not only drives its fairytale success forward, but which thoroughly insulates itself from attack. Apple has shown itself to be a true *Game Changer*.

The Beginning of a Counter-Revolution

A sure sign that you've got a 'highly infectious' product idea is when customers begin to change their thinking, attitudes and behavior. The iPod awakened consumers' need to have their complete music collection 'in the palm of their hand' – at any time and in any place – with the surprising consequence that many iPod enthusiasts have put their entire CD collections in the basement and listen to music at home through stylish mini-speakers. Herein lies the fundamental change in the Original Idea of the category: with the advent of the iPod, the category ceased to be a 'mobile substitute' for the home stereo system and became instead the heart and soul of your entire private music collection – even at home.

The music sector witnessed an historic attitude shift: billions in turnover suddenly migrated from record stores to the Internet. It is true that music exchanges already existed on the World Wide Web, but it wasn't until the iPod came along that Internet music sales began to flourish, something experts had previously declared impossible. Another consequence of the behavior change was that customers rarely purchased complete albums any more, opting rather for their favorite individual songs. The mega trend moved away from big stars and big hits to a broad spectrum of cult music far from the mainstream. The superstar of past years was on his way to extinction, an invalid in the music sector. The bosses of the music industry found themselves under massive pressure and struggled to re-shape their marketing strategies.

In the meanwhile, Apple prepared to enter the market for classical hi-fi stereo players with iPod music boxes. Over time, the iPod has evolved to become the true heart of music culture at home. Today you can even buy a modern computer-driven mini-studio for private use at home. And all this because of a device that is smaller than a packet of cigarettes.

Why Does It Take so Little to Cause an Earthquake?

The iPod story is one of the most famous business successes of our time. What was really new about it? The digital MP3 format had existed before, with MP3 players as well. Music stores on the Internet? Old news! Yes, sure, the revolutionary, award-winning design was different and so was the click wheel, which made navigating through even the largest music collections a delight. Both of these were without question important elements of the success – but only 'just' elements. At the end of the day, the iPod story is all about reinventing a well-known, established product category, breathing life into a new idea and exploding the limitations of the 'old' idea – *a Walkman, reinvented for the Internet age*. This is exactly like a drawing board experiment. There was nothing so exceptional, spectacular or technologically revolutionary about the iPod that a Sony manager couldn't have thought of it. But old hands in the market sometimes become a bit short sighted when they have dominated the business and ruled it without challenge over the course of many years. To be fair, in the beginning many were blind to the power of Apple's new idea. When Steve Jobs presented it to the public for the first time in October of 2001, he was greeted with sympathy, ridicule and derision. Many of them thought: *What makes this egomaniac think he's so important? The iPod is exactly like all other MP3 players, only with a bit more user-friendliness, more storage capacity and an innovative design.* Something was easily missed; even though the product and its technology closely resembled a large number of existing products even back then, what makes all the difference is breathing in that invisible and intangible new idea, with sufficient inherent strength to unleash a revolution.

WHY IT TAKES SO LITTLE TO CONTROL A CATEGORY'S EVOLUTION!

Markets find themselves in flux and are undergoing evolutionary transformations. From a Game Strategy perspective the notion of 'evolution' is a poor choice of words, because it misleads us to interpret developments in the market as things that 'happen' and not things that can be actively steered and managed.

In fact, sometimes evolution leads to a dead end: remember our friends the Neanderthals! Lots of normal players accept 'evolutionary' trends as inevitable: that's the way the market is and nothing can be done about it. But the Game Changer refuses to bow to anything as inevitable and knows how to take control of his market, even when it seems to be at a dead end. Our next case shows exactly that: a tired category that seemed to be going nowhere, until along came a true Game Changer.

Once upon a Time There Was a Dreary Little Coffee Shop on Every Corner

Coffee shops have existed in America as long as there has been coffee. A few years ago on every second street corner, pedestrians walked passed one of these small, dismal coffee stores. There, you would be served a bleak, watery brew of instant coffee in a paper cup, most of the time for less than a dollar. In the shop windows a colorful neon sign blinked 'COFFEE TO GO,' reducing the Original Idea of coffee shops at that time to the following:

> **Attempt to capture the Original Idea of traditional coffee shops: a coffee shop is like a 'transit station' which pedestrians rush through to pick up a coffee.**

Coffee shops were all about grabbing an occasional caffeine-kick without giving it a lot of thought. Coffee was robbed of all of its sensual experiential dimensions and reduced to a simple effect function. That is business at a Neanderthal stage – but nobody seemed to worry too much about it. X-thousand of these kinds of 'coffee to go' shops were strewn across the United States; they resembled each other like clones of a very joyless but fruitful species. The business model attracted only the bravest of small shop owners, who tried to keep their heads above water penny by penny and cup for cup. In all, the Game in this market was tired and gave little joy, but everyone played along, including the customers.

An Epiphany in Milano

In 1983 the American coffee trader Howard Schultz took a vacation to Italy. While enjoying a cup of espresso in a Milanese coffee bar, he asked himself why such incredibly seductive shops with high-class coffee couldn't also work in America. Why not simply borrow a good idea? Why not adopt the European success model for the American market? After all, there was no law of nature saying that Americans were doomed forever to drink watery instant coffee.

In 1984 Schultz opened the first Starbucks Coffee shop – with an idea 'borrowed' from Europe and a completely different business model. *From a rushed 'coffee to go' to an oasis of modern coffee culture* – the new paradigm could be described in these terms. Starbucks transformed the joyless coffee transit station.

> **The New Original Idea (as invented by Starbucks): with Starbucks, the new generation coffee shop becomes just the opposite of a 'transit station' – it is the customer's 'third place': a private refuge between work and home.**

With this new core idea of a coffee shop, Starbucks not only took the Competitive Game to a higher level but more importantly, they established a completely new business model:

At Starbucks, comfortable leather chairs invite people to stay a while. Guests are spoiled with a range of (pricey!) culinary delights, while reading their newspaper or surfing the Internet on their laptop, for which regular customers can purchase a monthly subscription. Starbucks attended to their 'third place' customers with a lavish buffet of fantastic coffee creations: Frappuccino, Caramel Macchiato, Vanilla Latte, White Chocolate Mocha. This is modern sensuality in a coffee cup, and with it, Starbucks was able to add value in ways and dimensions previously deemed impossible. Suddenly, customers willingly paid three to five times more than in the old 'coffee to go' age.

The idea struck a chord with the entire nation. Business boomed and Starbucks expanded with the speed of an epidemic: almost as if it had no competition. In New York City, you come across a Starbucks Café every 400 meters. In 20 years, over 12 000 operations have sprung up like mushrooms and the next 30,000 are already in the planning phase. One satirical magazine commented: 'A new Starbucks just opened in the restroom of an existing Starbucks.'

Currently, annual turnover is approaching the $8 billion range, and the capitalized value of the firm has climbed to over $23 billion on the stock exchange. All this happened in an established market in which nothing had happened for decades, in which everything seemed saturated to some and hopeless to others.

When a Market Strays into an Evolutionary Dead-End

The history of traditional coffee shops is far from unique. There are many markets that have become bogged down in stagnation. The market participants have become the prisoners of their own routine. They persist in doggedly following business models that have 'evolved' over time, despite significant limitations and weaknesses.

The 'coffee shop syndrome' arises when market participants continue to play the traditional game, even when the world has obviously moved on. This is the time for the Game Changers to bring in a new round and take the Game to the next level.

Consider this: How many sectors suffer from a more or less pronounced case of the 'coffee shop syndrome'? How many traditional markets need a man like Schultz, bringing fresh thinking to start a revolution?

Why It Doesn't Take Much to Drive the Category

With all respect to Schultz and his entrepreneurial achievement, he didn't invent either coffee or the coffee culture. He 'simply' gave back to coffee its own culture

– transforming a coffee shop into a 'third place' for the customer. How's that for a stroke of genius?

Every game lives on ideas, which are something anybody can come up with – anytime. People instinctively think this implies a creative 'tour de force,' one that can only spring from the soul of a gifted visionary. Wrong. All you need is a clear head, healthy common sense, a bit of courage and the openness to think freely. You don't need to be an intellectual or creative mastermind to think this way. Every manager can do it. Even those who have no technological innovation, no monopoly position or a fortune in the bank.

COURAGEOUSLY SLAY THE SACRED COWS!

Traditions give markets their depth, color and culture. There's no question that they make our lives richer, but they have no value by themselves. One may, should, perhaps must hold on to those traditions that have their own intrinsic value. At the same time, you must abandon traditions that do nothing more than cling nostalgically to old habits. These are nothing more than ballast that can slow down or frustrate the growth and expansion of a market. Knowing the difference between 'good' and 'bad' traditions is part of the Game Changer's art. A superb example of that art can be seen in the following case history of the Cirque du Soleil.

Flashback to a Dying Market

In theory, the circus market has been clinically dead for about 50 years, *in theory*. The business model is as old as ages and has the pungent aroma of horse dung and sawdust. One Philip Astley is supposed to have invented the circus in the late 18th century, originally as a theatre with horses. In 1831 the first acts with trained lions made their appearance; later came acrobats and clowns. Over the next 120 years, the traveling circus was in its heyday, up until the 1950s when the big circuses started their irreversible decline. Today a few hundred family firms scrape a living traveling through the provinces with their faded and tattered tents – most of them vegetating at the subsistence level, barely able to keep their heads above water. If there is one market for which there is in theory no room in the 21st century, then it has got to be the circus. As we said, *in theory!*

Attempt to capture the Original Idea of a circus: a circus is a traveling company of performers that usually features trained animal acts, clowns and various types of acrobatics.

A Troupe of Canadian Street Jugglers Reinvents the Circus

It was a troupe of jugglers, fire breathers, stilt walkers and magicians who gathered together under the leadership of the homeless Guy Laliberté to found the 'Cirque du Soleil' in Montréal. Laliberté had run away from home when he was 14 and learned the trade of juggling and fire breathing from other street performers. The young troupe called themselves a 'circus' but a circus that threw out just about every single tradition, convention and limitation. They radically upended the business model of the circus, reducing it to a slim, trim and up-to-date idea:

The new Original Idea of a circus (as practiced by Cirque du Soleil): 'Modern Life Entertainment of Superlative.' All of that – and nothing else!

Everything fitting that description is allowed. From Tarzan to Japanese drumming and breakdancing to Mozart's Magic Flute. Most recently, the Canadian circus has drawn its inspiration from trendy extreme sports: inline skating, BMX, free climbing, bungee jumping and the like. The Cirque du Soleil is open to everything, sucking up new trends like a sponge instead of losing itself in the old and dusty traditions of the circus trade. These street performers have nothing to do with trained animals, with the odor of elephant dung and old-school clowns.

A Circus Becomes a Global Player in the Entertainment Industry

With the reinvention of the circus, Cirque du Soleil advanced in just two short decades to become a global player in the entertainment industry with over 3000 employees. The concern presents 13 shows each year around the globe and draws over eight million spectators. Annually, a turnover of 500 million euros floods their box offices. It would be easy to double the business in just two or three years according to the firm's main office in Montréal. The insistence on maintaining absolutely state-of-the-art standards of creativity is the only thing slowing down their expansion. The juggler Laliberté has gone from a homeless person to the first ever circus billionaire, and with the same speed of a successful entrepreneur in the high-tech age.

Today in Las Vegas alone, the Cirque du Soleil has five stationary shows. The Canadians have even replaced Siegfried and Roy in the Mirage Hotel. The best seats go for $150 each. Could you imagine in your faintest dreams good old circus Roncalli making it big in Las Vegas?

The Cirque du Soleil is organized and operated like a modern global concern. The Canadians invest approximately $140 million in the creation of each new show. The company's data banks have files of 25,000 small, big and wannabe artists from around the world, with videos of rehearsals for the widest imaginable range of disciplines. Cirque du Soleil talent scouts scour the globe in the search for new artists. The company's set designers rigorously control every design and every fabric sample – and that over the course of decades. When the bamboo actor from a show named Dralion rips his costume during a performance in Europe, one of 300 employees in Montréal selects a sample with the number 01204-1219-61 from the archives, sews a replacement and sends it to the European location by overnight courier.

In brief, the good old circus is experiencing a renaissance with a totally rehabilitated business model. Within the limitations of the original circus idea, it would have been impossible to excite a modern audience, drive up the price of tickets dramatically and, finally, conquer Las Vegas.

'Good' and 'Bad' Traditions

Trained animal acts, clowns and acrobats were pretty much the Original Idea of the circus. What can be done when this Original Idea no longer has its old power, when a lot of dust has accumulated? How much tradition can be dispensed with? Where do you draw the lines? The best thing to do is go back to the drawing board, where you can compare the *fascination* and the *limitations* of each individual tradition.

Animal acts are great, no doubt about it, but they require enormous care, budget and transportation constraints. The costs are so high that they make it impossible to manage the circus business model as a modern industrial concern, geared to grow and expand. Furthermore, the core audience is limited to families with children. What about the clowns? Can they really excite a mass audience in the age of television and video games or are they little more than a romantic tribute to nostalgia? Of course, it's hard to say goodbye to cherished traditions. However, if you really want to enter the next era of growth, it's better not to let yourself be held back by some sacred cows.

TAKE THE LEAD WHEN A VALUE SHIFT HITS THE MARKET

Just as the world constantly changes, so people change their attitudes, value structures, needs and desires. Market researchers call this a 'value shift.' Most market participants recognize that they must *adjust* to a value shift, gradually adapting their products or services to the new value structure. However, a value shift can be a tricky beast. Sometimes people change so fundamentally that nothing short of a complete reformulation of the Original Idea of the product category is sufficient to avoid being overwhelmed by changing times.

What do 'value shifts' have to do with Game Strategy? Actually, quite a bit. Game Changers know when value shifts have occurred in their markets and know how to use those shifts to their own advantage. Let's take a look at a vivid example of how Game Changers have successfully exploited shifting values in the market for – hang on, here it comes – dolls. That's right: dolls, as in doll houses, as in children's toys. After all, dolls have values, too.

Flashback to the Children's Room of Yore

The first age of dolls began in 1815, when in Germany's Thuringia region of Walterhausen the first doll manufacturer came into being. Even back then, dolls made in Walterhausen were exported to over 30 countries. The most popular models sold under charming names like 'Skinny Bones,' 'Little Dreamer,' 'Little Miss Basket,' 'Tom Thumb,' 'Pudgy Boy,' 'Naughty Boy' and 'Dorli.' Over the course of decades these dolls gradually took on ever more realistic forms. Their faces acquired a life-like expression, their limbs became flexible and some of them even learned to speak.

> **Attempt to capture the Original Idea : A 'doll' used to be a 'baby cuddle toy.'**

With a 'Skinny Bones' or a 'Pudgy Boy' children's little hearts were driven to kisses and hugs. Over time, each and every doll manufacturer accepted this Original Idea, as if required to do so by an unwritten law. Innovation had been going wild over decades, but always within the thought path of the category's Original Idea.

The Grown-Up Fashion Doll Revolutionizes the Market

Recently, a woman by the name of Ruth Handler was acclaimed as one of the most influential personalities of the 20th century. Ruth Handler doesn't ring a bell? We are talking about the Mother of the 'Barbie' doll, the first grown-up fashion doll, born in the year 1959. While it is true Barbie was also a doll, inside her was a totally new idea:

> **After close to 150 years, the Original Idea of a doll transformed from 'baby cuddle toy' into a 'grown-up fashion toy,' which laid the groundwork for an entirely new business model.**

For the first time, the doll became a social and cultural entity. Barbie even engaged in a love relationship with a guy named Ken, who she later 'dumped' for a blond surfer type called Blaine. Barbie is now employed and career-oriented. She made it all the way to becoming an astronaut and later she was the first female American president. Someone so multifaceted naturally needs the right wardrobe for each occasion. Haute couture designers were hired to transform Barbie into a modern style icon. Most importantly, Barbie took the Game in the traditional market to a higher level by jumpstarting an entirely new business model, scarcely comparable with the old baby cuddle toy: *'The doll sells the fashion and the fashion sells the doll,'* Ruth Handler once said. The producing firm Mattel ascended to market leader, the first and only doll manufacturer with several billion dollars of revenues – successfully defending its position for almost 50 years.

Then a Value Shift Hits and the Business is Shaken

However, the world changes and along with it so do children. Some time around the turn of this century, more and more 'Tweens' between the ages of 4 and 14, began to discover a modern lifestyle for themselves. They started to pick trendy role models like Britney Spears, Lindsay Lohan, Kate Moss or Paris Hilton. The media observed a 'new coolness.' Meanwhile, even the first lifestyle magazines for children made their appearance. A further consequence of this trend was that children started to abandon playing with dolls – including Barbie – at the age of six. It's just not cool, this 'baby stuff.' The fashion doll business began to stumble and soon experienced over two-digit percentage sales declines.

The value shift was also very apparent to the makers of Barbie. Innovations were launched by the fistful: Barbie became younger, trendier and sexier. Her companion, Ken, was given a wardrobe makeover by star designers and then he even had a facelift, but in the end he was replaced by Blaine, the cute surfer. Nothing seemed to work.

Why It's Impossible for Barbie to Ever Become 'Cool' and Trendy

The fashion doll was conceived in the image of honest bourgeois society. With her, children played at being grown-ups, trying out different social role models. The fashion doll was a reflection of the consensus, the morals and the value system of 'bourgeois' American culture. That was a good thing, too, since the business model thrived on accompanying Barbie through all paths of life and all imaginable careers, always inventing new outfits for her – up to and including a spacesuit. Barbie fit in everywhere and was 'at home' in all life situations. Everything that was smooth, conformist and appropriate belonged to the essence of the original idea of the fashion doll. A rebellious, kinky or 'hip' Barbie couldn't be re-styled for alternative lifestyles. For over 40 years, that was just fine, but then the value shift occurred, making Barbie appear increasingly 'conventional' or 'arch-conservative' or even 'suburban.' Obviously, for someone who chooses Paris Hilton as their role model, a fashion doll seems as out of date as Doris Day.

One thing is clear: it's tough for someone who has stood out over a half century as utterly conformist to suddenly become 'cool.' Mattel's attempts to modernize Barbie and to make her 'trendier' were most likely doomed to fail from the beginning. The innovation motor was running at top speed, but every new development inevitably ran up against the limitations inherent to the Original Idea of the fashion doll.

The New Dolls: Party Chicks with a Tramp Look

In June of 2001, the doll was reinvented anew, this time by the Californian toy manufacturer MGA Entertainment. The fashion doll gave way to lifestyle dolls, all in the spirit of those glamorous stars of the party scene, Spears, Hilton and Moss. The new dolls were called Bratz – derived from the word 'brat' or 'naughty child'. These sexy little tramps didn't have bourgeois suburban names like Barbie or Ken, let alone 'Little Dreamer' or 'Pudgy Boy.' They were called Meygan, Sasha, Roxxi and Jade, appearing together in cliques and moving in the lifestyle scenes of London, Tokyo, New York and Hollywood. They dressed in a combination of sleezy punk rock, wore culty piercings and dark make-up on a pale complexion. The so-called 'Bratz Pack' founded their own rock and punk bands and lived in the present day of Japanese videogames, iPods, Boy and Girl bands and American Idol casting shows. The Bratz makers breathed a new idea into their dolls:

At the start of the 21st century, the new generation of dolls moved from being a 'fashion toy' to becoming a 'lifestyle toy,' laying the groundwork for yet another business model.

The 'lifestyle' doll is so much more than just a trendy new product design. For the first time, a doll adopted an important social function – for kids to express their 'coolness' and their belonging to the in-group of their peers. In a sense, the proud young owners of Bratz 'lifestyle' dolls could express their 'membership' in the highly aspirational 'cool' club.

That is something the fashion doll had never been able to do – and it was impossible to breathe that idea into a toy whose business model thrived on 'conformism.'

However, with Bratz dolls, 7- to 13-year-old children can express their own kind of 'cool' prestige, rebel a bit and shock their parents. That was certainly never the case with Barbie, and absolutely not with the original German baby dolls of the 19th century.

The Gateway to a New Business Model

This new image-building function for kids ('cool prestige') opened the gateway to a highly interesting business model. For the first time a doll brand can expand into other lifestyle markets. The children of today want to listen to Bratz CDs, see Bratz films, call each other on Bratz cellphones, order Bratz menus at McDonald's, experiment with Bratz cosmetic sets and above all wear Bratz fashions themselves. This type of business model was simply not possible in the pre-Bratz era. Starting at age 6, playing with dolls becomes embarrassing. For that reason, the previous generation of dolls was excluded from the 'lifestyle' concept, good old Barbie, too. Who wants to order a Barbie menu at Burger King? Who would make a phone call with a Nokia Barbie phone? The conformist fashion doll is simply incompatible with a business model expanding into lifestyle.

The Art of Breaking out of Old Thought Paths

The history of the doll illustrates the two types of innovation identified in Game Strategy. The early doll manufacturers were without question highly innovative, constantly developing new models and brands and working ceaselessly on a doll that ever more closely resembled a human baby. All subsequent developments occurred *within* the limitative idea that a doll had to be a baby-like cuddle toy. With the invention of the fashion doll came a *new Original Idea*: the toy doll as a modern cultural entity opened up whole new business opportunities. Then when the value shift occurred at the turn of the 21st century, doll manufacturers were unable for years to detach themselves from their Original Idea. They modified and adapted the fashion doll, apparently never recognizing that those adaptations were fully imbued with the genetic code of a socially integrated fashion doll. It is just not possible to suddenly make them 'cool,' 'trendy' or 'rebellious.' The Original Idea of the fashion doll contains so much conformity that all attempts to correct its image in the direction of a cooler lifestyle were doomed to failure.

The manufacturer MGA assumed the role of Game Changer and discovered the solution: reinvent the doll according to the demands of the present time. With remarkable success: by 2004 Bratz had already taken over market leadership from Barbie in England. Emboldened by this flourishing billion dollar business, MGA's boss Isaac Larian said: 'It's time for Barbie to retire.' A little too late, Mattel managers responded. Their new trendy doll collection called 'My Scene' bore a remarkable resemblance to the Bratz dolls. However, in this game, new rules apply and it appears that MGA has become the new *Game Master*.

Before we leave the success story of Bratz and MGA, we would be remiss if we did not mention the on-going legal battle they are fighting with Mattel. Mattel contends that the Original Idea of Bratz dolls was actually conceived of by one of their own designers who subsequently moved to MGA. This designer developed the Bratz concept for his new employers, but Mattel contends that he came up with the idea during his time of employment for Mattel, in which case the idea actually belongs to Mattel. This is the essence of Mattel's $2 billion lawsuit against MGA, which resulted in a jury recently awarding Mattel 'only' $100 million. The lawsuit continues, with Mattel seeking to block MGA from marketing Bratz dolls ever again. Our point has less to do with the trials and tribulations of intellectual property battles, and more to do with the power of an idea: the former Mattel designer's idea was, in Mattel's view, worth $2 billion. That says an awful lot all by itself!

WHEN THE MARKET NEEDS A COMPLETE OVERHAUL

Just as there are companies in need of a total re-fit, so do some markets, and just as the career opportunities are limited for even an outstanding employee in a 'broken' company, so is it difficult for first class firms to flourish in an unruly, unstable or shattered market. There are markets where nothing less will do than a complete overhaul. Our next case history involves one of those 'ailing' markets and shows how one firm used a classic Game Strategy in an attempt to redefine that market's Original Idea, aiming at taking a dominant position in a totally revitalized sector.

This case concerns the 'outsourcing' market. Here we are traditionally dealing with externalizing certain production processes to an outside partner, who is able to provide the same – or a better – service for a lower cost.

The Original Idea behind the traditional 'outsourcing' sector was primarily about 'economical provisioning.'

In everyday business life this usually boils down to a simple 'make or buy' decision. Which is more economical, making it yourself or outsourcing it? In the 1980s and 1990s outsourcing boomed. Especially IT functions, but also personnel management, real estate management and portions of financial management were hived off to external specialists.

During the 1990s the outsourcing market steamed into choppy waters. The big boom of data processing was past; market saturation had set in. The globalization wave continued to drive the market, but brought with it a lot of uncertainty. Citibank, for example, had been deceived by its Asian outsourcing partners, who had transferred customer funds to their own private accounts. Dell took back control of its service sector that had been transferred to India, much to the dissatisfaction of many of Dell's customers. Some major outsourcing deals soured and the media smelled blood. These were terrible weather conditions for the entire sector.

The leading outsourcing service providers such as Accenture faced the challenge of how to conclude large, long-term contracts with the global players while such an unstable situation persisted.

Evidently, it's not enough to think about your own Positioning in the market or how you can best differentiate yourself from competitors. When the market itself is ailing, it is not good enough to position yourself as the uncontested Number One. Your real challenge then is to reconsider the category's Original Idea.

Lobbying for a New Kind of Outsourcing

In the context of this turmoil, Accenture assumed the role of the Game Changer, becoming a lobbyist for 'the new outsourcing.' Here is a brief sketch of the Game Changing Idea:

> **New Outsourcing goes far beyond 'economical provisioning.' It is redefined as part of a megatrend in globalization: namely the 'Third Revolution in Value Creation.'**

Let's explore that new idea a little. The first revolution was the invention of the production line process by Henry Ford at the beginning of the 20th century. The second revolution in value creation occurred in the course of the last few decades: in the age of 'lean production' when 'vertical integration' of automobile manufacturers, for instance, went from about 70% of total value (still typically the case in the 1960s) down to on average 25% today. This means that 75% of automobile production is outsourced – with some manufacturers reaching 90%. Possible reductions in the vertical integration of industrial production have been largely exhausted. The logical next step is the reduction in vertical integration in all administrative functions of the enterprise and in the entire service sector. The third revolution in value creation is accordingly the logical, consistent and in many ways inevitable continuation of the first and second revolutions.

The Category's New Idea: Powered by Emotion

Something fundamental had changed about the outsourcing concept. The outsourcing idea transformed from being an 'internal' case-by-case decision of the firm into an 'external' megaforce, namely that third revolution. This implies that the 'new outsourcing' will sooner or later touch all companies – whether they like it or not.

Now, in what way could that new idea help Accenture – in their endeavour as a Game Changer – to take the troubled 'outsourcing game' to a new level? First of all, the 'new outsourcing' idea fundamentally reframes your options as a (global) player. It is not so much about the question: 'Should I or shouldn't I consider "outsourcing" certain business processes at this point in time?' Provided that you buy into the idea of the 'Third Revolution in Value Creation' your option suddenly presents itself very differently: 'Do I want to surf that new megatrend – or be buried by it?'

The new idea of the category is charged with substantial emotional power. The logic of that idea implies that it doesn't make a lot of sense to be 'against' outsourcing. How does it help you to be 'against' a major tectonic shift which you believe is taking external control of the market right now? It wouldn't be too much to say that the revolution in value creation suggests that *there is no escape.* Accepting the new idea means reconsidering all of your previous thinking, judgments and actions about the subject.

'Old' outsourcing had been a question of efficiency and effectiveness within the organization. 'New' outsourcing (if you buy into the idea!) is about exploiting the opportunities of an inevitable global megatrend – rather than being buried by it.

Accenture supported this sense of inevitability through an analogy drawn from the second revolution in value creation, namely from the automobile industry. Toyota today produces four million cars with 37,000 employees; General Motors needs 20 times (!) that many people to produce just eight million vehicles. Toyota is highly profitable; General Motors is deeply in debt and engaged in a life or death struggle. The same fate awaits those firms, Accenture would have us believe, that sleep through the third revolution in value creation.

Anatomy of a New Game Idea

Putting the new outsourcing idea under a microscope, four points become clear, all of which work to the future advantage of outsourcing providers like Accenture:

1. *The 'new magnitude' aspect.* The Original Idea of the outsourcing sector revolved around the notion of 'economical provisioning.' This is the kind of decision that would have been made on a 'case-by-case' basis by individual units of a firm, for instance in the IT department. With the new idea, outsourcing is catapulted to a far higher dimension. Now we are dealing with something that can affect the ability of the entire firm to compete over the long

run. As such, outsourcing rises to the top of the personal agenda of the CEO.

2. *The 'state-of-the-art' aspect.* The new outsourcing is nothing less than a modern *business philosophy.* In the beginning of the 21st century, global players have to focus 100% on their core competences. 'Any modern company should only do what they can do best – and have everything else done externally.' This is 'state of the art' in strategic thinking – propagated by professors of the world's most admired business schools and followed by CEOs that count as the 'elite' of globalization. In that sense, outsourcing is no longer just a matter of factual, pragmatic economic advantage. It rises to the ranks of an ideological decision of principle, for many even a question of honor.

3. *The 'inevitable' aspect.* Referring to the first and second revolutions in value creation suggests the following. The third round is going to be just as big, powerful and inevitable. Apparently, it has already started. Eastman Kodak has been working with the new outsourcing since 1989. Other big names have followed: Deutsche Bank, British Telecom, BBC, The Bank of America, BP, Nokia and many others. No one can opt out of this megatrend. The only choice is whether you want to be in the vanguard or just one of the followers. Again, there seems to be no escape.

4. *The 'innovation partnership' aspect.* Part of the 'new outsourcing' idea is also that your partner is doing a lot more than just 'handling' certain business processes for you. The idea is that they are always at the cutting edge of innovation in these areas – keeping your 'outsourced' functions and processes constantly at a 'state-of-the-art' level. If you outsource, let's say your 'buying department', your external innovation partner will always make sure that you benefit from the latest concepts, technologies and innovations. That is something your company might not be able to do by itself – given that 'buying' may not be part of your own core competences.

The new outsourcing makes the choice of an external partner much more demanding. You're going to need a generalist, someone competent in all of your firm's business sectors and categories. The advisors have got to be of the same caliber as the top management consultants. They have to be able to deploy effective infrastructures and resource plans in order to not just implement outsourcing but to really practice it on a full service basis. Finally, they must be able to work internationally in order to meet the globalized requirements of multinational companies.

In other words, the vast number of smaller, specialized or regional suppliers, who had previously shared a piece of the 'outsourcing' pie, have seen their day. Only those who are true international generalists are fully qualified for the new game – meaning service providers like Accenture. Within the logic of the new game, they take the role of the 'logical' winner.

Why Stage the New Idea as a Big Game?

Good question. Why did Accenture choose to stage a new game and invite the entire sector to play along? Why involve industry associations (like EICTA), the media (like the FT) and write books about it? What's the point of the firm becoming the Game Changer, permitting their closest competitors to profit from it?

Accenture deliberately stayed away from anything that seemed like they were trying to make the new idea their own property. They never presented themselves as the 'inventor' or 'spiritual father' of the Third Revolution in Value Creation, nor did they demand any form of 'exclusivity.' They never complained when someone else jumped on the bandwagon. Each and every imitator was welcome and extended an enthusiastic invitation to play along in the new game. That may seem a bit strange to those readers who for decades have devoured books on business strategy that advocate the exact opposite: 'Differentiate yourself. Seek out a USP. Conquer your own gap in the market. Establish yourself with your new idea as an innovation leader.' Accenture undertook – deliberately – the exact opposite, because in reality, Game Strategy thrives on its own popular acceptance. The more who play along, so much the better for the *Game Changer*.

When a USP is Just Not Enough

The outsourcing market was 'in need of major renovation' when the Original Idea became too 'limited' in the age of globalization. The notion of 'economical provisioning' restricted the development potential of the entire sector. The boom in outsourcing of IT functions had started to peter out. Globalization had given outsourcing a questionable reputation. At the same time, the idea was becoming confused with new concepts like 'offshoring.' In this generally bewildering environment, it was just not enough for a single company to concentrate on defining its own USP in the sector, based on its own strengths or points of difference. In an *unstable market*, the only way to win is to first clear the decks – with a powerful new idea.

RADICAL VISIONS AND THEIR PITFALLS

The drawing board experiment uses objective analysis to identify new opportunities for a future-oriented growth strategy. This raises the question of just how radical you should be when challenging the conventions, traditions and limitations of tried and trusted business models. There is always the risk of going too far if you don't reinvent the market on the basis of the demands and possibilities of the present, but are led astray by starry-eyed visions of the future.

Up to now, most of our cases have been about the successful use of Game Strategy. Which is what you expected, of course! However, sometimes attempts to employ Game Strategy go awry, and we think it is just as important to learn from mistakes. So here we go with a couple of attempts by world-class companies and their leaders, which didn't quite get it right.

The Daring Visions of the Coca-Cola Company

The legendary chief of Coca-Cola, Robert Goizueta, who led the company from 1981 to 1997, has been called a radical visionary. As an example, he was the one who challenged the entire complicated traditional distribution model of the beverage industry. First, put the soft drinks into bottles and then pack them in boxes. Then transport the boxes to the retail trade. From there customers pick them up and lug them back home. Just for good measure, all of the empties have to be disposed of at considerable expense. What a pain! Wasn't there an easier, more modern way? How would you reinvent that distribution process on a drawing board – for the 21st century and all the centuries to follow? One day Goizueta walked past a water faucet and dreamed that the 'C' for 'cold' could stand for 'Coca-Cola.' What a marvelous growth model: soft drinks from the faucet! In 1986 Goizueta proclaimed: 'The people of the United States already consume more soft drinks than any other form of liquid – including tap water.' So why not let Cola bubble out of the pipes? Goizueta's successor Douglas Daft even built a prototype for a Coke-from-the-faucet system – a kind of tank, filled with soft drink syrup, designed to fit under the kitchen sink. Daft, too, dreamed of reinventing his market with this fundamentally new device. The competition would be raised to a new level. Today brand switchers still have the choice of Coke or Pepsi; tomorrow, customers would be bound to Coke indefinitely through their investment in the new Coke-tank system. Coke would be able to build a fortress around its business that would be extraordinarily difficult to breach. On top of that, it was more than likely consumers would dramatically increase their consumption of Coke when the sweet brew started to flow straight from the faucet. Some of you are probably already getting goose bumps from this image. Don't worry, even ex-Coke Doug Daft had to admit: 'There's no market for it. People still want to buy things personally. But mark my words, the day will come when this idea will be reality.'

Even if you're not a soft drink fan, this story demonstrates how the accepted conventional wisdom of a market model can be put to the test by the drawing board experiment and how to discover new opportunities by challenging conventions and traditions. The trick, of course, is to be right in your analysis of the customer. Which brings us to our second example of how reinventors of their category can just be a bit too much ahead of their times.

A Brave Attempt to Reinvent the Automobile Market

Around the turn of the millennium, Jacques Nasser was CEO of Ford Motor, and he started thinking about how he could invent a car for the new century. What would you have done? What are the decisive and fundamental limitations that exist in today's automobile market and which you could cast aside in an attempt to gain global market leadership? Nasser was convinced that he had discovered this kind of limitation in the notion that people wanted to *own* cars, instead of using them as a service. Have you ever asked yourself the question: Why does it really make any logical sense for customers to own an automobile? Naturally, this is a convention to which we have become accustomed over decades. Henry Ford originally introduced this market mechanism and some 80 years later, Jacques Nasser asked himself whether it wouldn't be far more advantageous, functional and comfortable to redesign the automobile market as a *service business*. Just imagine, all you have to do is sign a leasing contract with Ford and throughout the entire year you can use precisely the type of vehicle that you need when you need it: a minivan for your vacation, an SUV in the winter, a convertible in the summer. Nasser figured that the average purchaser of an automobile generates one-time revenues of $20,000. A comprehensive service contract, on the other hand, would generate a total of $68,000 over the course of ten years: that includes the rental price, maintenance, repairs, replacement parts, gas and insurance. Based

FOURTH GAME STRATEGY 169

on that, Nasser wasted no time and in a fit of enthusiasm, he went out and bought Kwik-Fit, a chain of 2000 car service centers in England. In a particularly visionary mood, he also bought his first scrapyard.

Initially, everything went smoothly for 'Jack the Knife' as he was known at the time. In 1999 he was elected 'Executive of the Year,' but just a year later, he found himself summarily fired. Jacques was accused of neglecting the tough-as-nails business of today in favor of his dreams of the future.

Nasser's radical dreaming, by the way, had already been far surpassed by no less than Henry Ford: 'The cars of the future will have wings,' the auto-tycoon declared in 1940. Quite a picture: cars that glide over the countryside just like swallows. 'You may laugh now,' intoned Ford, 'but that's what's going to happen.'

These kinds of fantasies make for great anecdotes, but they really have nothing to do with a drawing board experiment. Indeed, they are more of a distraction than an inspiration for an achievable future growth strategy. They also demonstrate that Game Strategy, too, needs to be done carefully and on the basis of sound analysis of real marketplace needs.

THE ESSENTIALS IN OVERVIEW

Fedex, Starbucks, Bratz, Swatch, Cirque du Soleil, iPod – these are the brands and the companies about which people say 'They took the Game to the next level' and in so doing conquered a leadership position.

In each of these cases there are good reasons:

- A structural change in the general environment, as was true for Fedex
- A crisis in the sector, as for Swatch
- Limiting traditions, for Cirque du Soleil
- A far-reaching shift in values, for the doll industry
- New technological possibilities (MP3 and the Internet), for the iPod
- An evolutionary dead end, as was the case of American coffee shops

Extraordinary situations demand radical thinking. The normal processes of innovation are simply not enough, because they take place within the old thought corridors. Radical thinking means breaking out of those corridors and seeking innovation in a completely different direction. It means challenging that which the other market participants perceive without questioning to be the self-evident, fixed general conditions: namely the *Original Idea* and the *original business model* of the category. There are a number of ways in which this is achievable:

1. Discard limitations and broaden the market.
2. Create a new business model to generate new sources of revenue.
3. Displace competitors and redivide the market.

1. Discard Limitations and Broaden the Market

The Swiss watch industry had become stuck in the thought corridor where watches were conceived as timepieces and jewelry of lasting value. This notion of the market contains the inherent limitation that every customer only needs a single watch. With the invention of the Swatch (literally: 'second watch') the limitation is abolished and the market is significantly broadened. Collecting watches becomes a popular sport. In a similar way, the Cirque du Soleil profited by abandoning traditional animal acts. Those acts represented a link with the nostalgic romance of the circus, but also constituted a significant barrier to the company's goal of becoming a global entertainment concern. The classical circus was a family business. The Cirque du Soleil emerged as a global empire.

2. Create a New Business Model to Generate New Sources of Revenue

The Original Idea of a product category is usually closely connected to the business model of the market. As long as dolls were seen to be 'baby cuddle toys,' the business model was by and large reduced to the sale of individual dolls. With the invention of the grown-up fashion doll, a whole new range of business potential was unveiled. As a social and cultural entity, fashion dolls need companions, pets, a house, and naturally lots and lots of clothes. 'The doll sells the fashion and the fashion sells the doll.' This kind of vibrant and near-to-inexhaustible business was simply not possible for the 'baby cuddle toys.'

3. Displace Competitors and Redivide the Market

A recurring principle is that the brave guys who reinvent an 'old' market destroy the hegemony of the old leaders and create a fundamental power shift. Apple with its iPod not only displaced Sony as king of the hill, but also built an absolute position of dominance with a market share of 70 to 80%. Because customers have in the meanwhile invested millions in the 'iPod System,' Apple's fortress becomes ever more secure from attack.

In general, the following holds true: the reinventor of a market *extracts* himself – to a certain degree – from the competition with traditional market participants. The Cirque du Soleil doesn't compete with the Circus Roncalli. Starbucks isn't really competing with old-fashioned coffee shops. The iPod is not really competing with traditional portable music players.

Cultivate Your Own Professional 'Curiosity'

Reinventing an established product category requires neither a technological innovation nor outstanding creativity. The drawing board experiment is nothing more than a structured process that anyone can employ. Extract yourself from the day-to-day business. Put yourself at an analytical distance and then 'wonder' about all those things in the business model of your market that others accept as 'self-evident' and 'natural'. Cultivate 'curiosity' as a part of your profession. In this way you will be able to avoid those blind spots that plague the 'old hands.' As in the case of Fedex, it wasn't the giant of the sector, UPS, but an ambitious student with no preconceptions about what was 'right' who determined that the established business model was unsuited for modern logistical processes. He had the courage to wonder about those conventions that sector insiders simply accepted as self-evident.

It is often newcomers and outsiders who reinvent a traditional market. Apple was a computer company with no experience in entertainment electronics. The Cirque du Soleil didn't come from a traditional circus, but rather from a troupe of street artists. Starbucks was originally a coffee trader, not a chain of coffee houses. Newcomers and outsiders can learn a lot from the 'old hands,' but at the same time they enjoy a priceless advantage: they are not mired in the old, tried and trusted game, and can therefore more easily extract themselves from the tried and trusted rules.

How *your business* can profit from Game Strategy

Game Strategy is a provocative and inspirational way of thinking about how to grow and gain control in the marketplace. It involves the 'Level II' strategies that Game Changers use when they have exhausted conventional Positioning opportunities. The primary resource required is a 'Game Changing Idea' powerful enough to recruit 'voluntary' allies among the other players, including customers, the trade, the media and opinion leaders. In principle, equal opportunity applies here: anybody can assume the role of the Game Changer and change the conditions that stand in the way of success.

Game Strategy starts where most managers in everyday business stop, namely in front of the 'rules and laws' of the market, by going 'beyond Positioning.' Game Masters are ready to change what ordinary players are accustomed to respect as the 'factual' or 'given' conditions of the Game. We expect that, at this point, some readers will want to know what 'added value' they can expect for their own company if they venture 'beyond Positioning.' Is Game Strategy applicable for you, too, or is it something that only works for a few lucky companies under a few extraordinary circumstances?

This final chapter will demonstrate that Game Strategy is relevant for any company – *now*. But don't get us wrong. We are not suggesting to *replace* 'tried and tested' strategy tools that may have worked for you in the past and at present – rather, Game Strategy can always add something on top to spark a 'bigger' inspiration, to contribute new perspectives or to reveal an entirely different direction that perhaps had not occurred to you before.

Ultimately, the 'mission' behind Game Strategy is about adopting *the right mindset*. With everything you do in the marketplace, you have the choice to approach it with a *player's mindset* or with a *Game Master's mindset*. Are you looking at the so-called 'rules and laws' of the market as 'given' conditions or are you able to expose some to be the exact opposite, namely powerful levers for growth and market success? In that sense, Game Strategy is not just a thinking tool for contrarians, rebels and revolutionaries. It is all about attitude. Many managers will argue: 'Excuse me – why should I get involved with "game changing"? I've got to sell my boxes and that keeps me pretty busy.' Fair enough, but how comfortable do you really feel about that kind of 'player attitude' knowing that some of your immediate competitors are at this very moment exploring *their options to defeat you* with game changing strategies? In the long run, it is the right mindset that separates the 'logical' winners from the 'logical' losers.

Our plea for this final chapter is this: *explore your market from a Game Changer's perspective* – not every day, but once in a while, as part of your strategy-building routines. Take a different look at your market and explore carefully what *would be* or *could be* your options to gain control. After all, Game Strategy is a *mindgame, too.*

1. EXPLORE THE 'IDEAS THAT RULE THE MARKET'

Today more than ever, managers are used to back up decisions, plans and strategies by market research. *Know your customer!* Armadas of market researchers swarm out to explore the customer's beliefs and perceptions, values and attitudes, habits and practices. *Know your competitors!* An ever-growing number of companies install their own 'Market Intelligence' department to observe closely what the competition is doing – much like a secret service in the political arena. *Anticipate trends!* A whole market research industry has emerged trying to capture today's megatrends and to understand the tectonic shifts that slowly transform the marketplace reality.

Managers like to accumulate loads of facts to create a larger picture of their market or category. We call them 'framework conditions.' The vast majority is inclined to respect and consider these 'factual' conditions, for instance when defining their general course for growth or their competitive strategy. It sounds like a 'no-brainer.' *Of course* you want to base your growth on solid and well-researched facts.

Nevertheless, at this point Game Strategy comes in and introduces a fresh and provocative thought:

Beyond the bulk of 'factual' conditions that constitute market-place reality, there is an overlay of 'Ideas that Rule the Competition.'

This is an unconventional notion. It shows that at least part of what most people consider to be the 'rules and laws' of the market are not based on solid facts, but are rather 'made of ideas' that 'rule the competition' simply because there is an informal and implicit consensus about them among the players.

For instance, the prevailing measures of quality and performance are nothing but 'shared ideas' among customers and/or trade partners, the media, opinion leaders and investors. Consider parasiticides for pets. Here, we captured one simple and single idea that 'ruled' the competition: the belief that '100% killing power' is the 'ultimate' measure of parasiticide performance. It was that single idea which made Frontline the 'logical' winner and Advantix the logical 'second best' forever – or at least until you start challenging that *game-controlling idea.*

The 'structures' of the market landscape or even the existing 'models of the market' are also part of the 'idea overlay' that rules the market. We have discussed how the 'insulin barrier' in the diabetes market separates the 'good camp' (tablets) and the 'bad camp' (insulin). Is that 'factual' market reality? Not at all, it is simply a 'virtual model' that the players in the market have agreed to. For that reason, you can change it, too. Such structures and 'models' regulate and control the dynamics in any market, segment or category. One of the most extreme (and certainly grossly distorted) examples is the 'new economy versus old economy' game that dominated the global marketplace for several years. Again, it is nothing but an 'idea overlay' but one with absolutely 'real' repercussions on the global marketplace.

Remember how Game Patterns 'rule the competition' – and Game Patterns, too, are made of ideas. While experts argued that the premium league of 'mass-customized' homes are in all respects equal to 'architect-designed homes' they remain nevertheless firmly stuck in the Game Pattern 'cheap substitute versus the real thing.' As a very 'real' consequence of that pattern, mass-customized homes are unable to make it beyond 15% of the market, at least in Germany. In the UK, the same companies achieve prices in excess of one million euros per home, simply because the old-fashioned Game Pattern does not exist.

Finally, we have introduced the 'Original Idea,' which is also very much the 'implicit definition' of any market, category or segment. We have described, for instance, how the original 'outsourcing' idea (namely economic provisioning) became too narrow-minded in the age of globalization. The 'Original Idea' in any market can become limiting or go out of fashion – while it continues to 'rule' the competition. When you are the first to change, twist or modify that 'Original Idea,' you can expect a fundamental shift in prevailing power relationships, as we have shown with the watch market (Swatch), the doll market (Barbie, Bratz) and the market for mobile music players (iPod).

As puzzling as it may sound at first, the 'ideas that rule the competition' exist and they are well worth exploring. Consider the several thousand markets, categories and segments out there. There is an infinite number of 'games' being played right now. Each and every one of them adheres to certain 'laws and rules,' which we have now revealed to be virtual in nature. They 'only' exist in the imaginations of all the players. They are no more and no less than shared beliefs or perceptions among those players. That is exactly why there is always a very real opportunity to change them.

First key message: **Look beyond the bulk of 'hard facts' that seem to constitute your marketplace reality and you will discover an overlay of** *ideas that rule the competition.* **These ideas can be extremely powerful because they represent an** *informal consensus* **among the market participants (including customers, the trade, opinion leaders, media and investors). In principle, one single player (your company, for instance) can change them, if you achieve consensus for a 'Game Changing Idea.'**

2. NOTHING CAN BEAT A 'GAME CHANGING IDEA'

Once you recognize that the market is ultimately ruled by ideas, you automatically start thinking differently about *how to win the Game*, too. The conventional thinking is very much about looking for 'material' *advantages* over competitors, while Game Strategy pushes the 'Game Changing Idea' into the center of the stage.

When asked what are the most powerful levers or drivers for breakthrough success, many managers first reply: 'Product innovation!' By this, they usually refer to a *technological 'edge' or advantage*, which gives you a head start in the ongoing 'arms race' for quality, performance and service. The implicit conviction is that if you can offer customers *tangible added value*, you can bring the competition to its knees. In that sense, 'product innovation' is part of what we call the 'materialistic' strategies.

The second lever for breakthrough growth in conventional thinking is called 'value for money' or simply 'better price.' If you can offer quality for a better price, you gain an advantage in the market or even become market leader. Such conventional price battles also count as 'materialistic' strategies as they usually demand massive investments into price and advertising, while margins and profits melt away.

Finally, the third most frequently mentioned 'material' lever for break-through market success is massive 'Marketing and Sales Campaigns!' Consider two competitors like Coke and Pepsi that seem to be constantly engaged in a major 'match-up' across all media channels, or consider a politician who defeats his opponent through massive campaigning and superior funds, or think about pharmaceutical companies that dominate the competition simply by their overpowering salesforces and omnipresence at the doctor's practice.

In the conservative manager's mind it is some kind of a 'material' advantage that will ultimately separate the winners from the losers in the market game. Game Strategy is different. While we fully recognize and respect the power of 'material weapons,' we firmly believe that the most powerful drivers, levers and instruments for breakthrough market success are immaterial and virtual in nature, namely 'Game Changing Ideas'.

When Doctor Atkins declared the Number One food enemy (until then fat) to be your best friend and the previous Number One friend (carbohydrates) to be actually the worst enemy, he was introducing a 'Game Changing Idea.' Then 100 million US citizens started to change their shopping and consumption behavior. They completely turned on their heels and initiated a tectonic shift in the exact opposite direction. That kind of megadynamic or megaforce can only be unleashed with a 'Game Changing Idea'. Conversely, can you imagine a single company able to create a similar impact with 'material' weapons, like technological innova-tions, price advantages or massive advertising or sales campaigns?

When Bayer started to persuade vets that '100% protection against infec-tions' beats '100% killing power', they, too, relied on a truly 'Game Changing Idea' with the inherent power to destabilize their key competitor.

When Tim O'Reilly invented the 'Web 2.0' idea (which was originally nothing more than something he used as the catchy 'buzzword' for a conference) he changed the way the entire Internet sector ticks today.

Dove shifted the competition from a simple 'soap versus soaps' level on to a higher ideological level: 'true beauty versus the false beauty ideals.' This was more than just a 'positioning idea' because it changed the nature of the competition.

In principle, all it takes is one individual person or company (not even the market leader) to inspire the market game with new ideas. Perhaps the most intriguing observation is that these ideas often do not appear to be anything 'magnificent,' 'brilliant' or 'visionary.' They do not necessarily come with the sounds, the flavor and the fragrance of 'grandezza.' Quite the contrary, some Game Changing Ideas at first sight look so modest and inconspicuous that you can easily overlook their enormous inherent power. At the end of the day, the only thing that counts is whether the idea is convincing and powerful enough to recruit allies in the market.

Second key message: **'Materialistic wargames' prevail and will persist in the business world. Game Strategy posits that the most powerful tool of all is *immaterial* in nature, namely 'the Game Changing Idea', which anybody can come up with, anytime.**

3. GAME CHANGERS CAN TAKE A CERTAIN DEGREE OF CONTROL IN THE MARKET – AND OVER THEIR COMPETITORS

Most readers won't find it difficult to agree that the 'ideas that rule the competition' exist and that what is usually called 'the Game' is ultimately 'made' of these ideas.

Likewise, it is easy to accept that 'Game Changing Ideas' are very powerful instruments to win the competition. Now we are going to get a bit more specific and posit that with Game Strategy you can actually achieve *a certain degree of 'control'* in the market – and over competitors, even if they are a bigger and more powerful.

This statement may sound counter-intuitive at first, to put it mildly, and some readers may find it even grossly exaggerated. This is understandable because in conventional business thinking your 'scope of control' starts and ends with your own company. Managers control no more and no less than their own organization and how it acts in the marketplace. Yes, of course, you might be able to put your competition *under pressure* somehow (let's say through a price battle or a highly competitive media campaign), but that's pressure and not 'control.'

When talking about 'control' the first thing that springs to mind is often the illegal practices of power abuse. That is not our subject here. Game Strategy advocates a more elegant concept of control, namely the one that comes when you introduce new rules and which requires the 'voluntary' consensus of other players. Still, if you achieve that consensus, let's say among your customers, you can indeed gain some control over competitors. Let's now see how exactly the 'Mechanisms of Game Control' work.

Consider RTL. When RTL stepped on to the TV marketplace stage in 1984, the advertising industry divided the 'multibillion dollar pie' among the mass media by a single, simple criterion, namely *reach among the entire population.* RTL's boss Thoma defined a new performance standard, one that served the purposes of his channel and still sounded entirely logical, namely *reach among the ad receptive target audience aged 14 to 49.*

Okay, that is changing the rules, but how exactly does the concept of 'control' apply here? First, the new performance measure 'upgraded' RTL's own target audience, which was 'spot on' the age range from 14 to 49. Secondly, the new criterion *excluded* 70% of the audience of ARD and ZDF who were 50 or older. These millions of mature viewers did not 'count' any more in the Game; they were simply taken out of the equation as if they had never existed. In other words, RTL deliberately maneuvered to neutralize 70% of their competitors' power. This one move put them into position to dethrone stronger opponents and take market leadership themselves. In Game Strategy language, we call this an indirect form of control – one that works via the accepted rules in the market.

So if 'control' does apply, the next question is *how does it work?* What is the 'mechanism of control' in the Game? To start with, you have a 'Game Changing Idea' on paper, but it remains in the 'idea stage' until it is accepted by other players. Bit by bit, it then becomes part of the undeniable marketplace reality. There is only one way to do this: you need to recruit allies. As soon as they start playing by the new rule, it becomes a 'valid' part of the Game. That is exactly what Helmut Thoma did. First, he recruited allies among his customers, namely the key managers of the advertising industry, the ones who decide which media channel gets which portion of the multibillion dollar advertising pie. Then came the market research companies who increasingly tailored their analytical tools and data banks according to the new criterion. Finally, even his public broadcaster competitors ARD and ZDF no longer had a choice: they were obliged to bow to the new rule, even though it toppled them from their throne.

Strictly speaking, it is not the *single company* itself that exerts control here. By no means was RTL in any kind of position to challenge or confront ARD and ZDF *directly*, let alone put them under any kind of pressure. Ultimately, it was the advertising industry, acting as an 'informal ally,' that put RTL into power. When they decided to play by the new rule, ARD and ZDF had no choice but to go along. This is the principal 'mechanism of control' that makes Game Strategy a viable option even for players who don't rank as market leaders.

> *Third key message*: **In conventional business thinking, 'control' starts and ends with your own organization (apart from illegal practices). Game Strategy posits that you can indeed take a certain degree of control in the market and over competitors – if you are able to recruit powerful allies who start playing by your rules. In that way, you can ultimately impose new rules, even on stronger opponents.**

4. GAME STRATEGY AS A 'BEHAVIOR CHANGING' INSTRUMENT

When we speak to managers about Game Strategy, we are often confronted with a fair question: 'My job as a manager is to meet volume and growth targets – and not to "change the Game." How does Game Strategy help me to deliver growth?'

The straight link to 'growth' lies in the fact that Game Strategy can be regarded as a 'behavior changing' instrument. A greater measure of growth for your own company will only happen if your target customers change their attitudes, perceptions, preferences and purchase behavior. That is exactly what 'Game Changing Ideas' can do for you.

Let's go back one step. In any game, there is always a direct link between the 'rules' and the typical behavior patterns of the players. More specifically, you can always understand and explain the behavior of players by connecting it to the Game's rules. Just observe a couple of soccer games, and there is no denying that the players demonstrate very specific 'behavior patterns,' which are different from other games, like basketball, baseball or rugby. To explain this behavior, you do not need to subject each player to intensive psychological analysis – you simply acknowledge that they are adhering to and acting by the 'rules of the Game.'

Likewise, the myriad of games in the marketplace are all accompanied by typical behavior patterns. Look at your customers, your trade partners, the investors or the media in *your* market and you will find that they are not just individuals acting in their individual ways, but are all engaging in 'game-like' behavior. In the 'logic' of the Game, they are doing what they have to do. This is also part of what they call 'market dynamics.' As in the Dr Atkins example, where everybody moved from the 'carbohydrate' camp to the 'fat and protein' camp, or like the diabetes case, where one million customers stopped in front of the 'insulin barrier,' the players in the market usually display 'game-like' behavior.

This is where your company comes in with your specific volume and growth targets. If you strive for a greater measure of growth, it is obviously necessary to shift substantial market volumes or market shares from other categories, from other segments or from direct competitors to your own camp or company. In other words, you somehow need to interfere with existing customer behavior patterns; you need to break them up and change them. It all boils down to the question: 'Do you want to change behavior in the conventional way or try a different approach using Game Strategy?

The conventional way is to pull out your classic 'marketing instruments': product or pricing initiatives, new distribution or 'placement' strategies, brand communication campaigns, sales initiatives or 'promotional' strategies. To apply them in the most effective way, you wrap your instrument around compelling 'customer insights,' which emerges from analyzing his psychology, his inner drives and motivations, beliefs, values and habits.

Game Strategy takes a different approach: instead of understanding the customer's behavior as a result of his individual *'inner' conditions*, we focus on behavior patterns that 'crowds' of people display according to the *conditions of the Game*. Groups of customers orient themselves by the 'rules of the Game.' They simply follow the Game's 'logic.'

This it not an attempt to replace proven psychological research techniques, but it does add a new perspective on customer behavior and can help you to find compelling new ways how to change it.

The 'ideas that rule the competition' are at the same time the 'ideas that rule the customer's behavior.'

For example, we have shown how the prevailing measures of quality in the market impact customer behavior and establish very simple patterns. Consider digital cameras and 'megapixels.' Most consumers wouldn't be able to define what they are. Plus, it turns out to be a highly incomplete and misleading quality criterion. However, it was a 'valid' criterion that 'led' the purchase decision of millions of customers.

We have described how changes in the structures or the 'virtual model' of the market landscape bring about highly simplified behavior patterns, just like the political axis gives orientation to the parties themselves, the media and the voters, or how the purely virtual two-camp structure 'new economy/old economy' ruled the behavior of CEO's, investors, media, politicians and (to a certain extent) customers for several years.

Game Changing Ideas impact behavior also in the sense that they can 'reframe' your perceived options as a target customer. The original 'outsourcing' idea framed things much like this: 'Do I or don't I want to benefit from cost savings through economic provisioning?' Then, the 'new outsourcing' confronts you with an entirely different choice: 'Do I want to surf the inevitable global megatrend (the third revolution of value creation) or be buried by it?' Reframing the customer's options in the Game is impacting his attitude and behavior.

Finally, Role Games and 'Game Patterns' are powerful tools to influence attitudes, perceptions, emotions and the entire decision-making process. Remember how effectively they work, even in murder trials, to influence a jury charged with delivering a 'life-or-death' verdict, as we have seen in the O. J. Simpson case.

Those are just a few examples to illustrate why we regard Game Strategy as a 'behavioral tool' – and a rather unconventional one at that. To explain and predict customer behavior through the conditions of the Game (rather than through psychology) can inspire different strategies concerning how to change it and to grow your business.

The fourth key message: **In conventional business you understand customer behavior through psychological research ('customer insights') and try to change it with the instruments of classic marketing. Game Strategy posits that customers adopt 'game-like' behavior. By introducing a 'Game Changing Idea' you can achieve the radical shifts in customer behavior required for a greater measure of growth.**

5. FINALLY ... GAME STRATEGY IS A TRULY 'DEMOCRATIC' TOOL

The 'Game Changing Idea' is not only one of the most powerful tools in business, it also counts as one of those rare 'democratic' resources. In principle, ideas are there for the taking by anybody at any time. There is no evidence to support the suggestion that larger corporations have some kind of special privilege for better ideas – *why should they?*

Any company can unleash the power of the Game Changing Idea, because it is your informal allies in the marketplace that make you strong. Not even the most powerful corporations in the world can get around that basic principle of Game Strategy. Remember how the global power player DeBeers started to enforce the '4C' valuation criteria that would help them to control the diamond market. By no means could they have simply 'imposed' these criteria on to the world of diamonds. They, too, needed to recruit 'voluntary' allies, foremost among key opinion leaders in the academic field of geology.

You might argue that bigger corporations have better networks to recruit allies in the market than smaller companies or newcomers. Maybe so, but that is a poor excuse. Ryanair was on the verge of bankruptcy when CEO Michael O'Leary assumed the role as the Game Changer. Today, more than 50 other budget airlines play by the rules that he established. Together, they form a powerful 'informal alliance' imposing massive pressure upon the national carriers and driving the tectonic shifts in the entire airtravel industry. In a sense, even your most immediate competitors can be your allies in a 'larger' battle.

Make the media your allies. 'Game Changing Ideas' do not travel as much on advertising dollars or euros, but rather on genuine media attention. Dr Atkins didn't need a multinational corporation to cause an earthquake in the US food sector – he simply used his books and their publicity to recruit 100 million allies among consumers in the marketplace. Atkins would have never been able to pay for the media coverage he got for free. Tim O'Reilly owned nothing but a small publishing company when he launched the 'Web 2.0' idea, which spread around the world like wildfire through 'free' media support. When Sanofi-Aventis launched the new therapy 'BOT' they, too, achieved 'free' media attention they would never have been able to pay for. In general, media are much more inclined to report about 'game changing news' than about 'product PR' or 'corporate news.'

184 T H E   I M P O S S I B L E   A D V A N T A G E

The fifth key message: Game Strategy is a 'democratic tool,' first, because its primary resource is immaterial and ubiquitous, namely ideas, and, second, because 'Game Changing Ideas' thrive on genuine media interest – and less on your own company's advertising or public relations.

THE FIVE STEPS TO GAME STRATEGY

We are often asked to explain what Game Strategy is 'ultimately' all about. Is it primarily a *creative way of thinking* about growth – beyond the box? Or is it more like a systematic tool for *competitive analysis* that goes beyond the limitations of Positioning? Or is it, as the name suggests, first and foremost a different *kind of strategy* that is based on 'taking control' with the help of informal allies?

We reply that it is all of the above. However, it is important to note that Game Strategy is rather about structured and analytical thinking than about something wildly disruptive and creative. Look at the five steps below and you will find that it is very much a logical analysis of the Competitive Game that navigates your thinking straight to the 'ballpark' where you have to look for your 'Game Changing Idea.'

Take RTL as an example. Once you've determined that the biggest barrier to RTL's market success was the prevailing measure of performance ('reach among the total population'), you intuitively know your challenge: *to redefine that measure.* If you go through the four classic game strategies again, there are plenty of similar examples. Game Strategy analysis often casts an entirely different light on your problem and reveals an unconventional solution. Think of the Zeiss case. Game analysis revealed the true issue: that the competition was ruled by 'banal' quality measures, namely technical characteristics of glass processing. Think of the diabetes brand Lantus that couldn't break through the 'insulin barrier' until management understood through game analysis that the 'insulin injection' wasn't the key issue. The patients were simply scared to move from the 'PLUS camp' (tablets) into the 'MINUS camp' (insulins). That is the kind of 'game-like' thinking which inspires a different kind of solution. Think of QIKTEL, the telco provider that had identified their sales and distribution system (telco retailers) as their key issue, while their real problem was a negative Game Pattern ('complicated sideline product versus simple and profitable mainstream products').

Game Strategy suggested what they needed to look for: a dominant 'counter-pattern'. In the end, QIKTEL emerged as the pioneer of the 'inbound opportunity.' These are just random examples of how solid game analysis inspires game changing solutions.

Now, we'll take a closer look at the five steps that lead to a breakthrough Game Strategy. Let's keep one point firmly in mind. Since Game Strategy is supposed to inspire open, free thinking, it would be contradictory to try to force it into a strict, methodical structure. Schematic process routines and workflows simply do not apply to a thought process that at its core aims at breaking old, conventional templates.

Step One: Choose Your Game *(Explore Your Options)*

Before *changing* the Game in the marketplace, it is critical to understand that you usually have several game options to choose from. This is not as trivial as it may sound. Only a few decades ago, it was rather obvious what market game you were signed up for. If your product was a chainsaw, it was more than obvious that you were in the chainsaw market competing against other chainsaw brands. That was your game. Pretty straightforward, and not much of a choice here. Chainsaws against other chainsaws. Colas against other colas. Branch banks against other branch banks. The good old age of 'homogeneous' competition, when you simply played the Game against the same kind of competitors are long gone. Today, markets have become a lot more complex and you can battle against a whole range of 'heterogeneous' competitors. In other words, you can now choose your game – and you had better make it a very careful choice.

For example, you can select your game on a smaller or a larger scale. Coca-Cola can play the 'cola game' only against Pepsi and some Private Labels, or it can engage in the larger 'soft drink game,' or it can define 'cold beverages' as their primary competitors. However, even that could be too limited. For years, Coca-Cola also attempted to generate growth at the expense of 'hot beverages' like coffee and tea – on the breakfast table. Again, you had better make a carefully thought-through decision.

More specifically, you have a choice to enter into the Game being played in *neighbouring markets*, where you might be able to take a piece of a much larger pie: like an Internet bank that chooses to engage in the Game of branch banks, or when a mobile telecommunications provider opens fire against fixed-line telephony, or when a margarine brand declares war on butter.

Also, you may come to the conclusion that your choice is *not* to take part in a game that you seem to be 'signed-up' for. For example, Red Bull decided *not* to play the 'soft drink game' even though a food scientist would be very likely to classify it as a soft drink or Toyota and Honda decided *not* to engage in the SUV game but rather open up a new game (the XUV game) with different rules. If this is the way you decide to go, you may as well skip step two and move straight ahead to step three.

Step Two: Do Your 'Game Strategy' Analysis

The second step is the 'heart and soul' of the process. Once you have picked the Game you want to play, control and win, your objective is to detect *that one angle* in the market where you can make the biggest difference with a Game Changing Idea.

The guiding thought for your Game Analysis: In what specific way does the Competitive Game as it is played today curtail the growth perspectives of your own product, service, brand or company?

To get there, you go through the following analytical exercise, which mirrors the logical sequence of the chapters in this book.

1. Analyze the existing measures of quality and performance

As a reminder, in each category, market or market segment, certain standards of quality and/or performance crystallize over time. When you change these measures, you can expect a significant power shift among the competitors.

Now do your analysis. How do customers (or other target groups like retailers or opinion leaders) assess quality and performance in your category? What are their key valuation and purchase criteria? What is the accepted 'standard of excellence'? To what degree are these criteria 'valid,' i.e. accepted throughout the customer base and shared by dealers, opinion leaders, journalists and/or investors? Are they just 'valid' or also 'true'? Where do these criteria come from? How consistent, stable, durable and sustainable are they? In what way are they incomplete, one-sided, emotional rather than factual, based on misbeliefs or simply false?

Take a look at the big picture. How sophisticated or undersophisticated are the prevailing quality standards and, hence, are we dealing with a sophisticated or a 'low-level' game?

Finally, how do existing quality standards 'regulate' the power balance in the Competitive Game? To what extent do some players benefit from them while others are put at a disadvantage? How does your own product or your own company stack up when you're evaluated by the prevailing measures of quality and performance?

2. Explore existing 'models' and dominant structures in your market and determine how they regulate market dynamics

As a reminder, market structures 'regulate' the dynamics of the Game. These structures are based on ideas, concepts, images and models of the market land-scape and hence are 'virtual' in nature. Nevertheless, by changing them you can bring forth absolutely real changes in the dynamics of the Competitive Game.

Now do your analysis. First, is there a dominant 'virtual' structure or a prevailing 'market model' that the various players in the market have agreed on? Is there something like a 'two-camp model' or an axis (like in politics) or a 'pyramid' or a system of 'leagues' and 'classes' (like in the hotel business) or a sequence of generations (like Web 2.0 versus Web 1.0)?

Then, test and challenge the structures. To what degree are categorizations and classifications in your market based on indisputable facts? To what degree are they based on 'soft' criteria? Are these structures and classifications simply technical aids for market research companies or are they deeply entrenched in the customer's mind and 'regulate' his choices?

How are your own products or services (or your entire company) classified or categorized? What about key competitors? Are these 'category allocations' carved in stone or could you argue about them?

Finally, explore how (virtual) structures and 'market models' regulate the Competitive Game (so-called structural effects). How do 'category labels' in the larger market environment (like being allocated to 'good camp' or 'bad camp') impact on the market dynamics, the competitive confrontation and your chances to win?

3. Scrutinize Role Games and prevailing Game Patterns

As a reminder, note that wherever opposing parties in a market come up against one another, role plays or stereotypical Game Patterns emerge (like 'hightech' versus 'nature' in the running shoe business). By introducing new patterns, the Game Changer can dramatically twist the odds in the competitive confrontation.

Now do your analysis. Zero-in on the competition between yourself (your product, service, brand, company) and your key competitors. Would you say that customers (or media, investors, other target groups) tend to reduce that competition to a fairly simplistic or 'black and white' pattern? Try to describe them as precisely as possible.

Seek to understand where these Game Patterns are coming from. Did they simply emerge over time or were they deliberately introduced by your competitors, your own company, opinion leaders or media?

Make an analysis. How does this Game Pattern function? To what degree does it impact on the media and the public opinion (activation function). What kind of *relative status* is attributed to the opposing parties? How are the Game Patterns likely to frame the customers' thinking and decision making? What is the role of ideology and emotions in the pattern?

Explore to what degree these simplistic role definitions increase or limit the development potential of the individual players. What are the implications for *your* product, service, brand or company?

4. Capture and define the 'Original Idea' of your category with all its implications and inherent limitations

As a reminder, each product and service category is subject to 'implicit' definition or an 'Original Idea'. By alterting or modifying this idea, the Game Changer can establish a dynamic new business model and destabilize the old 'top dogs' in the market.

Now do your analysis. Take your category back to the 'drawing board' and determine which conventions and traditions constitute today's business model – as it has emerged over the past years and/or decades. What central common product characteristics (or service features) are respected by all of the market participants? What conventions beyond the product form part of the larger business model in your category, industry or business sector?

Then detect the inherent limitations. In what way or to what degree does the 'Original Idea' of your category limit access to your current target group or to new target groups, limit the frequency of purchase or usage occasions and limit the price the target group is willing to pay?

Test and challenge the 'conventions' that are part of the business model in your category. Work out the difference between 'good' conventions and traditions (which are truly 'constitutional' or add relevance, meaning and fascination to your category) and 'bad' conventions and traditions (the ones that do nothing more than curtail present or future growth perspectives).

Evaluate how the 'Original Idea' of your category would be different if it were invented today. How would it be defined if only the demands, conditions, opportunities, needs and possibilities of the present were taken into consideration – regardless of any past conventions and traditions?

That is a very rough summary of how game analysis works. Note that each of the four approaches above represents its own 'standalone' perspective. In this manner, the Game in the market is explored four times, each time in a different way. The four perspectives are largely independent of one another. One may be very helpful, while another may not get you much further in your current market situation. That is not a problem, because you obviously cannot (and shouldn't attempt to) change all aspects of the Competitive Game at once. All you want to do is to identify *that one angle* that helps you turn around the Game in your own favor.

Step Three: Craft Your 'Game Changing Idea'

We have argued that your game analysis will point to the 'ballpark' which shows where to look for your Game Changing Idea. However, the 'ballpark' is not yet a solution.

That is why you are now entering the 'experimental stage' in the process. You are playing with different Game Changing Ideas and trying to determine *what* they are likely to do for you.

> *Anticipate the change in the Game and its 'logical' consequences.* **Make a projection of the 'logical' implications of your new Game Changing Idea(s). How are they likely to impact on (i) the competitive situation and/or (ii) the behavior and decision making of other players, foremost the customer? And finally, how is your own company likely to benefit from it?**

Keep in mind that there is a direct link between the rules of the Game and the way the players act in it. The 'rules of the Game' are at the same time the 'ideas that rule the competition' and, more specifically, 'the ideas that rule the customer's behavior.' Consequently, it must be possible to anticipate how new rules are likely to change the marketplace conditions in your favor.

Nevertheless, we are not advocating that you engage in 'wild speculations' about what your Game Changing Ideas can do for you. We are talking about very logical projections. Imagine that the Formula One racing authorities – in their role as Game Masters – were to develop regulations that standardize the technology of the cars. Now, it is pretty logical to anticipate how 'homogenized technology' will change the competitive situation: the chances to win the competition increase for the 'best drivers' as opposed to the 'best engineers.' In other words, you can 'logically' expect a shift in the prevailing power balance to the benefit of smaller, private teams and to the disadvantage of leading global car manufacturers (who will no longer be able to exploit as much their high-tech advantage). There is nothing speculative about it. It is simply about projecting 'logical' consequences.

The same applies to new rules or 'Game Changing Ideas' in the market-place. To a certain degree, the Game Changer can project what is likely to happen – always provided that he succeeds in securing full acceptance and consensus among other players for his new rules. For example, you can 'project' how new measures of quality and performance are likely to change the competitive situation or impact the customer's decision making. This was true in our parasiticide case study. If you introduce a new 'ultimate' standard of performance ('100% protection from infections') you can make firm projections about how the competitive situation changes: how your key competitor compares to the new standard, how your own product does and what the implications are for the 'relative power' between the two. Of course, that is not saying that you will actually succeed in *securing full acceptance of* your new quality measure. However, at this stage, we are still simply assuming that you will.

Likewise, you can quite logically project how other possible game strategies are likely to turn the Competitive Game to your own favor:

– How will new measures of quality and performance impact currently prevailing power relationships (if you achieved consensus for them)?
– How are new structures, classifications or 'models of the market' likely to help your product, brand or company?
– How can alternative new Game Patterns shift the 'relative status' of competing parties or 'reframe' the entire decision-making process?

– How likely is your freshly defined 'Original Idea' to liberate the category of its inherent limitations and empower a new business model?

Of course, such projections are qualitative in nature. They simply enable you to compare the relative power of alternative options at a very early development stage.

Prepare the argument for your 'pitch.' **Define your conclusive argument through which you want to convince your future allies in the marketplace (customers, retailers, opinion leaders, journalists, investors) that your new rules apply – and why exactly they are more appropriate than the currently prevailing rules.**

In a sense, you are assuming the role of a defense attorney making his final plea to a jury. It is a piece of communication that you can put on paper and test its power with members of the target groups that you want to convince. Just try it with any of your 'tried and tested' market research partners.

Step Four: Design Your Strategic Masterplan

Before you start recruiting allies and take your 'Game Changing Idea' to the market, you need to define your (corporate) strategic masterplan. It is possible that you have identified implications for your products or product portfolio, for innovations or for the priorities of the research and development teams. You may want to change something regarding pricing, distribution or your general sales approach. Maybe you need to change your brand Positioning or communication approach in general. In some cases, it may make sense to introduce some overall organization changes.

Once you have defined your masterplan on the strategic level, it is usual to define with our partners, teams or task forces, each of which takes on responsibility for part of the strategic masterplan. We recommend designating someone to have overall responsibility, in order to keep the larger view firmly in sight and to serve as the 'steward of the idea,' so that compromises for the sake of expediency are kept to an absolute minimum.

Step Five: Start Recruiting and Winning over Allies

A 'game changing strategy' moves from the virtual 'idea stage' to becoming an uncontested 'rule of the Game' only when a substantial number of players agree to it and start playing by it. Your assignment at this stage is to define your allies. Who are the most important fellow players who must be won over to your side at an early stage? Are they customers? Opinion leaders? The trade press? Public authorities? Several parties or all of them? It is now time to go out and 'pitch' your argument to them. That could happen through very targeted 'idea lobbying' with selected key decision makers or opinion leaders. Alternately, you may arrive at a 'broader' mass-market communication and PR campaign, which can involve writing books and speaking at conferences and congresses.

When your allies are on board, the Game can really get going. Now you are playing according to your own rules and are able to unleash forces unknown to those players that rely exclusively on their own strength. Keep in mind it is ultimately these voluntary and informal allies who empower the Game Changer and not his own 'internal' resources.

IT'S TIME TO EXPLORE YOUR OWN GAME CHANGING OPPORTUNITIES

If you are the one responsible for market success in your company, you spend a lot of your time thinking about product initiatives and innovations, new pricing structures, handling distribution channels, unlocking new markets and target prospects, expanding into different regions and building your brands. However, never forget that all of this is still 'Level I' strategies. It is the level of direct competitive confrontation. You still experience the Game from an 'interior perspective' and that is no longer good enough. Being a 'first-class' player is only 'second best' if you can be the 'Game Changer.'

True, in everyday life, you won't be able to detect a striking difference between ordinary players and Game Changers. It is only once in a while that the Game Changers take off their 'jerseys,' move up to Level II and take an 'exterior perspective' view of the Game. We predict you will find this a worthwhile and 'mind-opening' exercise – even if you do not plan to revolutionize your market within the next 12 months.

Consider Google, where the following rule prevails: devote 70% of resources to the core business and the other 30% are free for creative thinking, new ideas and breakthrough experimentation. This is how we view the role of Game Strategy in the daily life of a manager. It is not thinking from dawn to dusk about how you can break or reinvent the rules and laws of the market, but it does make sense to devote at least a portion of your precious time and resources to a provocatively different kind of thinking.

Enough said. You want to find out what your chances are to go beyond Positioning and 'change the Game' out there. *Start today and give it a go!*

After the Game

The manuscript for this book was almost complete. We were on a transatlantic flight from Frankfurt to New York. As the evening grew late and time dragged on, we started up a conversation with a fellow traveler, who introduced himself as the CEO of a mid-sized American company. Our conversation was short but lively: 'OK, so you're writing something about "Game Strategy",' the man said. 'Interesting. Can you explain to me in one sentence exactly what that is?' Americans are well known for liking things crisp, snappy and to the point. Game Strategy in one sentence? Sure, why not?

> *Game Strategy is about changing the rules of the Game to your advantage – while you are playing it.*

Sure enough, that's the essence of it. The American was silent for a few moments, frowned doubtfully and then muttered: 'But that's impossible.'

Our new friend was actually completely correct and helped us to find the right title for this book. When one player takes control of the rules he enjoys an 'impossible' advantage over competitors that are content to 'play along.' That is why, in the long run, the Rule Makers and Game Changers will emerge as the 'logical' winners.

You'll like Game Strategy if you enjoy and have fun by thinking differently, freely and radically. We have used Game Strategy for years as a proven-effective professional tool, able to analyze the market in a radical fashion and identify major levers for growth. From practical experience we know how deeply and thoroughly you can actually influence marketplace and competitive events over the long term.

It is important not to lose sight of one key point. The more effective an instrument is, and the more powerful a lever it represents, then all the more respectfully should it be employed. It is in this spirit – and with confidence! – that we hope you will find our way of thinking useful. Have fun with it, but, above all, have success! If you have any questions, inspirations, ideas or case histories about Game Strategy, don't hesitate to contact us through our homepage: www.impossible-advantage.com. We look forward to hearing from you!

Postscript: how Game *Strategy* differs from Game *Theory*

Let's start with a brief explanation of what game *theory* is all about. We would request that experts in the field permit us a couple of deliberate simplifications.

Game theory was invented in the first half of the last century by the mathematicians John von Neumann and Oscar Morgenstern, who in 1944 published their classic book, *Theory of Games and Economic Behavior*. The two mathematicians observed participants in classic party games. They wanted to determine how the players – starting from identical initial conditions – came up with winning strategies. This exciting scientific challenge culminated in the question: 'How can I outwit a competitor who is also trying to outwit me?' This is the typical approach of attempting to second-guess the reaction of an opponent in advance. 'What does he think I'm thinking?' is the kind of question a strategic thinking player – for example in a chess game – has to deal with, or even more complex: 'What does he believe that I think he's thinking?' Pretty much an endless loop.

A typical example of a game theory problem with some economic relevance is the so-called 'icecream man' dilemma. Imagine there are two men selling icecream along the same 100 meter stretch of beach. Because both think in economic terms, one occupies the left-hand side and the other the right-hand side. Both select a position such that between the two of them, there is the smallest degree of overlap. One day, one of the two icecream men tries to outwit his competitor by moving a bit toward the center of the beach, thereby acquiring a concrete, objective advantage. This move restricts the territory of his adversary, pushing him back a bit. Unfortunately, he neglected to consider what his competitor was thinking. In order to compensate for this disadvantage, he, too, decides to advance toward the center.

Ironically, at this point, *both icecream men stand to lose*. First, they are locked in a bitter struggle for the center and, second, both lose business that should have come from the two ends of the beach, because now they are too far away for the swimmers out there. Now there's an opening for a third or even a fourth icecream man, which would make life for the first two more difficult. Wouldn't it have been smarter for the two of them to stick to their original locations? Perhaps. In game theory, it is all about figuring out an optimal behavioral strategy given the question of what your competitor thinks that you think that he thinks …

These kinds of artificially constructed game theory problems can be easily carried over into real life. Actually, we can compare the mathematically expected outcome and results of the icecream man dilemma with the behavior of the two major political parties in the German national election of 1998. At that time, the Social Democrats or SPD, historically positioned well to the center-left of the political spectrum, concluded under the leadership of Gerhard Schröder that they had to move closer to the middle of that spectrum if they were to loosen the 16-year grip on power by the Christian Democrats or CDU under Helmut Kohl. That is where the SPD, campaigning as the party of the 'New Middle,' could win over the greatest share of swing voters. The calculation was made, and just as game theorists predicted, the SPD won the election. Just as it was no surprise that, in response, the CDU decided to move more toward the center in order to compensate for their disadvantage. The result was that the two major parties were now engaged in a tooth-and-nail struggle from which they both emerged as losers. On the one hand they collide in the middle and on the other they abandon the opposite ends of the political left/right spectrum to new opponents like the Left Party. Previously, about 80% of the electorate voted for one of the two major parties. Today in the 'New Middle' they are contesting only 50 to 60% of voters, thereby creating significant free room for the new Left Party ('Die Linken'), which went from practically nothing to a two-digit share of the vote.

There are important similarities between game theory and Game Strategy. Both approaches attempt to explain *the behavior* of the players and seek to determine optimal strategies in the competition. But that is where the similarity ends. Game *theory* arrives at optimal economic behavior strategies by looking at things from the perspective of either 'both-try-to-outwit-the-other' or 'the-best-for-both' solutions. Changing the Game or any of the rules has *nothing* to do with game theory – but this is the *central, core theme* of Game Strategy that we present in this book for the first time. We regard this as the most important difference.

New discoveries in game *theory* have been awarded over half a dozen Nobel Prizes during the past 20 years. One of those prizes went to John Forbes Nash, whose story became famous in the popular movie *A Beautiful Mind*. But game theory is far too theoretical and abstract to be of practical use to managers who are trying to develop a success strategy for the marketplace. For *game strategies*, it is the reverse. You may never win a Nobel Prize, but you are likely to find some valuable inspirations about how to win in the marketplace.

Thanks!

The creation of this book took a bit longer than the usual pregnancy, about 10 and one half months. As is so often the case, this pregnancy passed through a seemingly endless range of phases, from anxious anticipation, to joy and on to euphoria, interspersed with mood shifts, sleepless nights and other discomforts. It was a very intense time and we would like to offer our heartfelt thanks to everyone who assisted, supported and counseled us.

Our first word of thanks goes to our longstanding business colleagues and partners Marion Beate Spinner, Thomas Schupp and Rainer Schüle. Together with them we developed the fundamental principles of Game Strategy thinking over the course of many years. Many of their thoughts, ideas and experiences have flowed throughout the manuscript. Our assistants Angela Christoph and Dorothe Mayer supported us with their research and tireless text editing, for which we are tremendously grateful.

Next, we want to thank our many friends who reviewed and critically examined the text, even in its earliest stages of development: Axel Baumhöfner, Holger Braun, Derek Brennan, Dr Hansjörg Gruber, Stefan Jost, Marcus Lüppens, Katrin Sachse, Harald Schäfers, Michael Steinau, Dirk Ullrich, Hans-Jürgen and Regine Walter. All of your experience, inspiration and stimulus ensured that our manuscript benefited significantly from better substance, freshness and value. Without you we would have had to be content with far less.

We thank our clients for the trust they have placed in us and for their openness to accept larger and sometimes 'radical' growth ideas. To all of you, we say that we fully recognize that a strong strategy is always only half the battle. You, however, have accepted the challenge to force through new ideas in your companies and to bring those ideas to the market. Special thanks goes to Thomas Steffens and Liska Vehling of BayerHealthCare and Dirk Ullrich and Regina Pfeiffer of Sanofi-Aventis. We take this opportunity to thank all our other clients whose case histories we were not able to include in the interests of keeping this volume slender, manageable and easy to read.

Not to be forgotten, thanks also go to those experts who helped us with the factually correct presentation of certain case histories, especially Prof. Helmut Braun, from whom we acquired a world of knowledge about diamonds and the market for precious stones.

A further word of thanks to Stephan Zech of Axel Springer AG, who distinguished himself through special understanding and support during the creative process, as well as considerable interest in serving as a test case for future uses of Game Strategy.

Last, but not least, a final thank you to Kathy Acton and Sui Sabine Wiley,[2] both of whom showed admirable serenity, understanding, tolerance and optimism throughout this book's creation. We are in their debt, but they know that already, and will demand compensation soon, no doubt ...

Wolfram Wördemann, Andreas Buchholz and Ned Wiley

Königstein and Berlin, January 2009

[2]Kathy Acton is the spouse of Wolfram Wördemann and Sui Sabine Wiley of Ned Wiley.

Index

ABC 45
Accenture 162, 163, 164, 166
activation function 109, 112, 114, 124, 132, 137
Adams, Judi 29
added value 50, 71
Adidas 111–12
Advantix 49, 50, 51–2, 53, 64, 175
'advertising receptive age group' 44, 45–6
'advertising receptive target audience' 45, 46, 47, 64
Aer Lingus 7, 9
Airbus 103, 118
Alltours 10
Alonso, Fernando 21
AMD 118
American Football 17
Apollo 61
Apple 170, 171
  iPod147–51
ARD 42, 44, 45, 64, 179, 180
Astley, Philip 154
Atkins, Dr 28, 30, 31, 177, 181, 183
  Dr Atkins' Diet Revolution 27
Atkins Case 30–1
Atkins Diet 28
Atkins Nutritionals 31
Aventis 83–4, 87, 88, 89, 183
'axis model' 68, 93

Balaxan 119, 120–5, 138
'ballpark' 189
Bank of America 165
'Barbie' doll 158–61, 176
barrier to resocialization 123

'basal-supported oral therapy,' (BOT) 88, 89, 98, 99, 183
Bayer 49, 50, 51, 52, 53, 63, 65, 177
BBC 165
Beautiful Mind, A (film) 199
Bertelsmann 113
'beyond positioning' 173
Blancpain 141
Blendax 72
BMW 19
Boeing 9, 103, 118
BOT therapy 88, 89, 98, 99, 183
BP 165
brand loyalty 137
Branson, Richard 25
Bratz 159, 160, 161, 162, 169, 176
Breadsmith 29
Bréguet 141
British Airways 9
British Telecom 165
bus industry 10
Bush, George W. 111, 118
business philosophy 165
business-to-business sector 49, 82

CBS 45
Central Selling Organization (CSO) 60
changing structures 71
Chicago Board of Trade 96
'Chicken or Egg' Dilemma 36–7
Chirac, Jacques 112–13
Circus Roncalli 156, 171
Cirque du Soleil 154, 155–6, 169, 170, 171

Citibank 162
classical game strategies 22–6
  redefining the measures of performance 23
  reshaping the market landscape 23–4
  restaging the competitive confrontation 24
  taking the game to the next level 24–5
Clinton, Hilary 115–18
Coca-Cola 25, 73, 74, 75, 76, 103, 107, 177, 185
Coca-Cola Company 98, 167–8
Cochran 135
Cola Wars 107
competition in the marketplace 15
competitive advantage 70, 118
competitive analysis 184
competitive game 2, 27, 93, 98
'confrontation' 108
core competences 165
correttezza commerciale 15
counter-pattern 125, 129, 130–2, 133
'creativity' 40
crossover vehicles 80, 81, 89, 98, 99
cultural revolution 90
custom-built homes versus mass-produced houses 103–4
'customer insights' 182
'customer Jury' 38–42
customer loyalty 128, 131

Printed and bound by CPI Group (UK) Ltd, Croydon, CR0 4YY

16/04/2025

14658820-0001